W9-BSK-677

BY THE SAME AUTHOR

JAMES MADISON

BENJAMIN FRANKLIN

FROM COLONY
TO COUNTRY

FROM COLONY TO COUNTRY

*The Revolution in
American Thought, 1750–1820*

RALPH KETCHAM

BROOKLINE PUBLIC LIBRARY

Macmillan Publishing Co., Inc.
NEW YORK
Collier Macmillan Publishers
LONDON

Coolidge

973.3
K49 F

copy 2

WITHDRAWN,
PUBLIC LIBRARY
BROOKLINE

Copyright © 1974 by Ralph Ketcham
All rights reserved. No part of this book may be reproduced or transmitted in any form or by any means,
electronic or mechanical, including photocopying, re-
cording or by any information storage and retrieval
system, without permission in writing from the Publisher.
Macmillan Publishing Co., Inc.
866 Third Avenue, New York, N.Y. 10022
Collier-Macmillan Canada Ltd.
First Printing 1974
Printed in the United States of America

Library of Congress Cataloging in Publication Data
Ketcham, Ralph Louis, 1927–
   From colony to country.
   Bibliography: p.
   1. United States—Intellectual life. I. Title.
E169.1.K417   917.3'03'3   73-18763
   ISBN 0-02-562930-1

FOR BEN AND LAURA LEE

Preface

THIS BOOK ARISES OUT OF MY READING AND TEACHING DURING THE LAST TEN YEARS OR SO IN THE FIELD OF EARLY AMERICAN THOUGHT, AND, LESS DIRECTLY, OUT OF MANY YEARS OF STUDY OF THE LIVES OF BENJAMIN FRANKLIN AND JAMES MADISON. ITS THEME, THE changing ideas of loyalty, purpose, and national character that were part of the transition from colony to country in 1750–1820, depends basically on my study of sermons, speeches, tracts, essays, letters, poems, novels, and historics written by Americans during those years.

Since changes in the *public* life of the colonies and then the nation were what preoccupied leading thinkers throughout the period, I have paid particular attention to the writings of the most influential statesmen: Benjamin Franklin, John Adams, Thomas Jefferson, James Madison, and Alexander Hamilton. I have for the same reason paid relatively little attention to artists, architects, scientists, and even literary figures, making use of them principally as they reflect the broader patterns of thought worked out by the more explicitly public philosophers. Writers and artists in this period had in general neither to "escape" and establish identity apart from politics nor to engage in crusades to transform American public purposes. Rather, they commonly sought to express in their art the new purposes and character of the new nation. The matter becomes clearer if one compares the concerns of intellectuals during this period with those of, say, Emerson's day, or Edmund Wilson's or Noam Chomsky's. I have, therefore, dealt with such figures as David Rittenhouse, Charles Willson Peale, and Washington Irving only as they reveal here and there the central trauma over the nation's political identity. Even religious writings, voluminous if not always creative during the Revolutionary era, are significant principally in their implications for the dominating public changes. The fact that Edwards predates and Emerson postdates the period covered in this study illustrates the point. More detailed, comprehensive studies of the novelists, poets, artists, and scientists of the period are listed in the bibliography.

I have throughout attended seriously to ideas themselves. If this seems abstract or elitist, I submit that there is more depth and therefore more intrinsic interest in the words of the intellectually talented and articulate than in such thoughts as survive of those who were less concerned with the life of the mind. Not only would I emphasize the intrinsic value of the study of ideas for their own sake (why else, indeed, do we read Plato, Burke, or Thoreau?), but I would also urge serious consideration of what the ideas mean as a *prerequisite* for understanding how they reflected social conditions and how they might in turn have influenced those conditions. Ideas are not separate from reality; they are *part* of it. We cannot have useful books about the role of ideas in society until we understand, thoroughly and critically, what the men who expressed the ideas were saying.

While depending basically on source materials, I have tried to synthesize and make use of the remarkably fine studies relating to American thought of the 1750–1820 era published during the last twenty years or so. The best of these books, of which I have made particular use, are Alan Heimert, *Religion and the American Mind* (1966), Bernard Bailyn, *Ideological Origins of the American Revolution* (1967), Gordon S. Wood, *The Creation of the American Republic, 1776–1787* (1969), and Winthrop Jordan, *White Over Black: American Attitudes Toward the Negro, 1550–1812* (1968). I have included in the bibliography other recent, important secondary works of cultural and intellectual history, but I have generally excluded the multitude of studies of the political, military, diplomatic, and economic history of the years 1750–1820. For primary sources, recently published, readily available anthologies and books of selected readings are listed, as well as multivolume collections of papers and writings. The bibliography, therefore, suggests the highlights for a reader interested in the intellectual history of the period, but it is not designed to go beyond that.

I am indebted to William Goetzmann who first arranged for me to write this book, helped with its design, and then evaluated the manuscript. Robert Cooke of Southampton College and Bruce Lohof of

Heidelburg College made possible opportunities to "try out" and discuss parts of the book. Many students, including especially B. F. Wilson, Kenn Peters, and William Bloodworth of the University of Texas, and Linda Biemer, Joel Friedlander, William Polf, Jack Heister, and Barbara Scott of Syracuse University, have helped immensely with their research and criticism. Conversations with Martin Diamond, Herbert Storing, Philip White, Gene Wise, and William Stinchcombe helped me overcome moments of error, lack of insight, and discouragement. Nelson Blake and Robert Crunden kindly but critically read the entire manuscript to my great benefit. Helene H. Fineman and my wife, Julia, have worked hard to improve the style and readability of the book. Mrs. Nancy Dore, Mrs. Jeanne Erwin, and Mrs. Marian Borst cheerfully deciphered my handwriting to produce a typescript. I have recorded my debt to the forebearance and high spirits of my young children in the dedication.

Silver Bay, New York
1974

Contents

I

The Colonial Mind

I

RITONS LIVING on the western side of the Atlantic Ocean in 1750 were, by and large, superpatriots. As with the nineteenth-century colonists, their zeal for British ways and words often seemed directly proportionate to their distance from the great abbey at Westminster. Devotion to the Crown, delight in the teatime ritual, and fascination with London fads were as intense in eighteenth-century Boston, Williamsburg, and Charleston as they were in nineteenth-century Bombay, Gibraltar, Singapore, and Sydney. A need for the protection of the Royal Navy and a fear of losing "Britishness" amid a wilderness or an alien culture were mainly responsible, but Benjamin Franklin noted other ties in a letter to his London bookseller in 1745:

Your authors know but little of the Fame they have on this Side of the Ocean. We are a kind of Posterity in respect to them. . . . We know nothing of their personal Failings; the Blemishes in their character never reach us, and therefore the bright and amiable part strikes us with its full Force. They have never offended us or any of our Friends, and we have no Competitions with them, and therefore we praise and admire them without restraint.[1]

British art, fashions, furniture, and architecture were as widely and as indiscriminately admired. In short, a web of nostalgia, shared tastes, psychic need, and habit, as well as geopolitical realism and political connection, bound the colonies to the mother country.

Dozens of other ties reinforced these bonds. Virginia planters mar-

keted their tobacco in London, Bristol, or Liverpool, and received in
return on their own Tidewater wharves the stores, implements, and
amenities they needed to survive *as Englishmen* in the New World.
Hundreds of colonials, especially those preparing for careers in law
and medicine, went to Great Britain for their education, and Anglican
clergymen went there for ordination. Many religious groups, like the
Quakers and the followers of George Whitefield, conceived of their
fellowship as a transatlantic communion. Mercantile enterprises commonly had branches or partnerships up and down the North American
coast as well as in the British Isles. Streams of British immigrants
provided a steady renewal of personal ties with the mother country.
The bonds were such that Franklin spoke fondly and unself-con-
sciously in 1751 of Britain as "a wise and good Mother," and of the
Empire as a "Family" where a weakening of any part diminished the
whole. In the middle of the eighteenth century the hyphenated form,
British-American, would have been absurd; the colonials considered
themselves Britons in America and still thought of journeys across the
Atlantic as "going home."[2]

Wherever one turned, the British pattern dominated. Patrick Henry
gained such book learning as he possessed through the tutelage of his
father, a graduate of King's College in Aberdeen, Scotland. Franklin,
David Rittenhouse, John Winthrop, and other colonial scientists were
or aspired to be members of the Royal Society, published their find-
ings in its *Transactions*, and, in time, used it as a model for their own
learned organization, the American Philosophical Society. The New
Light Presbyterian founders of the College of New Jersey (Princeton), though they abhorred the narrow, stultifying Anglicanism of
Oxford and Cambridge, turned for guidance to the English Dissenting
academies presided over by Philip Doddridge and other creative educators. John Adams, a fifth-generation American, nevertheless studied
the English common law as his own, and in court he found himself
surrounded by the procedures and paraphernalia of the King's Bench.
At least until his thirtieth birthday George Washington had no higher
ambition than to receive a commission in one of His Majesty's regiments. Thomas Jefferson's first draft of a state paper, written in the
courtly language of Georgian England, prayed for "his Majesty's
sacred person and government," and expressed "a lively sense of his
royal favor." Franklin's earliest memories were of the rejoicing in

New England occasioned by news of the death of "that wicked old Persecutor of God's People, Lewis XIV"—the same Louis against whom Old England had fought for a quarter-century.[3]

It was the Anglo-French wars of 1689–1763 that most stimulated British patriotism in the colonies. In North America they were called, with gratitude, not contempt, by the names of the sovereigns conducting them—King William's War, Queen Anne's War, and King George's War. The outcome meant literally life or death to the colonies, still in tender immaturity and threatened on all sides by what they rightly regarded as aggressive French or Spanish despotism. Thus Carolinians rejoiced exceedingly at the repulse of a Franco-Spanish attack on Charleston in 1706, and the capture of Louisbourg from the French in 1745 seemed to New Englanders a deliverance from the hands of the Devil himself. The national future of North America was very much in doubt until Wolfe's capture of Quebec in 1759. Before that, from Massachusetts to Georgia, the colonists displayed intense loyalty to the British Crown and its powerful protectors, the Redcoats and the Royal Navy. Though quarrels were common between colonies and mother country and important tensions persisted, these paled, at least on the conscious level, beside the constant, effusive, and heartfelt expressions of love for Great Britain.

The Seven Years' War, already two years old in North America when it was declared in Europe in 1756, intensified British loyalties among the colonials. From Lake Champlain to the Great Valley of Virginia the frontier seemed defenseless against roving bands of Frenchmen and their Indian allies. Farms were burned and pioneers murdered less than a hundred miles from Philadelphia, and all of Virginia west of the Blue Ridge had to be virtually abandoned. However tragic the effect of Braddock's humiliation and defeat (and however much Franklin and others, in retrospect, would see in him sinister signs of British arrogance and militarism), his heroic death on the battlefield was for the colonists a blood sacrifice by the mother country on their behalf. Later disasters at Oswego, Ticonderoga, and elsewhere only strengthened the need for all Britons to "do or die" together. *The American Magazine*, founded in Philadelphia in 1757 to stiffen patriotic ardor, followed articles signed "Antigallician" with a poem connecting all virtues and values with British nationality:

Reason's sov'reign empire, *Britons*, O maintain,
While Deamons yell, and Monks blaspheme in vain.
Hers is the regimen of civil good;
And her's religion, truly understood.

· · ·

But, oh, new dangers threat in hostile fields;
The savage sword, lo, devastation yields,
Ambition mounts *Bellona's* snake-whipt car:
Rome and her furies urgeth the infernal war!
Lo! to restore the reign of ancient night!
The potent monarchs of the globe unite!
Drown'd *Reformation* in a crimson flood,
And swim to empire in a sea of blood.
Genius of *Albion*, raise thy languid head;
Nor groan o'er mansions of the mighty dead!
Thy country calls! Rise, with recover'd force
To curb the insulting *Gaul's* impetuous course![4]

Then, as Pitt and his vigorous commanders organized and carried off the great victories at Fort Pitt, Louisburg, Niagara, and on the Plains of Abraham, joy and gratitude in America knew no bounds. Throughout the colonies the fame of the British warriors was preserved in the names of dozens of towns and counties: Amherst, Wolfe, Pitt, Forbes, and Boscawen. After the conquest of Canada, Franklin, in London and speaking "as a Briton," declared:

The future grandeur and stability of the British empire lie in America [where foundations exist] broad and strong enough to support the greatest political structure human wisdom ever yet erected. . . . All the country from the St. Lawrence to the Mississippi will in another century be filled with British people. Britain itself will become vastly more populous by the immense increase of its commerce; the Atlantic Sea will be covered with [British] trading ships; and [British] naval power thence continually increasing, will extend [British] influence round the whole globe, and awe the world![5]

In 1761 America joined heartily in celebrating the coronation of George III, the first truly British monarch of the House of Hanover.

Pride in British culture and confidence in the prosperity of the Empire reached an apex.

Though Franklin's emphasis on the *American* growth of the Empire might have alarmed some Englishmen, his theme was in fact part of an increasingly dominant geopolitics espoused by Pitt and other government leaders. They held that England's security and prosperity depended not on carefully managed dynastic connections with Europe, but rather on the growth of her trade, her navy, and her empire. Chesterfield, Bolingbroke, and other publicists popular in America trumpeted this position, which, following Pitt's lead, was generally adopted as the basis for British policy in the mid-eighteenth century. With this turning away from the continent of Europe, and the candid acknowledgment of the vital place of the New World in Britain's future, many colonials thought that a firm foundation had been laid for an expanding empire in which they were important, if not yet entirely equal, partners. Moreover, though this outlook had its imperialistic aspects, the new British concept of empire—within a context of the now subordinated dynastic ambitions and compared to the exclusive, tightly controlled Franco-Spanish attitude toward colonial possessions—was dynamic and freedom-extending. It depended on a growing, relatively free trade, prosperity in the New as well as the Old World, and a continuing flow of settlers both across the Atlantic and into the American West. This expansiveness, at first both loyally British and entirely committed to the growth of America, colored every aspect of colonial thought as the Great War for Empire drew to its victorious close.[6]

II

Beneath this seemingly pervasive, astonishingly uncritical Britishness, however, strong currents were moving the colonists toward a uniquely American outlook. Far more than the settlers at first realized, circumstances in the New World imposed not only novel ways of living, but also of thinking. Every effort to transplant an English idea or institution proved at best only partially successful. As Daniel Boorstin has shown, colonies founded with some special European purpose in mind were forced to adjust to the new American environment.

Thus Georgia became a slave-based plantation economy growing rice and cotton, not a haven where, as General Oglethorpe had envisioned in London, English indigents might raise silkworms. New England became a Puritan land where, of necessity, community growth replaced absorption with the intricacies of theology. Institutions also responded to the relative absence of Old World conventions. Lawyers became generalists skilled in many branches of law and leaders in public affairs, while their English counterparts, with their guildlike thinking, remained elaborately trained specialists little concerned with politics. Similarly, education and medicine developed flexibilities and a practical emphasis impossible amid the hoary, tradition-encrusted practices in Great Britain. In short, as "a disproving ground for utopias" and uncongenial to institutional rigidities, the American colonies had, willy-nilly and unconsciously, forged for themselves profoundly new approaches to life.[7]

The first portion of Franklin's *Autobiography*, describing his youth and young manhood and written in 1771 when he still considered himself a loyal subject of George III, wonderfully (but implicitly) displays the incipient Americanness of colonial life. His father and the household he established in Boston exhibited a self-reliance, a civic consciousness, and a sense of purpose uncommon among the still semi-feudal, primevally silent common people of Great Britain. After becoming a "freethinker" in religion and a critic (with his brother) of the Mather-dominated Massachusetts establishment, Franklin showed further independence of mind when he ran away from home rather than endure his brother's petty tyranny. In Philadelphia he found not only abundant opportunity for his own bursting energies, but also a new community ready to respond to his many ideas for civic improvement. Any part of this innovating life would have seemed an incredible deliverance in the Old World, but in America Franklin described it matter-of-factly as a development available in some measure to any man who displayed the qualities Poor Richard recommended to his readers. In the unformed, stimulating environment of the New World personal values, ways of making a living, and community organization were transformed, imperceptively and in many ways unwittingly, but in the long run decisively. The colonists were on the road to becoming what, after the Revolution, Crèvecoeur would celebrate as a new breed of men: Americans.

The colonial mind, then, in the mid-eighteenth century was in a scarcely perceived state of kinetic tension. Its outward forms, its avowed loyalties, its inbred predispositions, were overwhelmingly English. Yet the distance separating the colonies from England, and the novel circumstances of life in the New World, nourished dynamic new patterns. Though in every area of American life unique conditions were eroding transplanted Old World forms, in 1750 the push was subsurface, powerful yet largely unrecognized, an unsettledness beneath the visible calm of a model British plantation.

In science, for example, Americans collaborated eagerly with European investigators and published papers in British journals, but, significantly, they made discoveries especially relevant to the North American environment. Botanical collectors and observers, familiar with hundreds of plants unknown in Europe, became the most famous American scientists. John Clayton and John Mitchell in Virginia, Alexander Garden in South Carolina, Cadwallader Colden in New York, and especially John Bartram in Pennsylvania became valued colleagues of Linnaeus and the other great botanists of the eighteenth century. John Winthrop, a Harvard physicist, and others transmitted important astronomical data to the Royal Society in London, and at the time of the transit of Venus in 1769 American scientists published a volume of their own observations. In aiding these advances many American scientists, along with their European colleagues, came to adopt a basic view of reality that rejected long-hallowed superstitions and supernatural cosmologies. This new, secular world-view had momentous social and political implications which seemed especially meaningful in an environment where "nature" pressed in on all sides. Despite this general awareness of "the Enlightenment," though, Franklin's universally acclaimed *Experiments and Observations on Electricity* was the only major theoretical work on a level with European efforts. Even in his case, such practical achievements as the Pennsylvania fireplace, the lightning rod, and bifocal lenses were more characteristic contributions. Though often conscious of their special opportunities, American scientists for the most part conceived of their work as subordinate to European efforts and were painfully aware of the disadvantages imposed by their isolation and lack of sophistication.[8]

Lawyers, doctors, and educators were at least as dependent on Europeans as the scientists. Though Jefferson, John Adams, and others

proved that colonial lawyers could receive thorough, scholarly training in America and achieve notable intellectual independence, many of
the most prestigious lawyers (John Dickinson and the Lees of Virginia, for example) were trained in England. The unique demands of a
New World practice emancipated American lawyers from much of
the pedantry and stifling obeisance of English law, but *Coke on Little-
ton*, Viner's *Abridgment of Law and Equity*, and other British tomes
remained staples of the legal profession. For doctors, study at Leiden,
Edinburgh, London, Paris, or Padua was, until the Revolution, essential
to respectable standing. As such physicians (mostly Scots by background or training) gradually improved American practice, they encountered an assortment of home-grown medics ranging from absurd
quacks to skilled practitioners who combined Indian lore, native me-
dicinal herbs, and a knowledge of local conditions to form a useful,
indigenous basis for American medicine.

In education, the chasm between the intense need felt by the colonists (especially the Puritans) to establish their own schools and colleges and the immense practical difficulties in founding wilderness
centers of learning left a legacy of frustration and unevenness. By the
third quarter of the eighteenth century a half-dozen "colleges" existed,
but they consisted of only a few teachers and perhaps fifty to a hundred students struggling with the mixture of Christian teaching and
classical learning that had for three hundred years dominated higher
education in the Western world. Yet forces reflecting New World
demands impinged. Dartmouth recognized a special mission to educate
the Indians. In Pennsylvania, guided at first by Franklin's fertile mind,
the College of Philadelphia, aware of the religious diversity in Pennsylvania, pronounced itself nonsectarian (though not secular) and recognized New World needs by requiring the study of English, science,
modern languages, and even agriculture as well as Greek, Latin, and
divinity. At Princeton, New Jersey, "New Light" Presbyterians established their own college rather than subject their congregations to
what Gilbert Tennent called "The Dangers of an Unconverted Ministry." The comfortable system of parish control by one established
minister and the education of clergymen by narrowly orthodox, often
somnolent colleges were anathema to the zealots of the Great Awakening. Though the leaders of the colleges would have repudiated any
suggestion that they were either unorthodox or anticlassical, new de-

partures were evident that would in time give American higher education a character far different from that long hallowed at Oxford and Cambridge. Similarly, grammar school and preparatory school curricula began shifting as formal devotion to the disciplined study of Latin contended with the insistent demands for other kinds of learning.

Colonial literary efforts reflected the slavish admiration of English models Franklin had noted in North American reading habits. Insofar as eighteenth-century Americans attempted to compose essays and poetry (which, judging from printed remains, was infrequent), they imitated the polished works of Addison, the satire of Swift, or the heroic couplets of Pope. The literary circle that gathered around Provost William Smith at the College of Philadelphia about 1760 accepted London literary tastes as unreservedly as had James Franklin's little group of aspiring literati in Boston half a century earlier. American commemorative odes celebrating the great victories of the Seven Years' War often changed little more than the proper nouns of their English models. In *belles-lettres*, as Emerson's famous lament of 1837 accurately noted, Americans were entirely under the spell of "the courtly muses of Europe" until well into the nineteenth century. Only in travel accounts, sermons, and, increasingly, political polemics, in which the American environment so obviously called for new themes and new substance if not new forms, did a more indigenous literature emerge. The colonial newspapers, filled with reprints from the London press or imitations of it, were graphic reminders of the enthrallment, in 1750, of the American mind to the pervasive influence of English culture.

Even in the realm of political ideas, where, since the American Revolution, there has been a strong tendency to find origins of rebellion far back in colonial history, an observer in Boston or Philadelphia in 1750 would have found no disloyalty to Britain. Patriotic ardor aroused by the Seven Years' War, and the immense benefits derived by British America from it, heightened feelings of gratitude toward the mother country and created a generation of Americans who had fought beside or in the regiments of the King of England. The rhetoric of English revolution, including the radical justifications for the events of the 1640s as well as the more respectable apologies for the Glorious Revolution of 1688, was, of course, well known and revered in America, but no more so than within a segment of British opinion, and without any implication that the colonists would ever have reason to proclaim the right of revolution against the reigning British sovereign. Such long-standing resistances to British authority as the "quest for power" of the colonial assemblies, the evasion of customs duties, and reluctance to quarter English troops all appealed to legitimate British precedents and assumed that somewhere in the much-admired government of King, Lords, and Commons, officials would hear and heed just complaints.

In religion, the diversity of sects in the colonies, the dependent, often nominal status of the Anglican Church, the unsettling enthusiasm of the Great Awakening, and the dominant position of "Dissenters" in New England and Pennsylvania resulted in the most pervasive departures from English practice and, at least potentially, the most disobedient rhetoric. The enfolding, privileged, politically powerful position of the Church of England at home had no parallel in the North American colonies. Puritans, Quakers, and Presbyterians alike recalled their persecution by Anglican bishops in England, and each sect had among its most cherished and oft-repeated traditions accounts of finding in the New World a place where they could worship as they pleased. In the eighteenth century the colonies could not forbid Anglican worship, and they had to endure the activities of the Society for the Propagation of the Gospel in Foreign Parts; but at the same time tirades against an American Episcopacy and ridicule of Anglican attempts to assume a position of social superiority abounded. Even in Virginia and other places where the Church of England was established, its financial position was less secure, its services less revered, and its clergy less honored and less powerful than was generally the case in England. The words of Milton, Sidney, and others gave American Dissenters plenty of good English ammunition against Anglican pretensions, but the struggle against an American bishopric and other resistances to Anglicanism nourished resentments against, and at times provoked direct challenges to, an element of British authority highly valued by many powerful men in London.[9]

III

The American mind, then, in the pre-Revolutionary generation, was thoroughly, compulsively English in almost all its articulated manifes-

tations. To destroy the instinctive loyalty of the colonists would require profound, wrenching changes. Symbols of British nationality
covered the colonies: the Union Jack flew everywhere; prayers included petitions for the health and long life of the House of Hanover;
every legal transaction required the King's seal; British ships, including
awesome men-of-war, filled colonial harbors; and the actions and proceedings of the Ministry and Parliament in London received full
coverage in the American press. Place names, besides commemorating
British heroes or victories of the moment, reflected the names of members of the royal family (derivatives of Charlotte, Caroline, George,
William, and York, for example) or places familiar to settlers from the
British Isles. This British omnipresence, accepted unquestioningly and
even eagerly in 1750 by virtually all the colonists, formed a large
portion of their sense of identity. Could it be wiped out? If so, how?
And what might replace it? The answer to these as yet unasked questions would be of supreme importance in understanding the transformation in American thought sure to accompany any loss of loyalty
to the English nation.

Beyond that, once the old loyalty and the allied purposes and commitments were gone, new goals would be needed. How might a new
nation (if indeed there could be such a thing—all existing nations
having their roots in some dim, prehistoric past) develop the peculiar
purposes and policies time and circumstances had imposed on Great
Britain and the other nation-states of the eighteenth century? Beginning with a relatively clean slate, what might a new nation decide to
seek for itself? What kind of government would it devise to pursue these
goals? How would it relate to the rest of the world? How would it organize its public life to supply, *de novo*, the network of obligation,
habit, loyalty, and responsibility that guided the common purposes
of any stable, self-conscious state? Of greatest practical importance,
would the former colonies become one nation or many, would they
create a common national destiny or would divisive forces produce several nations or a loose confederation? In seeking answers to
these questions (itself a task requiring profound efforts in political and
social philosophy), what reformulations or new directions would be
indicated or mandated in other areas of thought? The more or less
overt, explicit effort to answer the political questions, and to understand their projections into other fields, seriously engaged American
intellectuals and concerned the American public from 1775 to 1789,

when "the creation of the American Republic," in Gordon Wood's phrase, took place.

But more was needed. A new symbolic loyalty, statements of national purpose, and even new constitutions were formal, mere skeletons, bones without flesh and blood. To *mean* something, a nation had to have a distinctive character, its people had to exhibit particular qualities, to travelers from abroad they had to convey a special impression that could be called American. Most ancient nations, from Japan to Ireland and from Russia to Ethiopia, had distinctive characters coloring the habits and attitudes of their peoples and giving distinctive attributes to their moral, intellectual, and aesthetic lives. What, then, would the character of this new nation be, and what would its people be like? What sense of the national future, the valued personality, economic growth, aesthetic tastes, and relationship to the environment would guide and inspire its development? Preachers, writers, philosophers, political leaders, and artists would be obsessed with these questions during the years of new nationhood. The effort to discover or create answers to them would constitute the first definitions of the American mind. The nature and widening significance of these successive, overlapping revolutions of loyalty, of purpose, and of character is the story of the growth of American thought from the dependence on Great Britain necessary before Wolfe's decisive victory at Quebec in 1759 to the national self-confidence that came with Jackson's equally decisive victory at New Orleans in 1815.

II

The Revolution in
Loyalty

JOHN ADAMS asserted in 1818 that "The [American] Revolution was effected before the war commenced. The Revolution was in the minds and hearts of the people; a change in their religious sentiments, of their duties and obligations." This statement is often cited to show that no real social change accompanied the American Revolution, that it was *merely* a change in national allegiance, but Adams meant to stress rather than to diminish the profundity of the Revolution. To him the change from the condition of his youth, when "the people of America had been educated in an habitual affection for England as . . . a kind and tender parent," to that of his manhood, when "they found her a cruel bedlam," signified a *"radical change in the principles, opinions, sentiments, and affections of the people [that] was the real American Revolution."* What Adams saw in his old age was the deep, pervading nature of national loyalty in the life of a people. In 1756, as a young lawyer in Worcester, Massachusetts, still near enough to the French and Indian frontier to fear actual attack, he wrote of the "brave, . . . expensive and very formidable preparations" of Britain to thwart French invasion and "to humble the insolent Tempers, and aspiring Prospects of that ambitious and faithless Nation." He remembered in old age that he had "rejoiced that I was an Englishman and gloried in the name of Briton" as he watched the armies of Wolfe and Amherst march through Worcester. John Adams was for one-quarter of his long life English to the core.[1]

To relinquish this affection and pride would be for him, as for many of his compatriots, a traumatic experience. His legal training had taught him to revere the English common law as the foundation of human liberty, and to admire, following Montesquieu, the balanced structure of British government as the surest bulwark against tyranny ever devised. His Christian education taught him that England, the land from which Elizabeth had repelled the Spanish Armada and William of Orange had defeated the Papist legions of Louis XIV, was the defender of the Reformation against the superstitions, tyranny, and cruelty of Rome. To a Puritan this was the central fact of two centuries of Western history. Furthermore, to one with Adams' strong sense of the complexity of human society and of man's need for symbols, ceremony, and such paraphernalia, the rituals of nationality were not mere show and pomp; they were rather the indispensable means whereby a *community* expressed its *common* feelings and offered obedience to the traditions and institutions that permitted civilized survival.[2]

Also part of Adams' bone-deep English consciousness was the love of a cultured man for the homeland of his spiritual and intellectual heroes. For him, Shakespeare, Bacon, Milton, Bunyan, Locke, Newton, and Pope had expressed, in matchless English, the ideas and values that gave meaning and purpose to his life. Without them he would be empty and adrift, and they seemed disembodied apart from the "blessed realm" of England where they had lived and died. To John Adams in 1758, to call himself an Englishman was no mere pledge of allegiance; it was to have a purpose, to revere a tradition, to possess a culture—indeed, it was his self-identity. Though Adams, as an exceptionally learned and thoughtful man, had a rare depth of intellectual commitment, an equally meaningful attachment, however subconscious and unarticulated, pervaded in some degree all levels of the colonial population. The revolution in the mind and heart of John Adams, from his exultation over the deeds of Pitt and Amherst in the 1750s to his bitter denunciations of Lord North and George III in the 1770s, is in microcosm a record of the traumatic change in loyalty, of the cultural bereavement, occasioned by the repudiation of English nationality.

Though John Adams was of the fifth generation of his family to live in Braintree, Massachusetts (where his ancestor, Henry Adams, had settled in 1638), and he proudly told George III in 1785 that he knew nothing of any English relatives, he was grown to manhood

before it ever occurred to him that he might be any less an Englishman than a resident of Bristol or Cornwall. Rather he described his
forebears as "all in the middle ranks of People in Society: all sober,
industrious, and religious"; that is, they exemplified the Puritan Ethic
taught by such Englishmen as William Perkins and John Bunyan.
Living as pious yeomen in Braintree, the Adamses supposed themselves to be fulfilling an entirely English life-style destined, they
hoped, to become characteristic for Britons on both sides of the Atlantic. The colony of Massachusetts, with relatively few non-British immigrants in 1750, felt itself peculiarly part of English history. Its
founders had been important figures in the Old World, and in coming
to the New they intended to *influence* English society, not escape
from it. There were always figures in English public life—Cromwell,
Algernon Sidney, Bolingbroke, and John Wilkes, for example—with
whom New Englanders could identify and who they could suppose
would "redirect" England onto paths entirely congenial to the men of
Massachusetts. Any sense of differing destinies, or that difficulties
could not be resolved within the realm, were products of only the ten
or fifteen years before 1776. Even Jonathan Mayhew's famous sermon
on "Unlimited Submission" in 1750, which Adams said made a "great
sensation" and was "a tolerable catechism" for future revolutionists,
was republished in England and denounced a tyranny as *potentially*
reprehensible in Old England as in New.[3]

At Harvard College, where Adams graduated in 1755, he studied
mathematics and natural philosophy under John Winthrop, an experi-
mental scientist, friend of Franklin's, and member of the Royal Society. Every aspect of this study strengthened his sense of Englishness.
At the same time, though, he listened to Mayhew's sermons and became disgusted at "a Spirit of Dogmatism and Bigotry" that harried to
death an "Arminian" minister in Braintree who had been Adams' admired tutor. After his graduation, as a fledgling teacher and apprentice
lawyer in Worcester, Adams lived among learned lawyers, physicians,
and clergymen. He read most of the books in their libraries and talked
at length about religion, history, and government—all in an English
context. Then, as a young lawyer in Boston amid the rejoicing over
the British conquest of Canada, Adams heard James Otis' stirring protest against the Writs of Assistance. Otis' arguments were disjointed

and perhaps inconsistent, but he did declare eloquently and categorically that such writs were "against the fundamental principles of
laws"; that is, they violated a higher, natural law than could be de-
creed in London and thus they had no legitimate authority. Adams left
the courtroom deeply impressed, "ready to take up arms against writs
of assistance." He later recalled as well that "the Child Independence
was born" at the moment of Otis' speech. Though Adams' recollec-
tions in old age doubtless exaggerated both the effect of Otis' speech
on him and its influence in stimulating colonial resistance to the
mother country, it seems certain a fateful issue had been raised—and
there could be no doubt of his side should he find *British* law profoundly contrary to *natural* law. It was dawning on him that national
loyalty was a complex thing which might, or might not, be in accord
with one's innermost convictions.[4]

In 1765, the year of the Stamp Act protests, Adams wrote a passion-
ate *Dissertation on the Canon and Feudal Law* (as it was titled when
reprinted in England) denouncing "a direct and formal design a foot
to enslave all America" through "an entire subversion of the whole
system of our fathers by the introduction of the canon and feudal law
into America." Adams played on the popular fear in New England of
Anglican bishops and the privileged position accorded the Established
Church in Britain, but he also invoked British tradition to resist the
schemes of the Grenville ministry: "Let us take it for granted that the
same spirit which once gave Caesar such a warm welcome, which [an-
nounced] hostilities against John till Magna Charta was signed, which
severed the head of Charles the First from his body and drove James
the Second from his kingdom . . . is still alive and active and warm in
England." In asking that "every sluice of knowledge be opened and set
flowing" to form a torrent of opposition to the iniquitous Stamp Act,
Adams called upon British radical Whig spokesmen: "The Brookses,
Hampdens, Vanes, Seldens, Miltons, Nedhams, Harringtons, Nevilles,
Sidneys, [and] Lockes." Proud of these and other writings against
British measures and of resistance throughout the colonies, he wrote in
his diary that 1765 was "a Year in which America has shown such
Magnanimity and Spirit, as never before appeared in any Country." It
was also a year such as John Adams had never seen, and would
scarcely have believed possible a few years before. He had examined
the acts of his British rulers against hallowed principles and put the

principles first in his allegiance. He still hoped the rulers would return to the principles, but he knew ultimately where he stood.[5]

Through the tumultuous decade 1765–1775 John Adams and his wife Abigail agonizingly completed the *"radical change . . . in principles, opinions, sentiments, and affections"* that constituted the first phase of the American Revolution. Events, harangues, and disquisitions combined to corrode their sense of Englishness and to nourish their sense of distinctive Americanness. When Adams defended the British perpetrators of the Boston Massacre, he did so not to save the Britons but to dignify the American cause by showing its fidelity to justice. Abigail wrote in December 1773 that "the Tea, that bainful weed is arrived" in Boston, and hoped its landing would be opposed in keeping with the flame of liberty which like lightning was "catching from Soul to Soul" throughout the colonies. A year later John wrote from Philadelphia that the experiment to "live without government" had, despite its perils, to be tried: "Let us Eat Potatoes and drink Water. Let us wear canvass, and undressed Sheepskins, rather than submit to the unrighteous, and ignominious Domination that is prepared for Us." Possessed of such convictions, the Adamses slowly recognized they were no longer loyal to England and thus were ready for the events of July 1776. When the Continental Congress adopted the Declaration of Independence, John, looking "back to the Year 1761," was "surprised at the Suddenness, as well as Greatness of this Revolution." It was the will of Heaven, it seemed, "that the two Countries should be sundered forever." He and his wife were now prepared to accept that. Though "well aware of the Toil and Blood and Treasure that it will cost us to maintain this Declaration," John saw "Rays of ravishing Light and Glory . . . [wherein] Posterity will tryumph." He could now consign himself and his family to the destiny of being *American*; he had a new loyalty.[6]

1. The Example of Benjamin Franklin

ENJAMIN FRANKLIN, FOR SIXTY YEARS A ZEALOUS ENGLISHMAN AND FOR TEN MORE A RELUCTANT, INCREASINGLY DISENCHANTED ONE, AFFORDS ANOTHER INSIGHT INTO THE TRAUMA OF LOST NATIONALITY. THOUGH FRANKLIN HAS BECOME, THROUGH THE PERSONA OF POOR Richard and the vividness of his *Autobiography*, the archetypal American, his mind and character can also be seen as the fulfillment of a "personality type" in development in England since the early days of the Reformation. Louis B. Wright has sketched for us "the middle class culture of Elizabethan England," the growth in English towns of a bourgeois class possessing attitudes of earnestness, self-help, hard work, upward mobility, and Puritan piety. Franklin's family, as he was proudly aware, came from this culture, which in England had produced men like John Bunyan and Daniel Defoe, both remembered by Franklin as of cardinal significance in his early intellectual growth. Bunyan's *Pilgrim's Progress*, sketching indelibly in clear, strong prose the qualities that sustained and those that blighted human life, was for Franklin a guide long after he had discarded Bunyan's theology. Defoe, a secularized Puritan who lived in England forty years before Franklin's time, bespoke the practical spirit of men joining together to solve community problems that later inspired Franklin's Junto in Philadelphia. Though Franklin and others stamped these qualities as "American traits," they had received mature expression by English authors and were solidly imbedded in a strand of English culture long before Franklin's birth.

[23]

I

In 1685, when Franklin's father emigrated to Boston, he brought with him a Puritan-bourgeois life-style that, as thousands of other Britons were discovering, found a most congenial environment in the New World. At the same time, despite the continuing sway of feudalism and privilege, the increasingly dominant spirit in England was that of the enterprising middle class, which, under Pitt's leadership, achieved the triumphs of the Great War for Empire. It was to this England, vigorous, expansive, Protestant, and progressive, that Franklin and other colonials gave such fierce devotion. They lived by its values, enjoyed its culture, thrived under its economics, and sustained its geopolitics. Whatever the difference between the Boston of Franklin's youth and the Philadelphia of his young manhood, as outposts of the British Empire both shared the hope and self-confidence (and arrogance) engendered by its dynamism.

For Franklin, as for most colonists with any substantial contact with the world beyond their own farms, every practical enterprise had important connections with the mother country. Franklin bought his press and typecastings from England. Most of the books he sold in his shop had been printed in England. He thus shared interests and did business with dozens of merchants in London, Bristol, and Liverpool. When he expanded his business he established partnerships in other English colonies on the mainland, and in such places as Nova Scotia and Antigua as well. As postmaster in Philadelphia he was part of a British Empire system. In 1753, when he became deputy postmaster general for North America, he received his appointment from the Crown and reported to a superior in London. At every turn, practice reinforced the commitment of precept and allegiance.

During the 1750s Franklin often revealed the substance of British loyalty. In *Observations concerning the Increase of Mankind*, written in 1751 and printed in 1755 and many times thereafter on both sides of the Atlantic, he proclaimed a heady vision of Empire destiny in North America: "What an Accession of Power to the British Empire by Sea as well as Land! What Increase of trade and Navigation! What Numbers of Ships and Seamen!" Soon the remarkable population growth in the New World would leave "the greatest Number of Englishmen . . . on this Side of the Water," where they would provide "a vast Demand

. . . for British Manufactures, a glorious Market . . . which will increase in a short Time even beyond [Great Britain's] Power of supplying, tho' her whole Trade should be to her Colonies." The government in London, therefore, if wise, would not restrain colonial growth, or even colonial manufactures, because the prosperity created at home and overseas by free expansion was infinitely greater than any that could be coaxed by a restrictive mercantilism. Franklin's Anglo-Saxon ethnocentricity even reached typical eighteenth-century heights when he complained of "Palatine Boors [German peasants] . . . swarming into our Settlements" where they might impose an "alien" culture, and of "black and tawny" races being brought to America, which otherwise might be blessed by a greater increase of "lovely White and Red" people. Though Franklin apologized that he was "partial to the Complexion of my Country [England]," he supposed "such Kind of Partiality is natural to Mankind."[1]

Franklin's loyalty to the Empire, though, was not at heart mere imperialism or bigotry. He believed in its growth because he thought that under the British flag was the best, perhaps the only, chance for free, self-reliant, and productive life to flourish. The despotic, stagnant French and Spanish colonies surrounding the rapidly growing English plantations were for Franklin and nearly all his compatriots conclusive vindication of the British system. He was sure that the fertile Mississippi Valley should be settled by independent yeomen like those in Massachusetts and Pennsylvania. "What a glorious thing it would be," he wrote George Whitefield in 1756, "to settle in that fine Country a large Strong Body of Religious and Industrious People!" He also hoped to limit luxury and privilege in the expanding settlements because they tended to reduce family size, which in turn diminished the thrift, industriousness, and self-reliance necessary for growth in freedom. He recognized, too, that slavery had no place in the development he envisioned. Any man, black or white, kept in slavery would, since he did not "benefit by his own Care or Diligence," be negligent, slothful, and dishonest. Furthermore, in addition to being oppressed and diseased themselves, slaves "perjorated the families that used them; the white Children becoming proud, disgusted with Labour, and being educated in idleness, are rendered unfit to get a Living by Industry." No conception more dominated Franklin's mind than his vision of the *kind* of people and the *kind* of settlement that should spread across the American West. Until he was sixty or so, he thought this vision possible *only* under the British flag—clearly his commitment to the flag would last only as long as he believed it stood for the virtues he sought. In countless ways the same reservation grew among his fellow colonials.[2]

Franklin's important role in intercolonial politics during the Great War for Empire further displayed both overt British patriotism and an underlying reservation. Responding to the French and Indian threat, he proposed at the Albany Congress in 1754 a "Plan of Union" comprising a "Grand Council" to be elected by the colonial assemblies and a "President General" to be appointed by the King. Legislation for defense or Indian affairs (including taxes) would be enacted by the Council and, if not vetoed by the President General or disallowed by the King, would become law and be carried out by the President General. In such a union, Franklin hoped, "the people of Great Britain and the people of the colonies would learn to consider themselves, not as belonging to different Communities with different Interests, but to one Community with one Interest, which I imagine would contribute to strengthen the whole, and greatly lessen the danger of future separations." But, in responding to a suggestion from the Royal Governor of Massachusetts that the colonial assemblies be excluded from power in the Union, Franklin made pregnant observations:

The people in the Colonies, who are to feel the immediate Mischiefs of Invasion and Conquest by an Enemy . . . are likely to be better Judges of the [armies] necessary . . . and of their own Abilities to bear the Expence, than the Parliament of England at so great a Distance. To propose taxing [the Colonies] by Parliament, and refusing them the Liberty of chusing a Representative Council . . . shows a Suspicion of their Loyalty to the Crown, or Regard of their Country, or of their Common Sense and Understanding, which they have not deserved, . . . and would be treating them as a conquered People, and not as true British Subjects.

"I look upon the Colonies as so many Counties gained to Great Britain," Franklin concluded, and asked why should it matter to "the general state, whether a merchant, a smith, or a hatter, grow rich in *Old* or *New* England?" If anything, he thought, the colonials, "who have most contributed to enlarge Britain's empire and commerce, encrease her strength, her wealth, and the numbers of her people . . .

ought rather to expect some preferment." Franklin was not inclined to be a second-class citizen.[3]

Resistance within Pennsylvania to the privileges insisted upon by Proprietor Thomas Penn and his supporters called forth an even more pointed statement of Franklin's political principles. "The People of this Province," he averred, "are generally of the middling sort, . . . chiefly industrious Farmers, Artificers, or Men in Trade; they enjoy and are fond of Freedom, *and the meanest among them* thinks he has a Right to Civility from the Greatest." To protect this freedom the people needed to elect their own legislative assembly, "by private Ballot . . . [to] best show their free Inclination and Judgment." In ridiculing the haughty, aristocratic airs of the Proprietary supporters who expected "the middling sort" to "stand cap-in-hand when they speak to the Lordlings, and *your Honour* begins or ends every sentence," Franklin showed again that a certain human dignity, a basic freedom, and even a measure of equality had become indispensable to his conception of a just society. That he still supposed Great Britain to be the bulwark of this kind of society was underscored dramatically in 1757 when he "went home" to England as agent for the Assembly to appeal to the British government for relief from the injustices of the Proprietor.[4]

In fifty years' residence in the New World, then, Franklin developed the life-style and social philosophy described so graphically in his *Autobiography*. This gave him a firm, unalterable conception of what was a good society and propelled him into a long public career to realize that vision. In the 1750s this dedication was entirely and uncritically contained within his British nationality. As "Poor Richard," the preceptor of thousands of Americans, and as the best-known colonial in England, Franklin represented the mainstream in American thought as the fateful pre-Revolutionary decades began.

II

During eighteen years (1757–1775) of almost unbroken residence in England Franklin lived in a remarkable laboratory for testing both his British loyalty and his American habits. Making his home in the city of Hume, Burke, and Dr. Johnson, Franklin embraced the social and cultural life of London. The famous writers, scientists, and politicians whose deeds and words had filled Franklin's paper in Philadelphia were now his frequent companions. He attended meetings of the Royal Society, went to Westminster Abbey to hear Handel's *Messiah*, visited the country estate of Lord Kames, traveled on the continent with the Queen's physician, received an honorary degree from Oxford, joined a coffeehouse club of political liberals, and otherwise enjoyed a society immensely richer and more cosmopolitan than any in the colonies. Nothing, he wrote in 1772, "can be more agreeable" than life in Britain. "I seldom dine at home in winter, and could spend the whole summer in the country-houses of inviting friends, if I chose it." During a brief trip to America in 1763 he wrote sentimentally to an English friend that "of all the enviable things England has, I envy most its People. . . . That little Island enjoys in almost every Neighborhood more sensible, virtuous Minds, than we can collect in ranging 100 Leagues of our vast Forests." Living in Great Britain made Franklin more aware of how much the colonies needed strong ties to the mother country to encourage "Embellishments [once] . . . the cares for the Necessaries of Life are over." To Franklin and other sophisticated colonials, primitive life had but limited appeal. Before they could throw off old loyalties or consider new ones, they had to think long and seriously about complexities of culture and nationality not easily acquired—or discarded.[5]

Along with his delight in social life, Franklin found what he hoped at first would be practical channels to work through in British politics. The great Pitt, whose wisdom, energy, and integrity had won a war, understood American interests, Franklin thought, and in both houses of Parliament there were "many . . . who are Friends to Liberty and of Noble Spirits." Franklin's strategy, then, as late as 1766, was to discourage "Excesses" in America so that the enemies of colonial freedom might be "disappointed," to support friendly ministries, and to *"thereby effectually secure* the American Interest in Parliament." His loyal predisposition caused him to underestimate, initially at least, the machinations of British politics hostile or indifferent to American interests.

His education in these political realities, however, soon began. He had not been in England a month before he heard from the president of the Privy Council, Lord Granville, the "alarming" doctrine that *"the*

King is the Legislator of the Colonies" and that his instructions "so far as relates to [the Colonies are] the *Law of the Land*." The other dominating member of the Council was "for carrying the [royal] Prerogative higher in all Respects," even in Britain. Hence, Franklin observed glumly, "one may easily conjecture what Reception a Petition concerning Privileges from the Colonies may meet from those who are known to think even the People of England have too many." Furthermore, Lord Halifax, president of the Board of Trade, had fathered one "military Government for a Colony" and thought that arrangement proper for other restless plantations. Among these "great People" who had the real power over the colonies, observed the knowledgeable Thomas Penn, "Franklin's popularity is nothing, . . . [and] he will be looked very coldly upon," whatever his fame among "electricians," moralists, and ineffectual philosopher-statesmen. Franklin slowly discovered that Penn was right and that the liberal currents of English thought so readily circulated to America, and the opinions of his enlightened friends, were far different from the attitudes of those in power. Lords, bishops, and magnates, seldom heard in Philadelphia, in London spoke loudly and acted decisively. To confront *this* England was for Franklin a traumatic and eventually transforming experience.[6]

At the same time, like a good reporter of humble origins, Franklin observed the harmful effects of the British social system. He noticed the utter degradation of the swarms of street cleaners, drovers, chimney sweeps, and footmen in London, compared with the relatively easy condition of laborers in the New World. Even starker was the contrast between the British countryside and that of America. "I have recently made a Tour through Ireland and Scotland," Franklin wrote a Connecticut friend in 1772:

In those Countries a small Part of the Society are Landlords, great Noblemen, and Gentlemen, extreamly opulent, living in the highest Affluence and Magnificence: The Bulk of the People Tenants, extreamly poor, living in the most sordid Wretchedness, in dirty Hovels of Mud and Straw, and cloathed only in Rags.

I thought often of the Happiness of New England, where every Man is a Freeholder, has a Vote in publick Affairs, lives in a tidy, warm House, has plenty of good Food and Fewel, with whole cloaths from Head to Foot, the Manufacture perhaps of his own Family. Long may they continue in this Situation! But if they should ever envy the Trade of these Countries, I can put them in a Way to obtain a Share of it. Let them with three fourths of the People of Ireland live the Year round on Potatoes and Buttermilk, without Shirts, then may their Merchants export Beef, Butter, and Linnen. Let them, with the Generality of the Common People of Scotland, go Barefoot, then may they make large Exports of Shoes and Stockings: And if they will be content to wear Rags, like the Spinners, and Weavers of England, they may make Cloths and Stuffs for all Parts of the World.

Farther, if my Countrymen should ever wish for the honour of having among them a gentry enormously wealthy, let them sell their Farms & pay rack'd Rents; the Scale of the Landlords will rise as that of the Tenants is depress'd, who will soon become poor, tattered, dirty, and abject in Spirit.[7]

In short, Franklin learned that while the surface of English society glittered and its liberal writers espoused Enlightenment ideals, the realities were often quite different. The England of his mind's eye, idealized through distance, had commanded his loyalty, but the social conditions and political views he encountered in the real England, when compared with life and thought in the colonies, were repugnant. Seen in this light, Franklin's well-documented disenchantment with England and its rulers in the ten years before 1776 becomes perfectly explicable and, in retrospect, at least, almost inevitable.

III

What then, more precisely, was the nature of Franklin's national loyalty in the 1750s, and what happened to it during the following two decades? His lodestar throughout was his vision of the future of North America: hard-working, prosperous, self-governing yeomen spreading across and cultivating the vast, immensely fertile Mississippi Valley—the same idea that transfixed every metaphysician of the American heartland from Thomas Jefferson to Frederick Jackson Turner. In Franklin's day the practical advantages as well as the emotional satisfactions of doing this under the British flag were great. England in the eighteenth century was, even her enemies agreed, the bastion of free government, obviously more fit than other nations to guide liberty-loving colonies. Also, the seeming invincibility of the Royal Navy made it the protector *par excellence* of exposed plantations far from home. Then, as a man proud of his culture and position in the universal brotherhood of learning and science, Franklin wished the colonies to be in touch with the center of Western civilization. Retaining English practices, using English institutions, and communicating with English colleagues was the obvious way to retain this connection. Altogether, the conception of a many-membered family acting cooperatively to extend what Jefferson would call an "Empire of Liberty" across the Atlantic and then across North America was overwhelmingly attractive. As long as there seemed any prospect at all that this growth might take place within the British Empire, there was no reason even to think about the perils of a new national loyalty.

Then, as Franklin lived through the Stamp Act, the Townshend Duties, the tea tax, and all the rest, he *adhered* to the *substance* of both his vision of the future and his American life-style, rather than to the *form* of his British allegiance. Back home in Pennsylvania in 1775, Franklin whistled bravely in the dark about the diligence, zeal, frugality, and industry he saw all around him—such a contrast to perfidious England, a mad shopkeeper that sought to increase its customers "by knocking them on the head; [and] of enabling them to pay their debts, by burning their houses." Such, he said, was "the difference between uncorrupted new states, and corrupted old ones." And yet, however much he admired the fortitude that could forgo three-course meals to subsist instead on "simple beef and pudding," and all the other plain virtues Poor Richard had encouraged, Franklin felt a deep loss. In willingly renouncing England, he disinherited, and thereby probably diminished, himself. Would he lose the richly furnished cultural home he had enjoyed for seventy years? Were Shakespeare and Milton, Blenheim and Wilton, Drake and Wolfe still "his" after he had forsworn allegiance to George III? In what relation would he stand to the land of his forefathers, he, the first Franklin who had ever thought for a moment about what his nationality was?[8]

IV

Winston Churchill has observed that the American colonists "had no common national tradition except that against which they were revolting." They had, self-consciously at least, no indigenous culture such as a conquered people maintain against their overlords, nor did they rebel because they had been captured by the thought of the French *philosophes* or by any other foreign ideology. No vision of a seductive new culture beckoned. If the colonials declared themselves to be no longer Britons, what were they? If they discarded the infinitude of customs, cadences, symbols, hardships, inflections, instincts, and reverences that for centuries had been England, what did they have? As the pre-Revolutionary debates show, the colonials often side-stepped this issue, at least until the Declaration of Independence, by proclaiming that they sought the rights of Englishmen as they were understood not only by Patrick Henry and Samuel Adams but by a host of men in Old England as well. And much of this claim was justified: the ideas and institutions they wanted were in large part derived from England, acquiring a distinctive American quality only gradually and often contrary to the intent of the Americans who at first pursued them. But as geography, war, pride, and logic exerted their decisive influence, Americans understood increasingly that a fast-growing people would soon project their thoughts and ideals far beyond those conceived of as being "English" in 1776. In declaring their disloyalty to Great Britain, then, Franklin and his compatriots confronted profound, pervading, momentous questions, even the asking of which, as John Adams understood, amounted to a substantial revolution.[9]

It is surprising, in retrospect, that the colonials could have become so distinct from Englishmen in Great Britain while so loudly proclaiming their own Englishness. Their failure to perceive any contradiction in their situation is largely explained by the operation of the Atlantic Ocean as a selective sieve for a hundred years or more. While it was true that what crossed the ocean—people, material, institutions, and ideas—was largely British, what reached America by no means represented a cross-section of Britain. The nobility were largely unrepresented, as was the class of the most powerful and successful men of affairs. For these Englishmen there was little motive to endure the uncertainty and hardship of migration. At the other end of the scale, the poorest, least enterprising Britons, if they knew of America at all, usually lacked the small means needed to leave home, and, more important, the self-confidence to conceive of themselves in a strange environment. The abundance of cheap land attracted many indentured servants, usually lower-class Britons, but one suspects that even the poor who came to America generally had above-average talents and initiative. Thus it seems likely that certain types of personality were found in disproportionate numbers in America simply because of the psychic and physical demands of a perilous thirty-five-hundred-mile voyage.

Furthermore, the Elizabethan and Stuart eras that spawned English exploration and settlement of the North American continent were times of extraordinary "conflict, crisis, and change," especially when compared with the rigid absolutisms that directed Spanish and French colonization. As a result, the English settlers brought with them be-wildering, contradictory instructions and intentions and experienced willy-nilly oscillations of policy and control—or lack of policy and control from home. The colonies began, for example, with such diverse preconceptions as those stated in the charter of the London Company that founded Jamestown in 1607 and those in the charter given to James Oglethorpe to found Georgia in 1732. Thus the colonists reflected the variety and tensions of a tumultuous age in English history that permitted them to think of virtually any ideology or doctrine or motivation or institution as "English."[10]

The realities of the sea passage and the needs of the New World also dictated what physical part of Great Britain would reach America. The immovability of Windsor Palace, Westminster Abbey, and Warwick Castle had an immeasurable impact on the way the im-migrants thought of themselves and their place in society. Without these familiar, imposing, perhaps intimidating structures, would men develop a different social and political philosophy? However much affluent colonials might yearn for the costly, the elegant, the superfluous, the paucity of shipboard space and the needs of New World enterprises dictated that they import the compact and the utilitarian. Thus, though Gainsborough paintings, Chippendale chairs, and Wedgwood china often crossed the Atlantic, compared with the fine houses of England, the houses of American gentlemen were sparcely furnished indeed. It was simply impossible to transplant en masse the luxurious paraphernalia of a hereditary nobility to plantations filling with yeo-men and artisans. Instead, a whole range of New World artifacts and landscape gradually appeared, producing such contrasts as, say, the planned elegance of St. James Park and the utilitarian disorder of the Boston Common.

Institutions underwent a no less profound, if less visible, change in crossing the Atlantic. Despite the determination of doctors, lawyers, printers, merchants, soldiers, and farmers to work by English stan-dards, new practices soon evolved. The guilds, traditions, habits, and privileges that dictated, often in anachronistic detail, occupational conduct in Great Britain did not exist in America, and efforts to transplant them proved largely unsuccessful. Certain usages woven into the fabric of English society were insupportable when removed from it. Doctors and lawyers soon found themselves detached from time-honored practices and restraints—luckily, as it proved, because the needs of their patients and clients were often different in the New World. Thus, again, novelty, improvisation, and unexpected possibilities became part of everyday experience. Mental habits resulted that had an incalculable significance for the development of the American mind. Whether desired or not, and only slowly recognized, everyday life in the colonies differed considerably from that in England, a fact that both explains much about emerging patterns of American thought and makes the coming of the American Revolution believable even amid the almost frantic continuing affirmations of Englishness.

2. The Great Awakening and Colonial Loyalties

RELIGIOUS BELIEF AND PRACTICE IN THE COLONIES ESPECIALLY RE-FLECTED THE SENSE OF ILL-DEFINED NEWNESS BECAUSE THERE WAS A WIDESPREAD, SELF-CONSCIOUS INTENTION TO DEPART FROM ENG-LISH ORTHODOXY. IN MOST OF NEW ENGLAND PURITAN "DISSENTERS" BECAME established. In two other colonies, Pennsylvania and Rhode Island, the memory of recent persecution was so vivid, and the implications of the privacy of conscience so faithfully accepted, that practices of religious toleration and diversity developed far beyond anything known or con-doned in Britain. Even in Virginia, where an Anglican Establishment received zealous official support, the position of the Church was unde-fined and tenuous compared with the deep roots of parson and parish in English country life. By 1750 religion in the colonies was vigorous and diversified, with habits of independence that were the continuing despair of emissaries sent by the Archbishop of Canterbury to assess the state of his Church in America.

I

The whole experience of the Great Awakening reveals its unpre-dictable qualities. Though it was part of a broad phenomenon also embracing German Pietism and English Methodism, and though George Whitefield's evangelistic tours were importantly stimulated by Europeans, its impact in America was far greater than in Great Brit-ain. In England John Wesley, as much as Whitefield or Tennent, preached the doctrine of personal salvation, but he could not conceive

[35]

of Christ's Church disembodied from the Church of England, while in America new churches, new branches, new synods, and new sects seemed to appear, as it were, every day. Indeed, the radicalism and enthusiasm of the Awakening, let loose in the New World, had a profound effect on the coming and course of the American Revolution itself.[1]

The essence of the Great Awakening, as Jonathan Edwards made clear in a series of powerful sermons and tracts, was a total dependence on what he called "the Holy Affections"—the transforming outpourings of the Holy Spirit. Edwards developed a radical extension of the empirical philosophy of John Locke that accounted for, and justified, his own traumatic experiences of "saving Grace." He held that "seeing God" and "feeling the Holy Spirit" were simply the most important of the sense impressions Locke argued were responsible for human growth. Thus he confronted his congregation in Northampton, Massachusetts, with the most vivid images of the terrible torments awaiting "Sinners in the hands of an angry God" and the ineffable joys infused by "the divine and supernatural light." The effect was remarkable. In the Connecticut Valley in the 1730s Edwards' graphic words moved whole congregations to alter their conduct and, ultimately, to reconsider their own nature and the nature of the society in which they lived. True "religious affections," Edwards argued, consisted of a sense, every moment, of God's presence and an infinite joy in doing His will. Without this sense, no more deductible through logic than the taste of honey can be described in words, a man would certainly be ineffectual, aimless, conventional, doomed. But once impressed with "the nature and necessity of our new birth," a great "work of redemption" was possible both in the individual and in society at large. The great evil for Edwards was "Arminianism," the comfortable theology of free will and spiritual self-help that encouraged men to be satisfied with themselves and their society as it was. This complacency, dominant in the Anglican Church, had already raised "wickedness of almost every kind . . . to the utmost extremity" in England, and would, unless the colonials were redeemed and vigilant, spread in America as well.[2]

In the next decade, as Whitefield preached to thousands upon thousands from Georgia to New England, as the Tennents evangelized the middle colonies, and as Samuel Davies and others broke in upon the complacent Anglicanism of the South, the colonies experienced their first mass, unifying movement. Congregationalists, Presbyterians, Baptists, and even some dissident Anglicans from Carolina, New Jersey, and Connecticut, inspired by the Great Awakening, joined "to make up a party for Jesus Christ" and proclaimed that all "particular churches, that are true Churches, make one general Church." Though this proposal might seem at first a reversion to the less diversified religious life guided in Great Britain by the Church of England, the basis of communion had been utterly altered. Ritual, tradition, nationalism, and inherited status had nothing to do with membership in the church of Whitefield and Edwards. A personal experience of the Holy Spirit, a commitment to the Kingdom of God, and a daily life of faith and charity were the vital, interconnected qualities. To one thus pledged (or "saved"), the work of the Kingdom was of transcending importance. Money, job, convention, parish, town, and state became matters of relative indifference subject to the transformations spiritual life would work upon them. And in the unfinished landscape and free air of the colonies the ferment produced by this radical doctrine had abundant opportunity to work.[3]

In 1740 Gilbert Tennent set the tone for a generation of evangelical assaults on comfortable, established parishes with his often preached and often printed sermon "The Danger of an Unconverted Ministry." He used the text "Woe unto You, Scribes and Pharisees, Hypocrites; for ye are like whited Sepulchres, which indeed appear beautiful outward, but are within full of dead Bones, and of all Uncleanness. Even so ye also appear righteous unto Men, but within ye are full of Hypocrisy and Iniquity." Tennent scorned the "cold, . . . sapless, unaffecting" discourses of the "Pharisee-Teachers" who, he alleged, cared more for their sinecure and their "hundreds of pounds per annum" than for the souls of their flocks. In characteristically graphic images, he thundered that "these Caterpillars labour to devour every green Thing, . . . [and] for all their long Prayers and other pious Pretenses, had their Eyes, with *Judas*, fixed upon the Bag." He accused Old Side Presbyterians (opponents of the Great Awakening) and other parish holders of spending their time at synod meetings talking of money, business, personalities, and organization.

"The minister's heart," Edwards insisted, must be "united to the people, not for filthy lucre or any worldly advantage, but with a pure benevolence to them, and desire to their spiritual welfare and prosper-

ity, and complacence in them as children of God and followers of
Christ Jesus." On Augustan rationalism, Edwards was sarcastic: the
"Ostentation of a very generous Charity" that granted that great spiritual leaders such as Luther, Calvin, Ames, and Hooker "did pretty
well for the day in which they lived," but that they "fondly embraced
. . . the most absurd, silly, and monstrous opinions, worthy of the
greatest contempt of gentlemen possessed of that noble and generous
freedom of thought, which happily prevails in this age of light and
inquiry." The great sin to Edwards was the smug rationalism that
belittled religious enthusiasm, that supposed men could gradually improve themselves and assumed existing society afforded reasonable sur-
roundings for such amelioration. Set beside this, the zeal and communal
millennialism of the Great Awakening seems very radical indeed.[4]

II

Insofar as Tennent, Edwards, and other preachers of the Great
Awakening invoked the prophetic voice of Judeo-Christianity, they
were within an ancient tradition and one which their contemporary,
John Wesley, bespoke in England. Their transcendental epistemology
had been extolled by poets, mystics, and philosophers around the
world from time immemorial. But the exceptional fervor of the out-
burst in the colonies in the 1730s and 1740s, and the deep and lasting
impact it had on American religious practices and institutions, revealed
again the malleable, unpredictable quality of life in the New World.
Though the Awakening had passed its peak by 1750, the receptivity to
change and the sense of communion of those who had experienced it
remained, and in the 1760s and 1770s, when Americans debated *national* loyalty and *political* purpose, the continuing impact of their
earlier religious ferment was everywhere evident. Tens of thousands
were used to the idea that a "New Birth" was possible, and even
necessary, and that old ways and formalities counted for but little in
the grand scheme of things. If, as Edwards once mused, the Kingdom
of God seemed destined to come first to New England, the founding
of a new nation might not be so impossible a task after all.

American evangelicals had, in fact, transformed the substance of
religious discourse. For example, they infused the word "union" with
the deep, spiritual meaning of community, communion in Christ's

kingdom on earth. Compared to this conception, Franklin's Albany Plan of Union, for example, seems mechanical, utilitarian, or additive —mere political dexterity. Edwards proclaimed:

How beautiful would it be for multitudes of Christians, in various parts of the world, by *explicit agreement*, to unite. . . . *Union* is one of the most *amiable* things that pertains to human society; yea, it is one of the most beautiful and happy things on earth, which indeed makes earth most like heaven. God has made of one blood all nations of men, to dwell on all the face of the earth; hereby teaching us this moral lesson, that it becomes mankind all to be united as one family. . . . A *civil* union, or an harmonious agreement among men in the management of their secular concerns, is amiable, but much more a pious union, and sweet agreement in the great business for which man was created, . . . even the business of religion; the life and soul of which is LOVE.

Inspired by such a glorious vision, preachers and hearers alike were willing to break the merely formal bonds of church organization. Indeed this was done in such numbers that alarmed established ministers warned parishioners that "you have no liberty, no right, to forsake the communion of our churches . . . you cannot do it without breaking the covenant . . . and incurring the awful guilt of schism."[5]

The Great Awakening ("New Light") preachers, then, were setting a noble ideal of a spiritual union in faith and love above temporal associations of existing churches and the parochial boundaries of individual colonies. Following them, tens of thousands of Americans had the experience of responding to "a higher calling," infinitely more precious, they were told, than the old, familiar institutional patterns. The obvious projection to the political realm, as the question of breaking the old bonds with Great Britain in order to form "a more perfect union" came to the fore, was not lost on the heirs of Edwards and Whitefield. To them, the great Continental fast day of July 20, 1775, when "not, perhaps, less than two millions of intelligent beings . . . engaged in the same public acts of religious worship," was the most glorious day of the Revolution. Six months later a follower of Edwards' hoped "that the dragon will be wholly consumed and destroyed; that . . . tyranny, persecution, and oppression, may be forever abolished; . . . that peace, liberty and righteousness might universally prevail; . . . and the kingdom of our God, and the power of Christ might be established to all the ends of the earth." In the middle of the war a zealous evangelical who had been a chaplain at Bunker Hill and Ticonderoga predicted that America would become "IMMANUEL's land, a Mountain of Holiness, a Habitation of Righteousness! The Lord's spiritual Empire of Love, Joy, and Peace will flourish gloriously in this Western World!" By 1776, then, Union had come to mean for many a grand, redemptive communion merging religious and political ideals that would, as in the Jeffersonian and Jacksonian movements, surge irresistibly beyond mechanistic balance-of-power concepts to seek a blessed life for all men. The New World seemed somehow to welcome and make practical such millennial dreams.[6]

Great Awakening rhetoric also affected the Revolution by projecting its vehement assaults on sin beyond the usual condemnations of "wantonness," debauchery, drunkenness, and "chambering." New Light ministers increasingly identified sin with the comfortable, privileged elements of society, focusing on the materialism of their way of life and their self-satisfied, rational religion. How could such smug people possibly be instruments for the strenuous crusade to bring about God's kingdom on earth, they asked. Using a text from Judges, "Curse ye Meroz, Curse ye bitterly the inhabitants thereof because they came not to the help of the Lord against the Mighty," preachers soon scolded not only those indifferent to community sin but those slow to support the Revolution as well. Denunciations of Toryism thundered from hundreds of pulpits in metaphors of sin familiar to congregations for a generation or more. "How provoking in the sight of God," Nathaniel Whitaker of Salem, Massachusetts, exclaimed, "is it to see some quite unconcerned for the good of the public, rolling in ease, amassing wealth to themselves, and slyly plotting to assist our enemies." In case anyone missed the point, these "idle spectators" were linked in infamy with "Pharaoh, Saul, Manasseh, Antiochus, Julian, Charles I . . . and George III."[7]

III

The Baptist revival in Virginia in the 1760s and 1770s showed further how evangelical churches projected their spiritual concerns into the temporal sphere and in the process developed a revolutionary social philosophy. Robert Semple, the historian of Virginia Baptists and himself a participant in the revivals, tells of confrontations in Chesterfield and King and Queen Counties about 1770:

Not infrequently the leading men would attend Baptist meetings, and would enter into arguments with the preachers: they insisted that their church was the oldest, and consequently the best: that their ministers were learned men, and consequently most competent to interpret scripture: that the better sort, and well-informed, adhered to them, whilst none, or scarcely any except the lower order, followed the Baptists: that they were all in peace and friendship before the coming of the Baptists; but now their houses and neighbourhoods were filled with religious disputes.

The Baptist preachers replied:

If the higher ranks in society did not countenance them, it was no more than what befell their master and his inspired apostles: that rich men in every generation, with some few exceptions, were enemies to a pure gospel: but that God had declared that he had chosen the poor of the world to be rich in faith: that it was true that most of their preachers were unlearned, yet that they had evidences that they were called to the ministry by the will of God: that this was the most essential qualification of a minister, the want of which all the learning of the schools could not supply. The Baptist preachers would often retort their own inconsistencies upon them: that while they professed to be Christians, they indulged themselves in the violation of most of the Christian concepts: that their communion was often polluted by the admission of known drunkards, gamesters, swearers, and revellers: that even their clergy [had not been born again]: that their public discourses were nothing more than moral addresses, such as a pagan philosopher, unassisted by the Bible, could have composed. . . . Most of the ministers of the establishment were men of classical and scientific educations, patronized by men in power, connected with great families, supported by competent salaries, and put into office by the strong arm of civil power. Thus pampered and secure, the men of this order were rolling on the bed of luxury.

These issues drawn in Virginia, of course, were much the same as those that had divided New England thirty years earlier: the complacent, learned, established Arminians on one side and the fervent, radical, populist evangelicals on the other side.

When persecution of the Baptists followed the "defeat" of the established spokesmen in debate, according to Semple, "the celebrated Patrick Henry, being always the friend of liberty . . . without hesita-

gentry style – loose-living [Anglican Clergy]

tion stepped forward to" defend the harassed clergymen. With "the power of God," the voice of Henry, and the bad example of the Anglican clergy on their side, the Baptists considered that they had accomplished "an important ecclesiastical revolution" as the Established Church crumbled during the political revolution of 1776. The Baptists saw close links between the two movements: the Established Church was "an inseparable appendage of Monarchy; one of the pillars by which it was supported. The dissenters . . . were republican from interest as well as principle; it was known that their influence was great among the common people; and the common people in every country are, more or less, republicans."[8]

Rhys Isaac has shown how the Baptist movement offered a profound challenge to the dominant social structure and mores of colonial Virginia—what he calls "the gentry style." This can be described as a "code of honor" where men had to prove their prowess, display their authority, and exhibit a kind of competitive self-assertion in every social exchange. The enormous vogue of horse-breeding, horse-racing, and cock-fighting rested upon these values, and even such things as the way the gentry strode ostentatiously into church, how they danced and caroused on court day, revealed the pridefulness and hauteur that pervaded gentry life—and was aped by the lower classes. These customs and values often implied aggression, hostility, and violence: horse races ended in challenges to duels, dances in near-rape, and elections in brawls. Slavery was both the root of the mores and the ultimate manifestation of the domineering style.[9]

The Baptists saw this entire complex of habits and attitudes as sinful and un-Christian, a mockery of the gospel of Jesus and the spirit of His church as described in the Acts of the Apostles. In contrast, they extolled humility, sobriety, equality of estimation (even for blacks), feelings of communion rather than competition, and a certain asceticism. To be "converted" meant not only to accept the theology of contrition, redemption, and salvation, but also to reject the sinful gentry ways and live in the new communion. John Leland called upon poor farmers to exchange the life of debt, excess, privation, and violence for one among "a congregation of faithful persons, called out of the world by divine grace, who mutually agree to live together, and execute gospel discipline among them." That such a spirit and such a community of faith gravely challenged the dominant culture is evident in the remark of a Loudoun County gentleman that the increasing Baptist influence was "quite destroying pleasure in the Country for they encourage ardent Prayer; strong and constant faith, and an intire Banishment of Gaming, Dancing, and Sabbath Day Diversions."[10]

In proclaiming such a deep chasm between themselves and the loose-living gentry society ministered to by the Anglican clergy, Virginia Baptists had formulated a social theory and an ideal for everyday life that was deeply radical. Their sense of purity within their own communion exemplified the idea of spiritual union Edwards had preached for so long. Their conviction that conventional society was hopelessly corrupt and un-Christian made it easy for them to take a revolutionary stance when the time came to challenge British authority. They were formulating, too, ultimate loyalties that allowed them to countenance loss of their British (Anglican) allegiance—indeed required them to set it aside unless it purged itself of iniquity—for to be "awakened" or "born again" meant to be willing to set aside *any* conventions or institutions and to seek instead a society transformed in its habits, values, and relationships.

IV

Though some evangelical ministers criticized the increasingly political tone of sermons during the 1770s, others set forth for their listeners some of the qualities of the Kingdom of Heaven on earth. To men propelled into political discourse by concern for the sins of greed and indifference, the Lockean concepts of "convenience" and of trusting the public good to the effects of enlightened self-interest (extended to economics by Adam Smith and others) were anathema. "Pirates and gangs of robbers," observed Nathaniel Niles in 1774, could "live in a kind of unity" if government, as argued, had as its main purpose the protection of personal property. In the *Treatise on Religious Affections* Edwards had insisted that mere prudential or intellectual adherence to a church was worthless and that only a heart-felt love, subsuming all a man's energy and transforming his every motive and impulse, was acceptable in God's sight. A similar commitment would be necessary politically, Niles insisted, because "just so far as [man's] affection is turned on private interest, he will become regardless of the common good, and when he is detached from the community in heart, his services will be very precarious at best." To those inspired by a vision of virtuous men in holy communion with one another, mechanistic, utilitarian, and, to them, ultimately cynical notions of public life and nationality would seem barren.[11]

Facing the difficult question of how to make political decisions, Awakened preachers persisted in their scorn for the Establishment. Persons of "a disinterested benevolent spirit," Niles felt, were generally "found among the lower classes of mankind, . . . [and only] a very small proportion of them among the great." In the will of the unpretentious majority, therefore, would most often be found the virtue essential to good government. These same preachers and their congregations, long convinced that true virtue consisted in the effects of the Holy Spirit spreading among the people, had no difficulty in discarding conventional wisdom about prerogative, aristocracy, and property. These hallowed props of stability, public morality, integrity, and national honor had no positive place in the evangelical vision of the good society—indeed, as zealous ministers increasingly pointed out, their effect seemed overwhelmingly prejudicial to God's purposes.

Though there was no tendency to equate majority rule with the general welfare or to disregard the possibility that cunning demagogues could mislead the masses, the heirs of the Great Awakening had sure grounds for turning expectantly *toward* "the people" as they discerned so vigilantly the greed and smugness of "the great." These perspectives, poured forth from hundreds of pulpits as waves of religious excitement surged through a new nation in search of new loyalties, had a profound if somewhat amorphous effect on the public philosophy.

V

The major public effect of the Great Awakening came directly, in ministers' exhortations to their congregations, but evangelical doctrines and rhetoric were also evident in the attitude of scores of the political leaders who had been influenced by New Light preaching. Patrick Henry, for example, came from a family divided and profoundly affected by the appearance of Whitefield in Hanover County, Virginia, in 1745. Henry's grandfather, Isaac Winston, had turned away from the staid Anglicanism preached by Henry's uncle in the local parish church, and Henry's mother had joined a Dissenting congregation. Patrick himself, as a boy of ten, probably heard Whitefield preach to a crowd so large that no church could hold it. More significantly, the eloquent Samuel Davies preached near Henry's home from the future revolutionist's eleventh to twenty-third year. Henry went regularly to Davies' services with his mother, repeating to her, as the family remembered, the text and substance of the sermon as they rode home in the gig. He always insisted, even after listening to the great speakers of the Revolutionary era, that Davies was the finest orator he had ever heard.[12]

Echoes of Davies' rhetoric abound everywhere in Henry's own speeches. The evangelical tone, the capacity to move men emotionally, the fervent commitment to a cause were hallmarks of Davies' style imitated by Henry. After seeing Davies "screw up the people to the greatest heights of religious-Phrenzy," as Henry's uncle reported ruefully to his superiors, young Patrick was made aware of the influence such oratory could have on an audience. Henry's famous exhortation to the Hanover volunteers, marching in May 1775 to confront Lord Dunmore, had overtones throughout of Davies' sermons twenty years earlier to Virginia troops going to war against the French. Davies had proclaimed "To Arms! . . . when ambition and avarice would rob us of our property . . . when they would enslave the free-born mind, and compel us meanly to cringe to usurpation and arbitrary power," while Henry asked "that God, who in former ages had hardened Pharaoh's heart . . . might show forth his power and glory in the redemption of his chosen people." The curses of Jeremiah called down by Davies on the heads of the French and Indians were invoked, almost verbatim, against the British by Henry in his "Give me liberty, or give me death" speech.

Henry also echoed evangelical rhetoric in 1763 while resisting efforts of Anglican clergymen to annul Virginia's Two-Penny Act. By thus trying to maintain their exorbitant salaries in times of hardship for the people, Henry charged, "instead of useful members of the state, they ought to be considered enemies of the community, . . . [and] very justly deserved to be punished with signal severity." Following this logic (as dozens of New Light preachers were doing), Henry observed that a king who would disallow such a "salutary" act as the Two-Penny one, "authenticated by the only authority which could give force to them for the government of this colony, . . .

degenerates into a tyrant and forfeits all right to his subjects' obedience."

The fervor, the defiance of the established order, and the invocation of the wrath of God that Davies and others had preached in the Virginia countryside had prepared Henry's audience to respond to appeals to take up arms against the enemies of righteousness. Though he later became a defender of state-supported religion, during the Revolution Patrick Henry's words and style of leadership derived from Whitefield and Davies and the Baptist churches' struggle for liberty of conscience under the colonial Establishment.

Samuel Adams also reflected the political effects of the Great Awakening. He came from a Puritan family that had long resisted the strong eighteenth-century tendencies toward secularism and "loose morals." At Harvard College in 1740 he experienced the Great Awakening, as brought by George Whitefield, that caused "Voices of Prayer and Praise" to be heard everywhere in students' rooms. His first wife, Elizabeth, was the daughter of the Reverend Samuel Checkley (1696–1769), minister of New South Church, which his family attended. Checkley was a moderate New Light who opened the New South pulpit to Whitefield in 1740 and again in 1745. His own sermons were said to be "serious, affecting, scriptural, plain, and useful," qualities notable in Samuel Adams' own character. Like Henry, Adams was early exposed to fervent New Light preaching, and though he seems to have been neither a close student of divinity nor a religious enthusiast, he was always a churchgoer and deserved his reputation as a man of faith and piety.[13]

In his public career Adams repeatedly linked political liberty with the need for moral regeneration, a revival of the spirit of the people, and a return to what he regarded as the religious purity of the first days of New England. John C. Miller has remarked that "Adams hoped to do by means of a political revolution what George Whitefield had done through a religious awakening." That is, he sought to stir and mobilize the people to resist evil, protect liberty, and create a godly, virtuous society. In his first attempts at political propagandizing (1748–1749) he deplored the moral decay in New England that he feared would bring in its train the "degeneracy" of "our Constitution, and our Liberties." Adams agreed with the followers of Edwards that "neither the wisest constitution nor the wisest laws will secure the liberty and happiness of a people whose manners are universally corrupt." Moreover, like Gilbert Tennent, Adams aimed barbs at the haughty, self-satisfied rich: "He that despises his neighbor's happiness because he wears a worsted cap or a leather apron, he that struts immeasurably above the lower size of the people, and pretends to adjust the rights of men by the distinctions of fortune" was not loyal to the public good.[14]

Through the crises of the Stamp Act and the Townshend Acts Adams drummed home the argument that Great Britain intended to debauch the colonies from the simple, pious ways of their forefathers: "Nothing but FRUGALITY can now save the distressed Northern colonies from impending ruin"; and five years later: "The religion and public liberty of a people are so intimately connected, their interests are interwoven, and cannot exist separately"; and in April 1776: "Our Enemies have made it an object to eradicate from the minds of the people in general a Sense of true Religion and Virtue, in hopes thereby the more easily to carry their Point of enslaving them." The same year he reminded Americans how their ancestors "threw off the Yoke of Popery in Religion" and exhorted them as well, in the spirit of Cromwell, to inaugurate the "reign of political Protestantism." In 1778, worried about the spirit of avarice in Boston and an "expensive entertainment" that had closed a militia review, he declared, "Luxury and Extravagance are in my opinion totally destructive of those virtues which are necessary for the Preservation of the Liberty and Happiness of the People." Adams' orations during the Revolution echoed, just as did Patrick Henry's, the cadences, the concerns, and the doctrines of the New Light preachers.[15]

This strain was so evident in Adams' character that friends and enemies alike took note of it. According to Tory Peter Oliver he always had "a religious mask" ready for his appeals to the people. Oliver even charged that Adams used the "good Voice and [mastery] of vocal Music" he had learned at New South Church to "inculcate Sedition among the Mechanicks" of Boston, whom he formed into "singing Societys." When Adams died, his fellow Jeffersonian, the Reverend William Bentley of Salem, wrote in his diary that Adams "preserved the severity of Cato in his manners, and the dogmatism of a priest in his religious observances." In his fervent, moralistic tone, in his insistence that virtue underlay any hope of a better society, and in his linking of "true religion" with political liberty, Samuel Adams reflected the doctrines and epistemology of the evangelical preachers he so often heard throughout his life. Though his announced ends were political, he never doubted their necessary connection with the piety and virtue of the people and thus had no trouble at all making common cause with the followers of Whitefield and Edwards.[16]

VI

Curiously, the evangelical preachers who spoke for separation from Great Britain and for new republican ideals were vehement critics of the rational clergymen, such as Jonathan Mayhew, often regarded as the religious spokesman for the American Revolution. Charles Chauncy focused upon this controversy in 1743 when he repudiated the transforming, millennial vision of colonial society that Jonathan Edwards had set forth in "Some Thoughts Concerning the Present Revival of Religion in New England." Chauncy was the complete Arminian, confident that reason was man's only sure guide in religion as well as in politics, comfortable in a congregational system that assured an established religion in a community, and content that social and political affairs be improved gradually as best decent men could in an admittedly imperfect society. He was, in short, humane, progressive, and liberal, convinced that the "ravings" of Edwards and his ilk arose "from Pride, Ignorance, Prejudice, Heat and Strength of Imagination." The followers of Whitefield, according to Chauncy's coworker Jonathan Mayhew, were "enlightened Idiots [who] impute all their ravings and follies and wild imaginations to the spirit of God; and usually think of themselves as *converted*, when the poor, unhappy creatures are *only out of their wits*."[17]

The dispute between the evangelicals and the rationalists (or New Lights and Old Lights, as they were called during the Great Awakening) was usually cast in doctrinal terms of "Calvinist versus Arminian," but the underlying issues were over epistemology and modes of social change. The rationalists, following the conventional interpretation of Locke, patiently gathered evidence and studied it reasonably to discover both religious truth and ways to improve human society. Their sermons were dispassionate, logical, and restrained in their promises for the future. They were often critical of existing society and were quick to challenge invasions of political or religious liberty, but they also accepted and defended the established order, both because their outlook was resolutely gradualist and because they themselves, by mid-eighteenth century, were well entrenched. Chauncy, for example, was minister of First Church in Boston for more than a half a century. In many respects the rationalists fitted the classic mold of liberals seeking a better future one step at a time, resentful of those who, foolishly and harmfully, distracted attention from these possible short steps by wild rhetoric and impractical visions.

To the evangelicals such a posture amounted to smug hypocrisy; it denied the Holy Spirit, the work of redemption, and true virtue. In adhering to empirical epistemology, the "Arminian" clergymen mistook the nature of religion and barred themselves and their followers from any real experience of God's grace. Thus the evangelicals and the rationalists debated the eternal question of whether mystical, suprarational, supernatural, transcendental experiences were or were not real. With different doctrinal substance, the issue arose fifty years later between Emerson and the Harvard Unitarians, one hundred years later between William James and C. S. Pierce, and a hundred and fifty years later between Reinhold Niebuhr and John Dewey. Benjamin Rush appreciated the political value of the spiritual when he wrote in 1802 that it seemed impossible to "produce political happiness by the solitary influence of human reason." He declared that only evangelical religion "affords *motives*; . . . agreeable, powerful, and irresistible . . . to induce mankind to act" upon the truths that might be discovered through reason. Religious experiences of the kind Edwards described so vividly not only were *real* and of transcending importance, but also provided the only firm motivation for a transformation of man and society. A century later Julia Ward Howe expressed Edwards' sense of the relation between religious affections and the commitment needed to cause real change (italics added):

> In the beauty of the lilies Christ
> was born across the sea
> With a glory in his bosom *that transfigures*
> *you and me.*
> As He died to *make men holy,*
> *Let us die to make men free.*
> His soul goes marching on. . . .

The patient rationalism of Chauncy not only could never provide such zeal, the evangelicals insisted, but its false doctrines of human nature actually delayed and stultified the vital responses.[18]

Within the context of the coming Revolution and quest for national identity, both sides of the religious debate lent substantial support to the movement for independence and nationhood, though they had profoundly different conceptions of the meaning, the potential *uses*, of these formal propositions. Thus the rationalists moved slowly toward the momentous step of renouncing a long-cherished loyalty to England and sought innumerable compromise resolutions to the crises of 1765–1776. The evangelicals were doubtless less subtle in their understanding of the complex issues at stake, but once they saw the British connection as diabolical, they condemned it utterly and moved quickly to explore revolutionary solutions. The rationalists commonly defended most of existing society as they sought to restrain this or that British oppression, while the evangelicals sought a society as radically transformed as they conceived a man to be when he experienced the Holy Spirit in his heart. These two groups, in fact, were defining the gradualist and the radical approaches to revolution, and were espousing attitudes toward national development and purpose that have remained in tension throughout American history. Both searched for ways to come to terms with the divesting of British nationality: Were the colonies to become an American version of Britain under a new flag, or was theirs a gloriously different destiny?

Jonathan Mayhew's famous sermon, *A Discourse Concerning Unlimited Submission and Non-Resistance to the Higher Powers: With some Reflections on the Resistance made to King Charles I* (1750), set forth the rationalists' view of revolution. Though less visionary than evangelical sermons, Mayhew's work was challenging enough to be "read by everybody, celebrated by friends, and abused by enemies," John Adams wrote in 1818. The argument was simple, and, by 1750, not in the least startling to a people who for a century had read Milton, Locke, Sidney, and other apologists for the Puritan and Glorious revolutions. Mayhew preached on the Apostle Paul's injunction in Romans XIII: "Let every soul be subject unto the higher powers. For there is no power but of God; the powers that be are ordained of God. Whosoever therefore that resisteth the power, resisteth the ordinance of God: and they that resist shall receive to themselves damnation." Thus using a text cited often by Christian ministers to urge obedience to earthly princes, Mayhew argued that the Apostle counseled obedience only to rulers who exercised "a reasonable and just authority for the good of human society." Rulers who "rob and ruin the public. . . . tyrants and public oppressors," were no more to be obeyed than "common *pirates* and *highwaymen*." The divine right of kings Mayhew ridiculed as "altogether as fabulous and chimerical as transubstantiation." Resistance to such a tyrant as Charles I, who "un-kinged himself" by his crimes against the people, was "a most right-eous and glorious stand made in defense of the natural and legal rights of the people against the unnatural and illegal encroachments of arbi-trary power." Such a doctrine, however legally or deferentially ex-pressed, was an unmistakable warning to would-be tyrants, and a clear call to resistance and revolution when oppression and suffering were severe and "there was no rational hope of redress in any other way." As Mayhew's paraphrasing (plagiarism, his opponents charged) of Bishop Benjamin Hoadly and other Anglican rationalists showed, he was following a line of thought familiar enough in England, but, as usual, one disproportionately dominant in America, because the tor-rent of reaction, represented in England by Falkland, Digby, Filmer, Laud, and a host of Tory High Church publicists, merely trickled across the Atlantic.[19]

Mayhew heaped his most virulent denunciations on the *religious* crimes of Charles I ("He married a French Catholic, . . . he supported that more than fiend, Archbishop *Laud*," etc.), on the "superstitions of Popery" allied with doctrines of unlimited submission, and on Bos-ton Anglicans, "very high in principles of *ecclesiastical authority*," who held up Charles I as "a great saint and a Martyr." "The true key for explaining the *mysterious* doctrine of King Charles's saintship and martyrdom," Mayhew declared, "was that he was a "good *church-man*" who died not "an enemy to *sin* but *dissenters*, who were railed against as schismatics, . . . traitors, . . . rebels, and all that is bad." Thus Mayhew had as his particular purpose not so much to remind New Englanders of their tradition of resistance to unjust civil authority as to expose the inroads of the Church of England in Boston and to set up a cry against the much-feared advent of an American bishop and other elements of an Anglican Establishment. In eighteenth-century political thought, of course, close and dangerous connections between religious and civil authority—and abuse of authority—were taken for granted.

Mayhew further revealed his moderate Whiggism by condemning Cromwell's hypocrisy, maladministration, and excessive ambition, by declaring the trial of Charles I "a mere mockery of justice," and by absolving the reigning House of Hanover from any hint that *it* was guilty of the usurpations for which the Stuarts had been rightfully deposed. He warned, also conventionally, against using liberty as a cloak for "maliciousness" or "licentiousness," or of being duped by those "who aim at *popularity* under the disguise of *patriotism*." "It is our happiness," he concluded, "to live under the government of a PRINCE who is satisfied with ruling according to law, . . . [and under whose] administration we enjoy all the liberty that is proper and expedient for us. It becomes us, therefore, to be contented and dutiful subjects."

In passing (though it did not go unnoticed), Mayhew turned his pen against his other enemies, the followers of Edwards and White-field, by equating the "absurd reveries of ancient or modern vision-aries" with the hocus-pocus of Rome. The argument of the *Discourse Concerning Unlimited Submission*, then, espoused the Lockean doc-trine of rebellion embraced by the English Whiggery, but it contained little of the ecstatic hope for a better world preached by the evangeli-cals. In fact, Mayhew was at pains to commend the Pauline doctrine of the Christian duty to obey rightful rulers. His use of such words as "proper," "fitting," and "dutiful" is a far cry from the rhetoric of the Great Awakening. The point here is not that the evangelicals dis-tracted men from earthly concerns by preaching fire, brimstone, and an unearthly kingdom, or that the rationalists were unduly subservient to the established powers, as each side was charged by its foes, but rather that both sides were, as British loyalty waned, working out differing concepts of American society. As the events of 1765–1783 proved, the concepts could often coexist and support a common program. Equally important, though, were the differing ideas, worked out in the debate over the Great Awakening in the 1740s and persisting as attention turned increasingly to politics, of the *kind* of change needed and the *nature* of the government and society that might as a result come into being.

The rationalists argued almost entirely as British subjects, seeking to maintain colonial privileges (including Congregational dominance in New England) within the Empire. The evangelicals, until shortly before 1776, showed no particular animosity toward Great Britain, but, significantly, they preached very little of Pauline obedience and they incessantly bespoke visions of a Kingdom of God on earth that required a radically altered society—whether or not the British flag waved over it. The rationalists, including Mayhew himself, continued to support the increasingly affluent and sophisticated colonial society, seeking only to prevent Jacobites, bishops, and others who were devils in Whig eyes from having power in North America. The evangelicals condemned these same devils, of course, but for being sinful in themselves rather than for merely symbolizing a counterestablishment that threatened the Congregational one in New England. The evangelical stance was less hostile to the British government as long as the sins of society were seen as permeating all levels equally, but once the followers of Edwards identified the executors of British rule as enemies of the communion of saints and the Kingdom of God on earth, they became fervent foes of Great Britain and proclaimed a vision of society far more revolutionary than that upheld by Chauncy and Mayhew.

3. Radical Whig Thought in America

JUST AS A PECULIAR OPPORTUNITY AND ORIENTATION IN RELIGIOUS THOUGHT MOVED AMERICANS, HOWEVER UNCONSCIOUSLY, TOWARD INDEPENDENCE, SO IN THE FORMULATION OF POLITICAL IDEAS THE INTERVENTION OF THE ATLANTIC OCEAN GRADUALLY NOURISHED A DIFFERENT emphasis in the British colonies. Caroline Robbins, Bernard Bailyn, and others have shown how political discourse in England during the seventeenth century furnished colonial thinkers with an array of brilliant arguments. From 1603, when Elizabeth's death and the ascension of the House of Stuart unsettled the English monarchy, through the cataclysmic events of the 1640s, to the crisis of 1688–1689, and even lingering into the dynastic changes and Jacobite rebellions of 1715 and 1745, fundamental questions of government agitated English theorists. Did kings rule by divine right? Was hereditary succession sacrosanct? What was the proper relationship between church and state? What were the rights of Englishmen? How should King, Lords, and Commons govern the Empire? Particularly, was Parliament, especially the House of Commons, to have decisive power? They even asked whether certain extralegal actions, perhaps even by throngs of "the people," were legitimate to resist tyrannical officials or governments. Britons in North America listened intently to these discussions, since the existence and nature of their unsettled plantations depended in some measure on their outcome.

I

The great source of political ideas was the debate over the very nature of English government that accompanied the epic victory of

the parliamentary forces at Westminster, on the battlefield, and in
the execution of Charles I. The words of the great parliamentary
orators—Parker, Pym, Eliot, Coke, Bacon, and Cromwell himself—
and the writings of Diggers, Levelers, and Independents—Prynne, Lil-
burne, Winstanley, and, most important, the legendary Milton—were,
to New World Puritans and others awakening to the logic of man's
quest for self-government, the words of heroes on the grand scale.
The hundreds of political pamphlets emanating from this period, especially those generated by the debates before Cromwell's army, often
reprinted (and more often quoted) as occasion required during the
next century or so, addressed such basic concepts as the nature of man,
the purpose of government, and the meaning of justice. Even during
the Restoration lull in political heroics, men wrote seriously about
continuity, order, and tradition in human society, and, most meaningfully, had a new cycle of degeneration from legislative supremacy to
military dictatorship on which to sermonize. Dozens of polemicists
cast Cromwell with Philip of Macedon and Caesar as murderers of
republican government, far worse than the most absolute sovereigns in
Europe, to say nothing of the limited English monarchs.

Then the speeches and pamphlets justifying the Glorious Revolution of 1688 furnished another round of more restrained, sophisticated
arguments resulting in the Whig orthodoxy that dominated English
thought during the eighteenth century: parliamentary supremacy, the
Protestant succession, the Bill of Rights, religious toleration under the
Anglican Establishment, and the leadership of the landed aristocracy.
Behind the polemics of the hour, readily accessible to colonial readers
of the London press, loomed the great theoretical works of Hobbes,
Harrington, Filmer, Sidney, and, of course, Locke himself. This body
of thought, added to the foundations in Thucydides, Aristotle, Cicero,
Plutarch, and Livy that Western men absorbed as they learned the
ancient languages, constituted the heritage of educated colonials from
the days of Cotton Mather and William Byrd to those of John Adams
and Thomas Jefferson.

Just as important as these original sources were the streams of elabo-
ration that flowed from English pens during the eighteenth century.
The British press, much the freest in the world, poured forth attacks,
apologies, and polemics that both gloried in the liberty already existing
in England (a chorus joined by a host of such Enlightened foreigners

as Voltaire and Montesquieu) and upbraided the Whig and Tory establishments for blocking the extension of free self-government implicit in the more radical of the seventeenth-century theorists. Writers urging this extension developed the so-called radical Whig tradition, seeking larger powers for the House of Commons, an expanded suffrage, abolition of Dissenter liabilities, wider freedom of the press, elimination of sinecures and official corruption, and the free-flowing rather than the mercantilist growth of the Empire. Gifted polemicists such as John Trenchard and Thomas Gordon (the "English Cato"), Phillip Doddridge, Isaac Watts, Benjamin Hoadly, Robert Molesworth, Francis Hutcheson, Thomas Hollis, Catharine Macaulay, Joseph Priestley, Richard Price, and James Burgh espoused these causes and influenced English thought—though they were opposed at every step by able conservatives and made only the most fleeting impressions on the stolid structure of British government.[1]

In the colonies radical Whig doctrines found a warm reception, while the opposition, in words and in social power, was but a pale reflection of its British model and somehow out of place in the New World. The arguments of Britons dissatisfied with the government of Robert Walpole, disgusted with the stagnant bigotry of Oxford and Cambridge, or frustrated by the privilege that still restrained enterprise at every turn, though but murmurs at home, in America resounded with obvious common sense, fully in tune with the needs and outlook of an unformed society. On the other hand, Tory apologetics, accepted as second nature in English rectories, country houses, and city clubs, if heard at all in America, were scorned as absurdly irrelevant. It was not that the experience of the New World generated novel thoughts unheard of in Europe; rather the New World environment proved a fertile field for testing in practice the more adventuresome notions of creative Britons. The community improvement projects Daniel Defoe proposed for English cities, for example, got nowhere at home, but Franklin, consciously using Defoe's approach and proposals, found Philadelphia ready and able to *act* on the multitude of civic enterprises suggested by the Londoner.

This pattern, evident for a century or more before the Declaration of Independence as the colonials thought about their government and social order, had produced in America a species of Briton less and less recognizable to visitors, royal officials, soldiers, and even emigrants used to the power structure and intellectual climate at home. Lord Loudoun, a tough Scottish peer with long experience of British officialdom who came to America as commander-in-chief of His Majesty's forces in 1756, found the practices and attitudes even among those zealously loyal to George II simply incomprehensible. Royal governors had been forced to give up the powers of the Crown to assemblies in return for their salaries, and the assemblies in turn catered to various ambitious interests among the people. Hence, Loudoun wrote his superiors, "there is no Law prevailing at present here, . . . but the Rule every man pleases to lay down to himself." He recommended that English authorities "pay the governors, and new model the governments," and, as long as the war with France lasted, depend only upon British regiments because "this Country will not run when the King calls." Twenty years later, another earnest official, Lord Dunmore, the last Royal Governor of Virginia, could see in the words and deeds of Patrick Henry only "a man of desperate circumstances! . . . [who] excited the People to join in . . . outrageous and rebellious Practices . . . in open Defiance of Law and Government." A section of British opinion, dominant in Westminster and Whitehall throughout the eighteenth century, had little use for doctrines of higher law and self-determination.[2]

Still, colonials seeking to extend their own self-rule (long before they had any thought of independence) were always able to invoke or quote some Briton whose views were at least as radical as their own. In 1722 Franklin concluded an attack on the Mather establishment in Boston ("hypocritical Pretenders to Religion") with a long quotation from the "English Cato" castigating "wonderful pious Persons" who were in fact "*publick Robbers*" plundering "a Fund of Subscriptions for charitable Uses." In 1735 lawyers for John Peter Zenger turned to the same *Cato's Letters* for support in their assault on the doctrine of seditious libel. Trenchard and Gordon had insisted, in an argument new in England, that truth was a sufficient defense against charges of libeling the government. James Alexander, one of Zenger's lawyers, paraphrased "Cato's" essay "Reflections on Libelling" before the court and in his account of the trial. William Livingston's *The Independent Reflector* (1752–1753), attacking privilege in government and authoritarianism in religion, was closely modeled on Trenchard and Gordon's *Independent Whig*. As noted above, Jonathan Mayhew lifted paragraphs virtually unchanged from Hoadly's *Measures of Submission to the Civil Magistrates* into his *Discourse on Unlimited Submission.* When the founders of the New Light College of New Jersey sought guidance in curriculum and educational philosophy, they received fruitful advice from Phillip Doddridge and other masters of English Dissenting academies. John Dickinson knew the works of Molesworth, Hoadly, and Burgh so well that quotations from them often overburdened his own discourses.[3]

Colonials indeed found doctrines expressed by British writers so exactly suited to their needs that they felt little cultural alienation from their mother country. What has been called "libertarian theory" flowed at least as readily from London pens as from Boston or Philadelphia pens. Writers on both sides of the Atlantic felt themselves part of a crusade to extend the principles of British liberty expressed by Milton, "Cato," and a host of others. No wonder, then, that writers in America gave little thought to their "uniqueness," or would not have conceived that their cause might be advanced by abandoning Hutcheson, Price, and Burgh. These radical Whigs living in Great Britain were disturbed by the same flaws in free government in the Empire as were their colleagues in America; some of them even flirted with schemes of dissent amounting to rebellion. Their loyalties—to a conception of free government long thought to be in the process of gradual realization in the British Empire—paralleled those of Franklin and John Adams. Only in opportunity to *do* something, to make an impact on the society in which they lived, and to see their ideas in some semblance realized, did the Americans differ from their English counterparts.

II

As the possibility of independence and its consequences increasingly occupied the American mind, projections looked forward, like the exhortations of Awakened preachers, to a new society with new purposes and character. With old loyalties shattered by a disgust on seeing the glorious England of 1758–1763 fall "from being the nursery of heroes, [to become] the residence of musicians, pimps, and panders," Americans began to consider the implications of this degeneration for their own national future. "Liberty," said John Adams in 1775, "can no more exist without virtue and independence than the body can live and move without a soul." Colonials seemed driven to ask what would happen if the logic of radical Whig doctrine were pursued in a land where there existed the unprecedented possibility of realizing "closet theories." The sense of this projection was caught in an exchange between the Swiss *philosophe* Isaac Iselin and his student Peter Ochs in 1777. "What do you think of the success of the Americans?" asked the pupil. "Might it perhaps be from [America] that we shall see the realization of what you have taught about the history of mankind?" "I am tempted to believe," replied the teacher, "that North America is the country where reason and humanity will develop more rapidly than anywhere else."[4]

The question of representation, for example, arose at first in the narrow, legalistic context of whether, according to the usages of the British Constitution, colonials were "represented" in Parliament. The House of Commons, a hodge-podge of rotten boroughs where there were no members from new cities such as Birmingham and Manchester, had no difficulty extending the idea of "virtual representation" to the colonies; that is, it was claimed that members of the House of Commons represented all commoners anywhere in the realm, not merely those living in their districts. This, of course, proved mere sophistry, since members showed little or no concern for American welfare. To whatever extent it might be true in England that members of the House of Commons were "affected by general dispositions" for the national interest or, at least, represented their "class" as opposed to the nobility, in America this was irrelevant—especially when contrasted with the generally "real" representation colonials knew in their own assemblies. Instead of the "virtual representation" of English cities justifying such representation for America, James Otis and others argued, it was clear that those cities themselves were entitled to *actual* representation. The colonials soon insisted upon the accountability of representatives to their constituents, and the need for binding instructions to delegates. It was insisted that government by consent must mean precisely that, as literally and directly as possible. Law was not something derived from "authority" divinely ordained or traditionally established, but simply the enactments of the representatives of the people responding faithfully to their expressed wishes.

This was what Americans in the Revolutionary era meant by "the pure republican principle."[5]

Since the sophistries about "virtual representation" were defended "as part of the British Constitution," that is, "that assemblage of laws, customs, and institutions which form the general system" of government, colonials soon questioned what the proper meaning of *constitution* was. As they sought to extricate themselves from British usages they found oppressive or arbitrary, the word came to signify *restraints* imposed on the government in order to protect the reasonable claims (rights) of the people. The capacity of clever writers to stretch the unwritten British Constitution to justify all sorts of absurdities diminished confidence in structures consisting merely of custom and precedent. The existence of the colonial charters, which Americans thought defined the privileges as well as the obligations of the settlers, further encouraged the idea that a written constitution would be the best guard against arbitrary government. Following such theorists as the Swiss Vattel and the Scottish Hume, Americans came to think of a constitution as a written frame of government for the legitimate enactment of law, and as a statement of the privileges of the people. It followed that routine legislation, acts of the executive, and even decisions of judges were subordinate to the terms of the constitution; if they contravened it, they were "null, void, of no effect." Since custom and even the common law were obviously inadequate foundations for colonial prerogatives, the way was clear, in the Age of Enlightenment, to enshrine reason as the definer of the natural rights of mankind. Radical Whig principles were thus increasingly expressed in universal language.[6]

As colonials examined questions of rights and representation, and as the possibility of independence loosened old ties of authority and obedience, the concept of sovereignty became central, especially the question: Was it divisible? Following the formulations of Bodin, Hobbes, and others, English political theory in the seventeenth century generally assumed that in any state there must be a single, supreme power which, in the final analysis, ruled. Such a theory was devised initially to justify monarchical absolutism or to preclude civil war and anarchy of the sort that had existed in England during the 1640s, but following 1641 and 1688 Parliament (King, Lords, and Commons), in Whiggish formulations, was held to be supreme. "There is and must be in all [forms of government] a supreme, irresistible, absolute, un-controlled authority," Blackstone intoned for all colonials to hear. In England it resided in Parliament, whose acts, therefore, "no power on earth can undo." As the Declaratory Act of 1766 put it, Parliament "had, hath, and of right ought to have, full power and authority to make laws and statutes of sufficient force and validity to bind the colonies and people of America in all cases whatsoever."

This declaration contravened long-standing practice in colonial government as well as widely revered notions of charters, covenants, and rights standing above mere statute. If Parliament meant to give full effect to the Declaratory Act (ending the so-called period of salutary neglect), and if it persisted in the fiction of virtual representa-tion, then, William Hicks wrote in 1768, Great Britain might "employ this unbounded legislative power for the horrid purpose of reducing three millions of people to a state of abject slavery." The situation of the colonies, he continued, "prevents their joining in the general council," so, to be free, they had to formulate their own "partial policy" in their own representative assemblies, subject only to the "restraining power lodged in the crown" which would assure "the general welfare of the whole." "Why," Hicks asked sarcastically, should "my being born in the island of Great Britain . . . vest me with a power to tie the hands of my American neighbour, and then justify me in picking his pocket?"[7]

Through the long, wordy debate over internal versus external taxa-tion, taxation to regulate trade or for revenue, taxation without repre-sentation, and all the rest, it became increasingly difficult to define an acceptable division of sovereignty. Able Tories held, as Thomas Hutchinson informed the Massachusetts House of Assembly in 1773, that "it is essential to the being of government that a power should always exist which no other power within such government can have right to withstand or control." Whig spokesmen finally agreed, but they claimed this unlimited power for the people living in the colonies —that is, they declared independence. In so doing they in one sense merely affirmed Locke, but in embodying this idea in a new nation shorn of the institutional encumbrances so evident even among British Whigs, the Americans gave the sovereignty of the people a purity and clarity of meaning it had not yet achieved in the Old World. The attempt to define a divided sovereignty, and the strong sense that somehow the scattered, diverse plantations in the New World required novel schemes of federation, survived the cataclysms of 1776 and was part of the experience of Americans when they undertook the strenuous consideration of the structure of their own national government. The projections of the debate over the British Empire and the awesome task of devising a new national loyalty had forced Americans to give their creative attention to basic questions of government.[8]

The colonists also extended English thought on extralegal measures necessary to resist tyranny, and had a chance to act out the implications. Radical Whig theory had long condoned measures by "the people" to resist oppression and thus regain their rights and liberties. However careful Whig writers were to profess loyalty to the King and to endorse the benefits of social order, they always left a way open for popular uprisings against any authority that became tyrannical. Algernon Sidney insisted that "the peace may be broken upon just grounds, and it may be neither a crime nor infamy to do it." Locke observed that "if the innocent honest man must quietly quit all he has for Peace sake, to him who lay violent hands upon it, [peace would be] maintained only for the benefit of Robbers and Oppressors." Thomas Gordon even argued that anarchy did "less harm" than tyranny because it was likely to "end sooner." "All tumults," he noted, "are in their nature, and must be, short in duration, must soon subside, or settle into some order. But Tyranny may last for ages, and go on destroying, till at last there is left nothing to destroy." With such theoretical support, the colonials had little difficulty in justifying acts to resist ministerial tyranny.[9]

This doctrine had sustained a series of popular uprisings and mob actions on both sides of the Atlantic during the eighteenth century, and in 1765 led to a model fulfillment of it in the colonial protest against the Stamp Act. Regarding that Act as clearly oppressive, the "Sons of Liberty" turned their attention to specific measures that would prevent its enforcement. They intended, particularly, to make sure that no person would be able to execute the office of stamp collector. Furthermore, they resolved to prevent royal officials from paralyzing colonial life merely because the hated stamps were not properly affixed to legal documents. To sustain these deliberate interventions, the resistance leaders were quite willing to call out "the Body of the People" to intimidate the enemies of liberty and even to commit measured acts of violence. A Rhode Island Son of Liberty, though, identified the critical limit of extralegal acts when he declared it essential "that on the one Hand we do not yield the Garden of God, and our Birthrights to the Sons of Ambition, and on the other that . . . in a day of Darkness and Difficulty, we do keep up by all Means in our Power as much of civil Government as all Mankind have ever found absolutely necessary for . . . the purposes of socal Life." In New York, after the repeal of the Stamp Act, the Sons of Liberty fulfilled their promise to dissolve "and let Government go on in its usual Forms." Properly undertaken and limited, then, acts of force and violence neither startled nor offended a large segment of colonial opinion by 1765. The resistance to the Stamp Act was thus in theory and in fact a movement *within* radical Whig conceptions of the British Constitution, not undermining but strengthening its essential qualities. The Sons of Liberty, though, had formed organizations and taken steps that were unlikely to happen soon or easily in Great Britain.[10]

In addition to extending radical Whig doctrines in unique ways, the colonials also had to confront quite different realities in their own public life. The great counterbalancing power centers of British society and government—the monarchy (symbol of unity and authority), the nobility (honorable defenders of stability), and the commons (vigorous, liberty-loving people of the realm)—simply didn't exist in the same relationship in America. The council, particularly, in most colonial legislatures was either the despised creature of the royal governor or the sycophant of the lower house, if elected by it. "The security therefore which the constitution derives in Britain from the House of Lords is here entirely wanting," concluded Richard Henry Lee in 1766, "and the just equilibrium totally destroyed by two parts out of three of the legislature being in the same hands." Faced with this deficiency and accepting Tom Paine's ridicule of hereditary succession and "the Royal Brute of Great Britain," some Americans thought about replacing King and nobility with an equitably proportioned unicameral legislature operating under a "continental charter." John Adams, however, spoke for most of his compatriots when he pronounced Paine "*a star of disaster*" who was bound to "produce confusion and every evil work" with such a simplistic notion of government. Adams then began a lifelong search for ways, in an essentially republican society, to structure into a government *real* checks on power. He soon discovered, as did James Madison and others, that without deep, traditional divisions in society, a "balance of powers" must depend on elaborate mechanisms that pitted self-centered, shifting "factions" against each other, thus giving American politics quite a different dynamic from that celebrated by Montesquieu as appropriate for the established societies of the Old World. In any case, Americans were aware that whatever path they took, toward Paine's unitary democracy or toward Adams' system of checks and balances, the British pattern could not be theirs.[11]

III

American social thought, too, responded to the absence of hereditary nobility and the loosening of ties implicit in the rejection of a national loyalty. Colonial society had been "distorted" by the failure of the British nobility to come to America in the first place, and then by the flight of Loyalists during the Revolution. Then, influenced by Great Awakening millennialism and by rational idealism, Americans asked a new question: Was a hierarchical society, prevalent everywhere in 1776, in fact desirable or necessary? If there were not to be inherited titles and structural privileges, what would guide the relationship between rich and poor, old families and new, farmers and merchants, town and country, clergy and laymen, governors and governed, and all the rest? Though few colonies entered upon the Revolution with any thought that such fundamental matters were at stake— to say nothing of having a systematic theory of social transformation —it soon became clear that discarding one nationality and establishing another raised all these questions. As Jefferson discovered in Virginia, after the Declaration of Independence new laws on land tenure, court procedure, crime and punishment, religious establishment, and education seemed necessary to "a foundation for a government truly republican." A decade or more of calculated defiance of a long-legitimized authority and a deeply ingrained loyalty, it soon became evident, was a prelude to, not a fulfillment of, a new order.[12]

Aware of these looming profundities, conservatives looked on with increasing alarm. To his own query, "whether some degree of respect be not always due from inferiors to superiors," Thomas Chandler answered, "the bonds of society would be dissolved, the harmony of the world confounded, and the order of nature subverted, if reverence, respect, and obedience might be refused to those whom the constitution has vested with the highest authority." As Chandler correctly and fearfully perceived, much of the talk he heard around him as New Yorkers pulled down the statue of George III had momentous implications. "Rank, at present, in America," wrote a Philadelphia revolutionary in 1776, "is derived more from qualification than property; a sound moral character, amiable manners, and firmness in principle constitute the first class, and will continue to do so till the origins of families be forgotten, and the proud follies of the old world overrun the simplicity of the new." Traditionalists and revolutionaries agreed on the extent if not the direction of change implicit in the broad confrontation of authority and the rejection of loyalty to England undergone by 1776.[13]

What Bernard Bailyn has called "the Contagion of Liberty" soon challenged other hoary institutions. Especially vigorous were the assaults on the traditional religious establishments—even by sectarians, such as New England Congregationalists and Virginia Anglicans, themselves privileged. Living in London and defending his native provinces, Franklin drew some pointed comparisons between "Toleration in Old England and New England." In the one, Dissenters were "excluded from all offices of profit and honor," while in the other "no test prevented Churchmen [Anglicans] from holding offices." In the one, "the benefits of education in the universities are appropriated to the sons of Churchmen," while in the other "the full benefit of the universities" was unrestricted. Finally, in the one, Dissenters were forced to pay a tithe but their clergy received no support from it, while in the other "taxes for support of public worship, when paid by Churchmen, are given to the Episcopal minister." Franklin touched upon the key to colonial hostility to an Established Church on the European model when he noted that Virginia Anglicans opposed an American bishop because it "must sooner or later saddle them with the great expenses to support it," and because the Anglican episcopate so ardently opposed any relaxation of the pervasive inequities imposed by their privileged status. The whole system and paraphernalia of princes and lords of the Church, social privilege, and episcopal control connoted to most colonials an exclusiveness, a smugness, and even an oppressiveness for which they had little use. They saw no reason, therefore, to plant it in their midst.[14]

The career of John Witherspoon (1723–1794) illustrates vividly this "contagion of liberty" in America. A devout clergyman entirely orthodox in theology and social theory, Witherspoon spent twenty-three years as a pastor in Beith and Paisley, Scotland, under the rigid authority of the Scottish Kirk. There he inveighed against drunkenness, Arminianism, and such frivolities as playacting, but at the same time fought stoutly against the hierarchical power of the Kirk. He insisted that local congregations, not synods and presbyteries, choose pastors and otherwise regulate crucial aspects of their spiritual life. As a hero of both orthodoxy and religious liberty, then, Witherspoon came to America in 1768 to become president of the College of New Jersey (Princeton). Under his guidance the college sent out a host of fervent ministers who evangelized the South and the West—and became a "nursery of sedition" for future leaders of the American Revolution, including James Madison, Aaron Burr, Light-horse Harry Lee, Aaron Ogden, Brockholst Livingston, and Philip Freneau. Witherspoon himself signed the Declaration of Independence and served for many years in the Continental Congress. In a pamphlet seeking to encourage students to come to Princeton, he proclaimed his pride in "the spirit of liberty [which] breathed high and strong" among students and faculty there and declared himself "an opposer of lordly domination and sacerdotal tyranny." He as readily taught Madison concepts of political liberty as he infused Samuel Stanhope Smith with a zeal to spread Presbyterianism in Virginia. There, the two Princetonians cooperated to found a college (revealingly named Hampden-Sydney), fight religious persecution, and inaugurate republican government. Meanwhile, Witherspoon's old parish in Paisley remained for generations under the domination of the Kirk he had unsuccessfully resisted, and we know nothing of the careers or influence of the young men to whom he had spoken in Scotland.[15]

In New England, faced with Anglican efforts to found a "mission church" in Cambridge clearly intended to become the center of a Massachusetts diocese, Jonathan Mayhew saw the seeds of tyranny. Anglicanism departed entirely, he charged, "from the simplicity of the

Gospel and the apostolic times . . . [with its] mitred, lordly SUCCESSORS *of the fishermen of Galilee* . . . [and an] enormous hierarchy [that ascended] by various gradations from the dirt to the skies." In Virginia Richard Bland confessed that though he was a "sincere" Anglican, he opposed the hierarchy because he knew it "to be a relic of the papal encroachments upon the common law." Disgusted by the persecution of Baptists in the Virginia Piedmont, and contrasting the attitude there with Witherspoon's preaching at Princeton and the religious freedom of Pennsylvania, James Madison declared that "religious bondage shackles and debilitates the mind and unfits it for every noble enterprise, every expanded prospect," and took the lead in securing full protection for "liberty of conscience" in the Virginia Declaration of Rights in 1776. Dissenters in Prince Edward County signed a petition thankful for deliverance by the Declaration "from a long night of ecclesiastical bondage," but asking further that the Virginia Assembly "raise religious as well as civil liberty to the zenith of glory, and . . . that without delay all church establishments might be pulled down, and every tax upon conscience and private judgment abolished." Anglican suspicion of hierarchy, Dissenter zeal for "private judgment," and rational ridicule of "making laws for the human mind" all had an influence on Madison, and resulted, in 1786, in the passage of Jefferson's Virginia Act for Establishing Religious Freedom. This famous statute expressed fully and categorically the doctrine of religious liberty and separation of church and state which, though scarcely thought of in 1750, seemed forty years later to be an obviously logical part of free government.[16]

Predictably, New Light enthusiasts extolled religious liberty even more fervently. During the Great Awakening they fought especially against the "ecclesiastical tyranny" of Old Lights who sought to exclude others from their pulpits, because such restriction thwarted the conversion and union of souls the evangelicals held was the only true religion. This attitude, of course, also made them determined foes of an American episcopate. Complete religious freedom, including abolition of parish lines, Jonathan Parsons said in 1774, was essential if Christians were to be able "to sit down with their brethren" in communion. Applied to the state, this concept precluded any form of establishment, religious tax, or privileged status. "Equal and exact liberty granted to all denominations," Parsons insisted, "would naturally tend to beget affectionate union," which could come only through the free working of the Holy Spirit. Levi Hart asserted at the same time that "ecclesiastical liberty gives every member opportunity to fill up his place in acting for the general good of that great and holy society of which the true church of Christ belongs, and of which they are the part." For the evangelicals, then, religious liberty was necessary not only to prevent civil interference with churches, but also to encourage the kindling of religious affections that were the foundation of Christ's kingdom on earth. They were working out the proposition of Roger Williams and others that the religious experience required, in its purity and beauty and holiness, absolute freedom from civil restraint. The ancient doctrine that religion needed state support for its own sake as well as to sustain public morality was denied: such a connection poisoned true religion and founded public virtue on hypocrisy. It is no accident, therefore, that such New Light zealots as Isaac Backus and John Leland were as notable in the fight for freedom of conscience in America as Jefferson and Madison.[17]

IV

The same projection of liberty that worked so powerfully against established religion came in time to be applied, though with much less practical effect, against the most obvious and intractable affront to the words of the declarers of independence—Negro slavery. To be a slave, to be "wholly under the power and control of another as to our actions and properties," was the antithesis of the human freedom so admired in the eighteenth century. John Dickinson declared in *Letters from a Farmer in Pennsylvania* that those taxed without their consent were "*slaves*" who should resent and resist their servitude. How much more oppressed than subjects of a sultan or czar were blacks kidnapped from their homeland and, often under the harshest conditions, forced to work forever for someone else? Nor, as slavery was viewed in Whig rhetoric, was kind treatment a sufficient apology. Anyone "who is bound to obey the will of another is as really a slave though he may have a good master as if he had a bad one," Stephen Hopkins noted while demonstrating how the Stamp Act "reduced [Americans] to the most abject slavery" because they were "taxed at the will of others, without any bounds, without any stipulation and agreement, contrary to their consent and against their will." In choice of words and, less frequently, in direct comment on the state of slavery in the colonies, many tracts protesting colonial bondage to Great Britain recognized that the appeals for liberty applied equally well to blacks held in servitude in North America.[18]

If some proponents of colonial liberty failed to note the discrepancy between their pleas for themselves and the condition of their slaves, their critics quickly pointed it out. Richard Bland said that under an English government "all *men* are *born free*," and John Camm asked him to look at his own Negroes—they were men, yet they were born slaves. Bland's actions spoke louder than his words. Other Southerners soon acknowledged the same discrepancy, though they appealed to "the general inconvenience of living here without them" as an apology for not freeing their slaves at once. Jefferson embodied all the inconsistencies when he noted in 1774 that "the rights of human nature [are] deeply wounded by this infamous practice" and at the same time blamed slavery in America on England for introducing it here. Later, in often-cited passages in *Notes on Virginia* (1782), he accepted the assumption of Negro inferiority to explain the existence of slavery, but then confronted the inescapable contradiction:

When arguing for ourselves, we lay it down as fundamental, that laws, to be just, must give a reciprocation of right; that without this, they are mere arbitrary rules of conduct, founded in force, and not in conscience; and it is a problem which I leave with the Master to solve, whether the religious precepts against violation of property [real estate and rights] were not framed for him as well as his slave? And whether the slave may not as justifiably take a little from one who has taken all from him, as he may slay one who would slay him?

Through a long life Jefferson lived uncomfortably with this affront, unable either to justify or to renounce slavery.[19]

Northern pamphleteers, however, scored slavery most unmercifully. James Otis asked whether " 'tis right to enslave a man because he is black," or whether "any logical inference in favor of slavery [can] be drawn from a flat nose, a long or short face?" "Every dealer in [slaves]," he said, is "a tyrant." According to a Massachusetts Election-day preacher in 1770, Americans holding African slaves "dishonored the Christian name, and degraded human nature." A Baptist preacher,

John Allen, was more scornful: "Blush Ye pretended votaries of freedom! Ye trifling patriots! Who are making a vain parade of being advocates for the liberties of mankind, who are thus making a mockery of your profession by trampling on the sacred natural rights and priorities of Africans." The same Connecticut New Light, Levi Hart, who had declaimed on the link between ecclesiastical and religious tyranny—noting that Americans seized Africans "or bribed them to seize one another, and transported them a thousand leagues into a strange land, and enslaved them for life"—asked, "When shall the happy day come when Americans shall be *consistently* engaged in the cause of liberty?"[20]

Another New Light and student of Jonathan Edwards, Samuel Hopkins, made the most complete argument against slavery in 1776, in a sixty-three-page pamphlet, *A Dialogue Concerning the Slavery of Africans; Showing It to Be the Duty and Interest of the American Colonies to Emancipate All the African Slaves*. Hopkins followed the by then well-known indictment of the slave trade, the nature of plantation slavery, and its corruption of masters as well as victims with a biting rebuttal of the various classical, Christian, and cynical apologies for slavery. The slavery to Great Britain protested so indignantly by self-proclaimed Sons of Liberty, Hopkins concluded, "is lighter than a feather compared to [the Africans'] heavy doom, and may be called liberty and happiness when contrasted with the . . . inutterable wretchedness to which they are subjected." The vengeance of God, he was sure, would fall upon any people who practiced such "gross, barefaced inconsistency." He pleaded that the nation about to be born repent, shed its sinful indifference, abolish slavery, and make restitution to the blacks.[21]

The logical extension of the doctrine of liberty to include all men, white and black, led to the general abolition of slavery north of the Mason-Dixon line during the Revolution (see Chapter 16) and placed the burden on those who would seek to explain how the phrase "all men are created equal" excluded black men. The undeniable link between the quest of Americans for liberty and the obligation to free their slaves, pointed out so forcefully by Otis, Hopkins, and others, has remained for two centuries a basic ideological weapon against the continuing oppression of blacks in the United States. But the contradiction between the moral clarity of the case against slavery and its persistence for so long was evidence that the new ideals created to replace the rejected loyalty to England needed new laws, new conceptions of the national interest, and new customs and attitudes to be fulfilled. The long-standing habits, entrenched institutions, economic benefits, and pervasive attitudes that sustained slavery, embedded in British nationality (though morally at odds with its professed ideals, as English abolitionists were beginning to proclaim), could not be done away with by a rejection of that nationality or a declaration of human equality. Again, new nationhood proved to be a beginning, not a fulfillment.

V

In the years before 1776, then, as loyalty to England diminished, the colonials engaged in a great debate not only over a legal break with the mother country (a relatively narrow question), but also over the much larger question of what would replace the discarded sentiments and commitments. If, for example, James Otis denied that British admiralty courts had jurisdiction over certain American cases (a specific point, apparently made in the interests of a client), he had to propose where these cases should be decided. And to do that he was forced to elaborate on sovereignty, federalism, and justice. Similarly, Richard Bland's argument that royal disallowance of Virginia's Two-Penny Act (1758) injured certain taxpayers of the colony quickly widened into discussions of church-state relationships, meaningful representation, and the nature of the British Empire. Though it is certain that the various disputes leading to the Revolution arose over specific economic grievances, it is equally certain, judging from the course of the controversies, that ideologies were invoked that aroused and sustained far more profound inquiries. The colonies began with standard English authorities such as Coke and Locke, but in instance after instance the fluidity of American circumstances and the freedom to follow logic where it would lead resulted in a "contagion of liberty." By 1776, not only was the quantity of American political writing remarkable, but its quality and speculativeness had developed to the point where new forms of government seemed necessary as well as possible —and where even attitudes, values, self-identity, and other facets of national character seemed due for reassessment and perhaps transformation.

4. American Thought in 1776

DAVID RAMSAY, A LEADING SOUTH CAROLINA DISSENTER, GRADUATE OF THE COLLEGE OF NEW JERSEY (1765), AND ARDENT PATRIOT, WROTE IN 1789 THAT "PREVIOUS TO THE AMERICAN REVOLUTION THE INHABITANTS OF THE BRITISH COLONIES WERE UNIVERSALLY LOYAL. That three millions of such subjects should break through all former attachments, and unanimously adopt new ones, could not reasonably be expected." To explain this extraordinary transformation, Ramsay reflected on the sorts of people who had supported the Revolution. Most important, he thought, were the "numerous independent whig yeomanry," especially plentiful in New England where, consequently, the Revolution received almost universal support. In New York and Pennsylvania already crystallized political factions took different sides during the Revolution. In each case, though, the more Whiggish, less dominant party, "the Livingston interest" in New York and the anti-Quaker group in Pennsylvania, supported the patriot cause. The Scotch-Irish, having "fled from oppression in their native country" and being mostly Presbyterians, and the Germans, possessing "industry and other republican virtues, . . . were generally determined whigs," too, Ramsay noted.[1]

Presbyterians (including Congregationalists) and Independents (Baptists, Methodists, and others) "were almost universally attached to the measures of Congress," Ramsay observed, because "their religious societies are governed on the republican plan." Even Anglican clergymen in the South were often "warm whigs"; in contrast to the middle colonies and New England, "in general . . . their church was able to support itself." Furthermore, the graduates of the colonial colleges, two thousand or more from Harvard and Yale and perhaps three hundred from the College of New Jersey, Ramsay thought, were, "with few exceptions . . . active and useful friends of independence." These men furnished the "knowledge and abilities" that guided "the great body of the people . . . [in] opposing the encroachments of Great Britain." Finally, Ramsay noted, "the age and temperament of individuals had often an influence in fixing their political character. . . . The active and spirited part of the community, who felt themselves possessed of talents that would raise them to eminence in a free government, longed for the establishment of independent constitutions. . . . The young, the ardent, the ambitious and the enterprising were mostly whigs." The only group Ramsay placed among the friends of independence for whom he could ascribe no particular motive, and who thus seemed something of an anomaly, were "the opulent slave holders in Virginia, the Carolinas, and Georgia."

On the Tory side were "placemen [officeholders] in Boston," aristocrats in New York who benefited from "the practice of entailing estates," those with "intermarriages and other connexions [with] . . . British officers and some of their first families," and Anglican clergymen in the North who were "pensioners on the bounty of the British government." The Scots in America, though contributing some of the "best officers" in Congress and in the Army, were "generally disposed to support the claims of Great Britain," Ramsay supposed, because "their nation for some years past had experienced a large proportion of royal favor." Noting that the dominant Delancey faction in New York and the Quaker party in Pennsylvania "were adverse to independence," Ramsay concluded that "revolutions in government are rarely patronized by any body of men who foresee that a diminution of their own importance is likely to result from the change." The pacifist Quakers, too, "could not be friendly to a revolution which could only be effected by the sword." Dealing with a situation puzzling and unwelcome to himself, Ramsay supposed that Carolina frontiersmen were largely Tory because, having experienced the harsh suppression of their Regulator movement, they were unwilling to support a Congress whose measures, so much "like their own regulating schemes." seemed destined to "terminate in the same disagreeable consequences." Finally, Ramsay counted as opponents "old men . . . [who] could not relish the great changes which were daily taking place, [and who were] attached to ancient forms and habits," and "the very rich."

For Ramsay, then, the explanation of the remarkable "break [of] all former attachments" in the British colonies by 1776 arose largely from qualities existing among the people in America. Republican institutions (that is, those not entirely controlled by an authoritarian hierarchy), the experience of fleeing from oppression in Europe, industrious habits, a New World education, religious dissent, and a spirit of ambition and enterprise were to him the generative factors. A society thus constituted would not long endure oppression and would have the initiative and energy to resist it successfully. Franklin had warned as early as 1767, that America, where "the seeds of liberty are universally found, [is] . . . an immense territory, . . . must become a great country, populous and mighty; and will, in less time than is generally conceived, be able to shake off any shackles that may be imposed on her."[2]

Just as the Great Awakening appeal for transformation of the individual and society produced a more radical response in the colonies than in England, so, too, radical Whig doctrines found a special destiny in America. Believing themselves the heirs of Milton, Bunyan, and the militant host whose Puritan Revolution had been stunted by the Restoration, New Englanders especially were a ready audience for those Englishmen who thought the moderate settlement of 1688, in its authorized Augustan and Georgian versions, left liberty unfulfilled. Every threat of arbitrariness, from the suppression of Leisler's Rebellion and Zenger's trial to the Parson's Cause and the Coercive Acts, found colonials echoing, elaborating, and then extending the doctrines of Algernon Sidney, Trenchard and Gordon, Benjamin Hoadly, and Joseph Priestley. At the same time, Tory rebuttals, for the most part, died over the Atlantic. Consequently, while in Great Britain the debate was the ancient one over the need to retain certain aspects of traditional society, in America the most vital discussion centered on the *application* of radical Whig ideas to an environment ready to receive them. Finally, as new possibilities were perceived, Americans began to formulate notions that looked forward to a new kind of man, a new society—and a new nationality.

The loss of loyalty to England formalized in 1776 left the American mind diminished and bereaved, of course, but also expectantly receptive. Everywhere, whether with hope or fear, a sense of portentousness pervaded the colonies. What did it mean for a people to declare they no longer possessed their birthright nationality? Could it be eradicated legally or practically? Beneath the legal and constitutional wrangling that filled the colonial press from the days of Mayhew, Otis, and Bland to the era of Adams, Jefferson, and Paine lay this agonizing question. As it impinged on the full consciousness of men from Massachusetts to Georgia, the habit of probing fundamentals became more widespread. Science, literature, religion, education, and art, as well as government, felt its impact. Since British loyalty and nationality had embodied habits and attitudes in all these areas, a new nationality, sufficiently rich to be a worthy replacement, would also have to "amount to something" across a similar spectrum. The taunts of Englishmen—from the army officer who boasted to Franklin in 1775 that "with a thousand British grenadiers, he would undertake to go from one end of America to another, and geld all the males, partly by force and partly by a little coaxing," to Sidney Smith's humiliating question in 1820, "Who reads an American book?"—indicates both the skepticism of Europeans that such an achievement was possible and the magnitude of the task Americans faced.[3]

To have come to this awesome prospect by 1776 was, as John Adams declared, a substantial revolution. The past had been challenged beyond the point of no return. Even if Great Britain reimposed her rule by force of arms (a strong possibility in 1776), she would never regain the union of sentiment and sympathy symbolized by Franklin's Englishness in 1750. America might, like Ireland, be *ruled* by Great Britain for a decade, a generation, or even a century, but she would, after the revolution of loyalties undergone by 1776, never again *be a part* of England. The intellectual energies called forth by one generation as it made its way toward the Declaration of Independence (an act of rejection) would need to be turned, in subsequent generations, to formulate purposes and establish governments, and ultimately, to mold a character and achieve a culture that would, as Jefferson hoped, convey "a decent respect to the opinions of mankind."

III

The Revolution in Purpose

IN THE Declaration of Independence, almost offhandedly, Americans made their first formal statement of the purpose and objectives of their new and uniquely originated nation. "The history of the present King of Great Britain is a history of repeated injuries and usurpations" so insufferable, Jefferson wrote, that the United Colonies "are obsolved from all allegiance to the British Crown, and . . . all political connection between them and the State of Great Britain is and ought to be totally dissolved." Under the "Laws of Nature and of Nature's God," Americans, equally with the rest of mankind, possessed "certain unalienable rights, that among these are life, liberty, and the pursuit of happiness," to secure which they would "institute new government, laying its foundation on such principles, and organizing its powers in such form as to them shall seem most likely to effect their safety and happiness." In this sketchy statement of purpose Jefferson included only a phrase about the mode of government; its "just powers [derived] from the consent of the governed." Precisely what the "unalienable rights" were, in what the "safety and happiness" of the people consisted, and what its "foundation principles," presumably the "Laws of Nature," prescribed were not set down, although, as Jefferson wrote in old age, the "American whigs" who signed the Declaration were all of "one opinion" on these substantial matters. Their manifesto rested on "the harmonizing sentiments of the day" gleaned from "the elementary books of public right, as Aristotle, Cicero, Locke, Sidney, etc."[1]

In their general enthusiasm the signers bypassed such difficulties as the basically different conceptions of the purpose of government found in Aristotle and in Locke. Moreover, in a single sentence of their Declaration they committed themselves to two propositions unlikely, as they themselves soon saw and readily admitted, ever to co-exist easily: their government was to guarantee "unalienable" rights and also to rest on the consent of the governed. That is, it was to ensure eternal verities but it was also to act as the people decided. What if the people, however organized to register their consent, agreed to an abridgment or suppression of one or all of these rights for most or even a few of the people? Though Jefferson's words make clear that he thought no government could justly deny "unalienable rights," he nonetheless left uncertain how this principle would be safeguarded under the also inviolable principle of government by consent. So at the time of the Revolution not only were the details of future government unsettled, but serious tensions were implicit in the words of the Declaration of Independence itself.[2]

5. The Spirit of 1776

OTHER EARLY, INFLUENTIAL STATEMENTS OF PURPOSE OFFERED NO FIRMER PROSPECT THAT EASY OR UNANIMOUS ANSWERS WOULD BE FORTHCOMING. THE MOST FAMOUS REVOLUTIONARY TRACT, PAINE'S COMMON SENSE, WHICH IS GIVEN MAJOR CREDIT FOR INSPIRING THE colonists with the courage to declare their independence, made the problem seem deceptively simple. "Government even in its best state is but a necessary evil," Paine asserted, because "were the impulses of conscience clear, uniform, and irresistibly obeyed, man would need no other lawgiver. . . . Government, like dress, is the badge of lost innocence; the palaces of kings are built on the ruins of the bowers of paradise." Hence, once the oppressions and irrationalities of "the royal brute of Great Britain," descended from "a French bastard" who had conquered the Anglo-Saxons with "an armed banditti," had been thrown off, a just government pledged to the safety and happiness of the people might be instituted. Then, turning to particulars which he had just implied were hardly to be taken seriously, Paine proclaimed, "I draw my idea of government from a principle in nature, which no art can overturn, viz. that the more simple anything is, the less liable it is to be disordered, and the easier repaired when disordered." At the outset of American debate on the purpose and nature of their new nation, then, the liberating effects of the painful divestment of loyalty to England made reliance on fundamentals seem the logical starting point. What else was left?

Paine rather offhandedly and with none of the intensity or assurance he used to condemn the British monarchy began to collect what he called "the straggling thoughts of individuals" on the structure of government that "wise and able men [might] improve into useful matter." Following his principle of simplicity, he proposed a grand continental assembly that would elect its own president (rotating by lot among the states) and frame a "Continental Charter" enshrining the liberties of the people. It would also, vaguely, fix the "manner of choosing members of Congress" and define its powers. Though these hints give little indication of how Paine thought government would in fact operate, it is clear that he had in mind a straightforward process: honest, earnest representatives of the people, working amicably together, would decide the relatively few questions that a good (simple) government needed to attend to in order to ensure public happiness. Then, moving back to rhetoric more congenial to him, Paine perorated, "O ye that love mankind! . . . Freedom hath been hunted round the globe, Asia, and Africa, have long expelled her—Europe regards her as a stranger, and England hath given her warning to depart. O! receive the fugitive, and prepare in time an asylum for mankind."[1]

Following Paine's lead, Americans enjoyed an exuberant, often radical, even millennial round of republican theorizing as they began the more sobering task of establishing new governments. A Trenton, New Jersey, versifier expressed the fond hope:

> Here Governments their last perfection take.
> Erected only for the People's sake.
> Founded no more on Conquest or in blood,
> But on the basis of the Public Good.
> No contests then shall mad ambition raise,
> No chieftains quarrel for a sprig of praise,
> No thrones shall rise, provoking lawless sway,
> And not a *King* to cloud the blissful day.

Americans, in setting aside royal authority, came gradually but excitedly to understand how novel it was to rest a society on the authority of *the people*. Frightened Tories agreed. Without obedience to the Crown, the Church, and all the other traditional symbols of authority, "the bonds of society would be dissolved, the harmony of the world confounded, and the order of nature subverted." As advocates of independence saw that *old* bonds were gone, *old* harmonies confounded, and an *old* order subverted, they searched for *new* foundations and *new* cohesions.[2]

The root realization was that in a republic the character of the society and of the government depended, ultimately, on the character of the people. Republicans agreed with defenders of traditional authority from Filmer to Blackstone that the source from which power emanated guided the destiny of the nation. Just as an absolute monarchy drew its alleged legitimization and virtue from the holy anointment and wisdom of the king, and a constitutional monarchy from the alleged sense of responsibility and obligation inherent in the lords and commons of the realm, a republic had no choice but to find its salvation in the alleged goodness of the people themselves. The Adamses and Paine and Jefferson accepted the centuries-old platonic postulate that justice in a society depended on the virtue of those who ruled. Their radically new problem was how to find, or to cultivate, and then to institutionalize this virtue and yet retain fidelity to the republican principle of government by consent.

To accomplish this, the people, or their representatives, would have to achieve the disinterested, unselfish concern for the public good that eighteenth-century political theory ascribed to "benevolent" despots. How was this to be done? A just society could come into being, it gradually appeared, only if everyday occupations, social arrangements, the distribution of wealth, education, access to political power, and all the things that regulated daily life were remodeled to nourish virtue in the people, the new rulers. Newspapers, pamphlets, and letters from Boston to Charleston were filled, in 1774–1776, with speculations about the revolutionary dimensions of the shift of authority from the Crown to the people. John Adams wrote a week after the Declaration of Independence that "Capacity, Spirit, and Zeal in the Cause" would have to characterize the new rulers in America. Throughout the colonies, but especially in Pennsylvania, he observed approvingly, the old, privileged leaders are "all fallen, like Grass before the Scythe, notwithstanding all their vast Advantages in Point of Fortune, Family and Abilities." A Virginian noted the vital, new dynamics: "It is the principle of equality which alone can inspire and preserve the virtue of its members, by placing them in a relation to the publick and to their fellow-citizens, which has a tendency to engage the heart and affections of both." That is, to achieve virtue, people had to have responsibility, and to assume responsibility, they had to be, in substantial ways,

equal. Pages and pages of resentment at "fawning parasites and cring-
ing courtiers" who gained power through royal favor attest that
American Whigs recognized that to fulfill the logic of their newly
based authority, sweeping changes were in order.[3]

Nothing short of a moral revolution was needed if the new American republics were to avoid the instability and viciousness so often
associated with rule by the people. To many, the corrupting effect of
the connection with England, complained of so bitterly by Franklin
from his London vantage point, was already far too prevalent in
America. "Notions of honour, rank and other courtly Ideas [had
been] so eagerly embraced" by many Americans, Charles Thomson
noted in 1776, that "had time been given for them to strike deeper
root, it would have been extremely difficult to have prepared men's
minds for the good seed of liberty." Not only was the general connection with a society as vice-ridden as that of England dangerous, but
the effort, increasingly obvious to Americans after the Declaratory
Act, of the British ministry to impose a tyranny in the colonies further threatened their moral character. "Wherever Tyranny is established," Samuel Adams wrote, "Immorality comes in like a Torrent. It
is in the Interest of Tyrants to reduce the People to Ignorance and
Vice." It was necessary, therefore, to cut the tie to England that
sustained the flow of poison into colonial life, and to replace the
British-induced immoral society with one in which the people might
achieve virtue and the other requisite republican qualities. The prospect, as John Adams wrote his wife the day after Congress had
adopted the Declaration of Independence, was perilous—and glorious:
"The new Governments we are assuming, in every Part, will require a
Purification from our Vices, and an Augmentation of our Virtues or
they will be no Blessings. The People will have unfounded Power.
And the People are extreamly addicted to Corruption and Venality, as
well as the Great. I am not without Apprehensions from this Quarter.
. . . Yet through all the Gloom I can see the Rays of ravishing Light
and Glory." Abigail replied with fervent hope: "May the foundation
of our new constitution, be justice, Truth and Righteousness."[4]

Americans increasingly understood the complexity of the challenge.
"Men became virtuous or vicious, good commonwealth men or the
contrary, generous, noble, and courageous, or base, mean-spirited, and
cowardly," said Samuel West in the Massachusetts election sermon of
1776, "according to the impression they have received from the gov-

ernment they are under." Freed of the baneful effects of British rule—
and of the consequent circle of privilege and corruption surrounding
the royal governors—Americans might abolish the *vicious* cycle and
instead energize a *progressive* cycle whereby personal virtue, public
education, and good government might sustain one another to build
the kingdom of righteousness envisioned by sacred and secular preachers alike. Though grim warnings made all aware that the task would
not be easy, in 1775–1776 the actual possibility that human personality, government, and society could be transformed filled the air and
intoxicated ordinarily sober considerations of public affairs. Americans
took their first steps toward definitions of national purpose and establishment of governments with a visionary idealism always pointing
toward what might be, always illuminating opportunities not to be
missed, even though the pressures of reality and the power of evil sometimes intervened to chasten fond hopes.[5]

Reflecting both the exuberance and the sobriety of this atmosphere,
and in part reacting against Paine's *Common Sense*, John Adams, in
the spring of 1776, set down his *Thoughts on Government* in the new
nation. "The divine science of politics is the science of social happiness, and the blessings of society depend entirely on the constitutions
of government," Adams asserted, thus denying Paine's supposition that
society, "in every state a blessing," could be good without government. "The greatest lawgivers of antiquity," Adams declared, would
have wished to live in 1776, when "three millions of people [had] full
power and a fair opportunity to form and establish the wisest and
happiest government that human wisdom can contrive." Agreeing
with Paine and "all speculative politicians . . . that the happiness of
society is the end of government," Adams went on to outline a much
more complex framework than that offered by Paine. Insisting on a
republican form and a government of laws, not of men, Adams proposed that the people of each state elect a legislative assembly that
would then elect a council, or upper house, having a "negative" on the
laws. He also called for a governor (preferably also chosen by the
assembly) with extensive executive authority as well as a veto power,
and a judiciary "distinct from both the legislative and executive, and
independent [of] both, that so it may be a check upon both, as both
should be checks upon that." Such checks, Adams hoped, would "control" the "fits of humor, starts of passion, flights of enthusiasm, partial-

ities, or prejudices" to which a single assembly, like an individual, would be subject. In fact, he quoted six reasons, each somberly taking into account the "vices, follies, and frailties" of mankind, for rejecting Paine's single assembly idea.[6]

Thus, in the early months of 1776, Jefferson, Paine, John Adams, and many other former subjects of George III sought to overcome, as Adams put it, "the greatest obstacle" to declaring independence: "agreeing on a government for our future regulation." The experience of colonial government, especially as understood by such veterans as Franklin, Samuel Adams, Roger Sherman, and Edmund Pendleton, would be invaluable, and the radical Whig tradition so well known in America would furnish many useful principles. John Dickinson, James Wilson, James Madison, and others also ransacked the histories of the ancient world and the records of other republics and confederations to discern applicable precedents. But how to make sense of it all would be a great challenge. As Ezra Stiles had written Catharine Macaulay before the Revolution, "England had been struggling under diseases for ages. It has at Times and in some parts received a temporary cure—but the Disorder is so radically seated as will at last baffle every political physician." The United States would therefore have to "originate new Constitutions . . . [and her] Men of Genius and penetrating Observation . . . [would have to] take a large and comprehensive view of the politics of the States and Countries around the Globe, [including] the Lights of Orientals and Asiatics, of the World itself both in ancient and modern Ages."[7]

The actual business of forming new governments required, as Washington observed a month before the Declaration of Independence, "infinite care, and unbounded attention. . . . Too much time . . . cannot be bestowed in weighing and digesting matters well. . . . [It] cannot be the Work of a day," he added. Similarly impressed with the awesome task, John Adams advised that it was "safest to proceed in all established modes to which the people have been familiarized by habit." Such caution found immense practical reinforcement from the innately conservative, substantial men who in every colony faced independence with trepidation and desired to retain as much of the old structure as possible within the new sovereignty. These men—James Bowdoin in Massachusetts, John Jay and Robert R. Livingston in New York, John Dickinson in Pennsylvania-Delaware, and Edmund Pendleton in Virginia, to name a few—though American enough to seriously participate in the task of constitution-making, held traditional notions of government and society that made them reluctant innovators. Pendleton, for example, wanted to retain the old land tenure system in Virginia, "which custom has made easy and familiar," changing only the reservation of privileges and revenues "from the Crown to the Community." He also favored a Senate "holding their Offices for life, unless impeached and . . . chosen out of the people of great property to secure their Attachment" to the stability of the state. Apropos the tendency in Jefferson's proposed penal code to "relax all Punishments [for crime] and rely on Virtue and the Public good as sufficient to prompt obedience to the Laws," Pendleton retorted that to do thus "You must find a new race of men to be the Subjects of it." He fought to retain an established church in Virginia in order, as centuries of social thought had held, to give formal, steady support to a holy religion whose strength was vital to the discipline and virtue of the community. Altogether, Pendleton was, as Jefferson found, "more disposed to acquiesce in things as they are, than to risk innovations." Such a predisposition to the status quo among men likely to have great influence in forming the new constitutions made it certain that these would reflect conservative as well as radical conceptions.[8]

6. New State Constitutions: Pennsylvania, Virginia, and Massachusetts

SPORADICALLY IN 1774 AND 1775, AS BRITISH AUTHORITY IN THE COLONIES DIMINISHED, AD HOC GROUPS, MOSTLY AT THE LOCAL LEVEL, CAME INTO BEING TO SUSTAIN GOVERNMENT. TOWNS AND COUNTIES, LARGELY CONTROLLED BY THOSE HOSTILE TO BRITISH RULE, CONtinued day-to-day affairs with little sense of traumatic change. Committees of Safety, formed all over the colonies, carried out such explicitly Revolutionary activities as enforcing nonimportation agreements and training the militia. The royal governors fled or were shunted aside, and the colonial legislatures founded on their authority passed out of existence, though the *members* of these bodies, often almost to a man, transferred readily to the Revolutionary conventions called to replace the old assemblies. Beginning with New Hampshire in January 1776, the states undertook to draft new constitutions ignoring British authority. Congress encouraged the movement on May 15, 1776, by advising the colonies to "adopt such government as shall, in the opinion of the representatives of the people, best conduce to the happiness and safety of their constituents in particular, and America in general." Within a year of the Declaration of Independence each state had a new constitution it regarded as fundamental law, appropriate to its new status as an independent republic. (The corporate colonies, Connecticut and Rhode Island, without royal governors, had merely to delete all reference to Great Britain in their existing charters).[1]

This, to John Adams was "the last Step, . . . a total absolute Independence" from England, because he believed "that no Colony, which shall assume a Government under the People, will give it up. . . . An whole Government of our own Choice, managed by Persons whom

We love, revere, and can confide in, has charms in it for which Men will fight." In church, listening to the Reverend George Duffield "run a Parallell between the Case of Israel and that of America, and between the Conduct of Pharaoh and that of George," Adams felt "an Awe upon my Mind, which is not easily described." To Americans who had absolved themselves of loyalty to Great Britain, the decisive act of reaffirmed loyalty and of renewed political bonds was the creation by the people of the states of their own republican governments. "Confederation will be necessary for our internal Concord, and alliances may be so for our external Defence," Adams noted, but "the Resolution for instituting [state] Governments" was the vital step in providing for the people the blessings of self-rule. Attention, energy, and devotion at the peak of republican enthusiasm in the former colonies focused on the constitutions issuing from the state conventions.[2]

I

In Pennsylvania, because the old colonial assembly had fought stubbornly and in the end lost on the issue of independence, the entrenched leaders were in despair and disarray. The victorious radicals thus controlled the convention that met in Philadelphia during the summer of 1776 to draft and adopt a new constitution. More than in any other state projections of pure republicanism infused the proceedings, occupied the public, and filled the newspapers. The Pennsylvania radicals sensed a unique opportunity to *really* institute government by consent. They meant to discard all the traditional notions of magisterial authority and even legislative power that imperiled the ordinary rights and happiness of the people. An anonymous pamphleteer, appropriately calling himself "Demophilus," urged the convention to accept Paine's dictum that good government was simple government and to restore the supposed ancient Saxon practice of intimacy between the people and public authority in order to abolish the oppressive distinction between ruler and ruled. A broadside declared that "a government made for the common good should be framed by men who can have no interest besides the common interest of mankind." Hence, "great and over-grown rich men . . . too apt to be framing distinctions in society, because they will reap the benefits of all such distinctions," and men in the learned professions, "generally filled with the quirks and quibbles of the schools," would be of little use in writing a republican constitution. "Honesty, common sense, and a plain understanding, when unbiased by sinister motives, are fully equal to the task," the broadside concluded.[3]

The preamble of the Pennsylvania constitution of 1776 proclaimed that "all government ought to be instituted and supported for the security and protection of the community as such, and to enable the individuals who compose it to enjoy their natural rights." To accomplish this, the delegates promulgated a *Declaration of Rights* and *Frame of Government*, to be the Constitution of this Commonwealth." The first clause put in extreme form the moral imperative for society already hallowed by Locke, Jefferson, and others: "All men are born equally free and independent, and have certain natural, inherent and inalienable rights, amongst which are, the enjoying and defending life and liberty, acquiring, possessing and protecting property, and pursuing and obtaining happiness and safety." The rest of the declaration enshrined the usual freedoms, but always with a categorical emphasis on the intimate control of the government by the people: "All power being originally inherent in, and consequently derived from the people; therefore all officers of government, whether legislative or executive, are trustees and servants, and at all times accountable to them." Thus, "the common benefit, . . . [not] the particular emolument or advantage of any single man, family, or sett of men," ought to motivate the government. Furthermore, elections and offices were to be open to "all free men having a sufficient evident common interest with, and attachment to the community." That all officers of the state "may be restrained from oppression," they would periodically be "reduced . . . to a private station." Since "standing armies in the time of peace are dangerous to liberty, they ought not to be kept up," and the military should always be kept "under strict subordination to . . . the civil power." Those "conscientiously scrupulous of bearing arms" were not to be compelled to do so. Finally, since to "keep a government free" required "frequent recurrence to fundamental principles," the people would maintain a steady surveillance over all "legislatures and magistrates." Starting from such propositions, Pennsylvanians would have to "clear away every part of the old rubbish . . . and begin upon a new foundation." The populist ethos was even more evident in a clause proposed but not adopted at the convention: "That an enormous proportion of property vested in a few individuals is dangerous to the rights, and destructive of the common happiness, of mankind, and therefore every free state hath a right by its laws to discourage the possession of such property."[4]

The center of the frame of government was a unicameral legislature "of persons most noted for wisdom and virtue" elected annually by all male taxpayers (and their sons) over twenty-one years of age. The representatives were to be residents of their districts, to hold no other civil offices while in the legislature, and to serve "no more than four years in seven" as representatives. Though these provisions were aimed at particular corruptions in Parliament or in the colonial assemblies, they reveal as well that the people intended their rulers to be extensions of themselves, not remote "philosopher-kings," professional officeholders, or even perpetual representatives. It was this dawning possibility that most captivated the Pennsylvania radicals and took them furthest from traditional conceptions of government. The legislature was given wide authority over appointments, had impeachment powers, and in designating delegates to Congress was to limit their term to two years with ineligibility for the next three. Since "representation in proportion to the number of taxable inhabitants is the only principle which can at all times secure liberty, and make the voice of a majority of the people the law of the land," there was to be a septennial census to be used as a basis for reapportionment. The debates in the House of Representatives were to be open to the public, its votes and proceedings published weekly, and the grounds for members' votes entered if they so desired. Finally, "all bills of a public nature shall be printed for the consideration of the people" before final debate in the assembly, and to prevent "the inconvenience of hasty determinations," passage by *two* annual assemblies would be necessary for final enactment.

For "executive" power, the frame of government provided a Supreme Executive Council of twelve members chosen by districts for staggered terms of three years. From this council there would be chosen annually, by joint ballot with the assembly, a president and vice president, who, acting with a quorum of at least five councilmen, would carry out carefully limited executive functions. Throughout, the intent was to prevent excess and tyranny rather than to enable positive action. Powers of pardon and trade regulation, for example, were limited to periods when the Assembly was not in session, and the president, though "commander in chief of the forces of the state, . . . shall not command in person." If executive and judicial officers took fees other than "as future legislation may grant," they were to be forever disqualified "from holding any office in this state." Salaries were to be "adequate but moderate" for all officials. Sheriffs and justices of the peace were to be appointed by the president in council, but from a short list elected by the people of a city or county. Sheriffs were to be chosen annually and were to hold office only three years in seven. Finally, all elections were to be "by ballot, free and voluntary," and electors or candidates who gave or received "meat, drink, monies, or otherwise" for votes would be disqualified. These clauses implied that a multitude of barriers and purifying devices were necessary to transform the immemorial impositions of rulers on the people into relationships of trust and utility.

Besides the built-in mechanisms to assure certain moral qualities in the commonwealth, the drafters provided explicitly for public virtue. Legislators were to be faithful, honest guardians of the people, and to declare their belief in "one God, the creator and governor of the universe, the rewarder of the good and the punisher of the wicked," and in the "Divine inspiration" of the Scriptures. They were, that is, to be earnest men devoted to God's purposes as revealed in His Word, not aimless, selfish profligates likely to lead the commonwealth to perdition. Imprisonment for debt was abolished, penalties were to be "proportionate to the crimes," and prisons were to be publicly inspected workhouses rather than places of hidden "sanguinary punishment." Foreigners "of good character" were to be welcomed and quickly granted "the rights of a natural born subject." Schools and at least one university were to be supported by the public so that all youths could be instructed "at low prices." Lest these specific provisions prove insufficient, "laws for the encouragement of virtue, and prevention of vice and immorality, [were to] be made and constantly kept in force," and religious and learned societies were to be "encouraged and protected."

The framers concluded their work with a hedge against both their own lack of wisdom and the machinations that might pervert their government. Every seven years a specially elected twenty-four-member Council of Censors would "enquire whether the constitution has been preserved inviolate in every part; and whether the legislative and executive branches of the government have performed their duty as guardians of the people." They would then punish offenders, and, if "absolutely necessary," call a convention to amend the constitution.

Only thus could "the freedom of the commonwealth . . . be preserved inviolate forever."[5]

Despite its novelty, much of the constitution still reflected old usages and principles in "Penn's province." Protection of religious liberty and conscientious objection had long been part of the public life of the Quaker colony. Many other parts of the Declaration of Rights, as well as basic elements of self-rule, paralleled the Charter of Privileges granted by William Penn in 1701. Even the unusual unicameral legislature was a carry-over from the colonial assembly in which Franklin and other framers of the 1776 document had served for years. Altogether, the Pennsylvania constitution of 1776 was a notable example of the *extension* of republican ideology, a fulfillment at a propitious moment of significant but incomplete beginnings in self-government. Under the spell of speculations induced by the overthrow of British authority and the sense of new prospects, radical conceptions of human society and government flowered, and, in Pennsylvania at least, received substantial enactment into fundamental law. Though the 1776 constitution lasted but fourteen years and by the time of its demise was widely condemned even by radical republicans, it and the spirit that produced it were significant parts of what Edmund Morgan has termed "The American Revolution Considered as an Intellectual Movement."

Attacks on the new Pennsylvania constitution began almost before it was promulgated in September 1776. Much of the thrust of John Adams' *Thoughts on Government* was directed against the notion of a "single assembly." All his life he scorned the Pennsylvania document as a "System of anarchy, . . . so democratical, without any restraint or even an attempt at any Equilibrium or Counterpoise, that it must produce confusion and every other Evil Work." As the convention sat, one moderate Whig termed its members "honest well-meaning Country men . . . hardly equal to the Task to form a new plan of Government," while another simply called them "numsculs." When the new constitution reached General Arthur St. Clair, who was serving in the army at Fort Ticonderoga, he thought it like "Ovid's description of matter before the Creation." Benjamin Rush declared that the constitution "substituted a mob government to one of the happiest governments of the world." The special target of the moderates was the test oath which, by pledging officeholders to not "directly or indirectly do any act or thing prejudicial or injurious to the constitution or government thereof," virtually excluded foes of the new constitution from serving under it and made difficult any opposition at all. This bothered the radicals very little, however, because their idealized conception of commonwealth unity required setting aside old notions of factional politics and rallying behind the sovereignty of the people.[6]

James Wilson, as learned in principles of government and law as any man in America, led the fight against the constitution. The root difficulty, he guided a mass meeting of opponents to resolve, was that the frame of government, since it provided for "no distribution of power into different hands, that one may check the other, . . . [violated] all principles of government laid down by such authorities as Montesquieu." To Wilson, as to John Adams and many others accustomed to Montesquieu's idealized conception of the "balanced" British Constitution of King, Lords, and Commons, the Pennsylvania constitution, since it ignored the sober needs of human government, was simply unworkable. Familiar usages, checks on popular power, and energetic execution of the laws were in their view essential to an orderly society composed of imperfect men. It was furthermore necessary to recognize, at least implicitly, that divergent interests and diverse stations in life gave men different perspectives, which stable government would somehow have to reflect. Though Wilson and many other "anticonstitutionalists" were sincere friends of independence and government by consent, they were appalled at the "democratical whimsies" imposed upon them.[7]

The conflict has remained fundamental. The anticonstitutionalists accepted the more traditional idea that wisdom and pursuit of the public good were to be achieved by a system of government protected in some way from *both* arbitrary authority and popular passions. Thus they thought in terms of restraints *within* the government on the power of its officers and of mechanisms that would refine or modulate (though not exclude) the influence of "the people" in the government. Such intricate controls, Wilson and others thought, provided the best, perhaps the only, chance of wise and just rule. The really radical aspect of constitutionalist thought, on the other hand, was to place the critical check in the hands of the people to prevent rulers from becoming corrupt, tyrannical, or self-serving. If enough power were invested in the people, they assumed, liberty and the public good would be preserved. Almost every provision of the 1776 constitution

—annual elections, rotation in office, a virtual referendum on laws, a wide franchise, extraordinary restraints on the executive and judicial branches, and the Council of Censors—expressed this conviction. The vital control was to enable the people to be sure that *their* government and *their* representatives would act in *their* interest. To the radical republicans the usual notion of checks and balances resting on orders and hierarchies in society had been swept away by independence. Thus they saw, with mounting excitement, that the *new* society might provide for government based on *one principle only*, that is, the will of the only remaining interest in the society, that of the public. Full debate on this point in Pennsylvania exposed the most crucial theoretical question underlying the search for new national purposes.

II

In Virginia the same forces were at work, but in different enough degrees to yield quite different results. The "radicals"—Richard Henry Lee, Patrick Henry, and Thomas Jefferson—who pushed Virginia toward independence and who gave her, with Massachusetts, the leadership of that movement, were less "democratical" than their Pennsylvania counterparts, and, since the issue of independence did not so sharply divide Virginia, her radical and conservative spokesmen more often compromised with each other. In the tumults surrounding the decay of British authority and the flight of Lord Dunmore, the last royal governor, extremist and moderate opposition was evident, but the widespread disgust at Dunmore's high-handedness had made most of the colony's established leaders—Richard Bland, Peyton Randolph, Robert Carter Nicholas, and Edmund Pendleton—earnest if cautious foes of Britain. Thus, though young James Madison thought Tidewater gentlemen of property "pusillanimous" in the face of Dunmore's threats, and though Thomas Ludwell Lee complained of "a certain set of Aristocrats," in general what Charles Sydnor has called "the political practices in Washington's Virginia" contained and accommodated animosities.[8]

Nonetheless, Virginians speculated grandly about the unique prospects for human government opened to them, and their early documents and laws reflected a firm republicanism. The Virginia Convention of 1776, after instructing its delegates in Congress to lead in declaring "the United Colonies free and independent states," turned to frame a state government. Let by its foremost republican theoretician, George Mason, the convention adopted a declaration of rights embodying the basic principles of government: "that all men are by nature equally free and independent, and have certain inherent rights, of which, when they enter into a state of society, they cannot, by any compact, deprive or divest their posterity . . . ; that all power is vested in, and consequently derived from, the people . . . ; that a majority of the community hath an indubitable, inalienable, and indefeasible right to reform, alter, or abolish" an unfaithful or unjust government; that the people cannot be bound by laws passed without their consent; "that the freedom of the press is one of the great bulwarks of liberty, and can never be restrained but by despotic government; [and] that no free government, or the blessings of liberty, can be preserved to any people, but by a firm adherence to justice, moderation, temperance, frugality, and virtue, and by frequent recurrence to fundamental principles." This Declaration of Rights, published throughout the colonies before the Declaration of Independence and soon translated and widely reprinted in Europe, became the prototype for such statements during the period that has been called the Age of Democratic Revolution. Though Mason and his colleagues drew from earlier English statements for their document, they gave the principles fuller and clearer formulation than had generally prevailed in the past.[9]

Debate over particular clauses, however, revealed that circumstances could bring about both limitations and extensions of "fundamental rights." The "set of Aristocrats" complained of by Thomas Ludwell Lee, for example, stalled the convention over the first line of Mason's original draft of the Declaration of Rights. If "all men are by nature equally free and independent," they asked, what would prevent slaves from claiming their freedom? "Civil convulsion" might ensue, they warned. Pendleton came up with a saving sophistry. He suggested adding the clause "when they enter into a state of society" after "all men." Since according to usage at that time slaves were held to be outside "a state of society," this would exclude them from the privileges of the declaration and thus preserve what Lee termed Virginia's "execrable system" of human bondage. The convention accepted Pendleton's cleverness, obviously intending, for the time being at least, not to tamper with the system basic to the Virginia economy and embedded in the attitudes of its people. This debate, as well as the antislavery sentiments in Jefferson's first draft of the Declaration of

Independence, reveal, though, that honest Americans were well aware of and embarrassed by the flat contradiction between the proclaimed ideals of their own revolution and the debased condition of their black slaves.[10]

Those ideals received more consistent treatment in the clause defining freedom of religion. Mason had simply incorporated the Lockean language that "all men should enjoy the fullest *Toleration* in the Exercise of Religion, according to the Dictates of Conscience" (italics added), reflecting circumstances in England where the Established Church held a privileged position but *granted toleration* to Dissenters. James Madison, however, who had read such radical Whig theorists as Joseph Priestley and Philip Furneaux and who had come to appreciate "the free air" of the middle colonies where there was no established church, objected to the invidious implications of "toleration." It was, as Thomas Paine later put it, "not the opposite of intolerance, but the counterfeit of it. Both are despotisms. The one assumes to itself the right of withholding liberty of conscience, the other of granting it." Thus, if liberty of conscience was inalienable, applying to all men as a natural right, the idea of toleration was an inadmissible fraud. Madison proposed instead categorical language: "All men are equally entitled to the free exercise of religion, according to the dictates of conscience." When the convention accepted this substitute, the definition of freedom of conscience was lifted beyond the idea of social convenience and official indulgence prevailing in England to the level of an absolute right, where it would subsequently build "the wall of separation" between church and state and protect nonbelief and heresy as well as varieties of orthodoxy.[11]

Though the effort to use Revolutionary idealism to abolish slavery in Virginia ended ignominiously in 1785 when the legislature overwhelmingly rejected a Jefferson-Madison plan for gradual manumission, in other areas the two men labored more successfully to "republicanize" Virginia's laws and institutions. After the Continental Congress had declared independence, Jefferson left for Virginia in September 1776, persuaded that "our whole code must be reviewed, adapted to our republican form of government; and now that we had no negatives of Councils, Governors, and Kings to restrain us from doing right, it should be corrected, in all its parts, with a single eye to reason, and the good of those for whose government it was framed."

His first targets were the semifeudal laws of entailment and primogeniture, which in his view "raised up a distinct set of families, who being privileged by law in the perpetuation of their wealth, were thus formed into a Patrician order." Jefferson proposed that property descend unentailed and be divided equally among children, thus annulling privilege, "and instead of an aristocracy of wealth, of more harm and danger, than benefit, to society, to make an opening for the aristocracy of virtue and talent, which nature has wisely provided for the direction of the interests of society, and scattered with equal hand through all its conditions."[12]

To further break up ancient inequities and to affirm the principle of reason, Jefferson drafted a sweeping law that would give full meaning to the clause guaranteeing liberty of conscience implanted by Madison in the Declaration of Rights. Jefferson began with a series of "self-evident" axioms: "that almighty God hath created the mind free, that all attempts to influence it by temporal punishments or burdens, or by civil incapacitations, tend only to beget habits of hypocrisy and meanness, . . . and that truth is great and will prevail if left to herself, that she is the proper and sufficient antagonist to error, and has nothing to fear from the conflict unless by human inter-position disarmed of her natural weapons, free argument and debate, errors ceasing to be dangerous when it is permitted freely to contradict them." Therefore, he concluded, "all men shall be free to profess, and by argument to maintain, their opinions in matters of religion," as a natural right forever inalienable by civil authority. When in 1785 the Virginia Assembly first rejected a bill sponsored by Patrick Henry to pay "teachers of the Christian religion" from tax funds, and then adopted Jefferson's statute for religious freedom, Madison, whose efforts had been crucial in these events, wrote with justifiable pride, "I flatter myself [we] have in this country [Virginia] extinguished forever the ambitious hope of making laws for the human mind." Though the *practice* of liberty of conscience might often fall short of this ideal, in at least one area Revolutionary principles had raised a standard of immense significance for the future. A key purpose of republican government was to free the human mind and conscience so it might seek and find truth.[13]

Having remodeled the legal code, abolished feudal privileges, and established freedom of conscience, Jefferson sought as well a "bill for a general education, [through which the people] would be qualified to understand their rights, to maintain them, and to exercise with intelligence their parts in self-government." He proposed elementary schools in each locality to be open to all children, intermediate schools in each region for the more able students, and then, as a capstone, a state university where republican principles would be sustained and leaders trained in them and in the branches of science and humane learning vital to a liberal civilization. Jefferson explained the intimate bond between his plan for education and the republican governments founded in 1776: "Every government degenerates when trusted to the rulers of the people alone. The people themselves therefore are its only safe depositories and to render even them safe, their minds must be improved to a certain degree. . . . It has been thought that corruption is restrained by confining the right of suffrage to a few of the wealthier people; but it would be more effectually restrained by an extension of that right to such members as would bid defiance to the means of corruption," that is, to all people educated for republican citizenship. Virtue in rulers—once kings, hereditary nobles, and rich men were regarded as uncertain sources—could be achieved only if the legitimate rulers (the people) were educated for their difficult new task. For centuries the academy or the church or the court tutor had been the carefully sustained means of training in principles of good government. Now, with all these institutions discredited as "unrepublican," an immense reformation was needed—nothing short of a vast system to transform the people and thus find in them the very wellsprings of virtue for so long thought to exist only in a tiny, privileged portion of mankind. Though the state of Virginia did not adopt Jefferson's plan for education, the rationale behind it and its projection of a public school system for all children remained on the agenda of the United States and came to be one of its vital purposes.[14]

As the defeat of the Jefferson-Madison plans for public education and for the gradual abolition of slavery, and even the closely contested ten-year battle over religious freedom reveal, the enactment of "republicanized" laws in Virginia was neither swift nor easy. Pendleton and Nicholas, "honest men, but zealous churchmen," even after defeat on church establishment, managed to preserve some of the old privileges. On the revision of the laws, Pendleton proved a learned and often useful colleague, but he was, as Jefferson noted, "zealously attached to ancient establishments." He was also an able debater, "full of resource, and never vanquished; for if he lost the main battle, he returned upon you, and regained so much of it as to make it a drawn one, by dexterous manoeuvres, skirmishes in detail, and recovery of small advantages which, little singly, were important all together." You never knew, Jefferson concluded wearily, "when you were clear of him." A man with such a conservative outlook and with numerous able allies was thus able to preserve in Virginia many of the old ways and establish there, as was true in the other states, a persisting tension between tradition and the new republican ideals. Nonetheless, as Jefferson's writings and career show so graphically, innovating ideas had been set in motion and would henceforth prod those in places of power.[15]

III

In addition to the thrusts to vitalize "government by consent" evident in Pennsylvania, and to reform the laws on a republican pattern undertaken in Virginia, the new states struggled to give meaning to the idea of constitutionalism itself. What was a constitution—a collection of precedents such as the Constitution of Great Britain idealized by Montesquieu, or a written document such as the charters of many of the colonies? Furthermore, if a society had no constitution, or sought a new one, from whence could it legitimately come and what was its relation to subsequent statute law? Finally, if a constitution was somehow "higher law," was it to be considered codified "natural law," and thus "unalienable" or immutable—even if the people consented to its abridgment?

In Massachusetts the search for a new constitution began in 1774 when word arrived that Great Britain, reacting to the Boston Tea Party, had abrogated the colony's charter. There had been dubiously legal town meetings and even sessions of the legislature before, but the colony's situation in 1774 seemed uniquely precarious: If the old government was defunct, and if, as all but a few Tories in the colony were determined, mere military government was unacceptable, what remained? To some students of Locke and the radical Whigs, the answer seemed to be that Massachusetts had reverted to "the state of nature." It was a familiar moral conception, but it was *in fact* unprecedented and frightening to many to be bereft of government. Also, towns in the western part of the state worried that eastern interests would use the lapse of government to impose some some kind of arbitrary control. When Boston groups tried merely to reestablish the colony's abrogated charter, Berkshire towns declared that they preferred a state of nature to an "antient Mode of Government . . . we so much detest and abhor." In May 1776 the town of Pittsfield insisted that "what is the fundamental Constitution of this province, what are the undeniable Rights of the people, the power of the Rulers, how often to be elected by the people, etc. . . . [are] things [not] yet ascertained." The workings of the courts, legalization of documents, and so on, were all "nothing whilst the foundation is unfixed, the Corner stone of Government unlaid." A constitution "*de novo*," the town meeting declared, was needed. Obviously there was much to do in theory and in practice to establish legitimate authority in Massachusetts.[16]

With government virtually suspended in parts of the state, and with more or less ad hoc bodies conducting the Revolution, the Boston town meeting insisted on a fundamental new start: The form of government "includes our all—it effects every Individual; every individual therefore ought to be consulting, aiding and assisting." It repudiated constitution-making "restricted or confined to any particular Assembly however respectable," while other towns asked that the constitution be formed by "electing persons for the expressed purpose of forming the Plan of Government." Only thus could "the wisdom of the whole State" be collected. The House of Representatives refused to call such a convention; but in 1778 it did submit to the people for ratification a constitution it had drafted. Partly because no constitutional convention had been called, the electorate rejected the proposed document, five to one. A year later the legislature bowed to the growing force of the "fundamental law" argument: the constitution of the "new state" of Massachusetts would be drafted by a convention especially elected for that purpose and would not become legitimate until ratified by a two-thirds vote of the people. This deliberate process affirmed the special place "constitutionalism" had come to occupy in an evolving American political theory.[17]

The document drafted by the Massachusetts convention under John Adams' leadership in the fall of 1779 not only defined *how* to legitimize a constitution but also *what* its basic qualities should be. The people, the preamble declared, "deliberately and peaceably, without fraud, violence, or surprise, [entered] into an original, explicit, and solemn compact," to frame "a constitution of government, to provide for an equitable mode of making laws, as well as for an impartial interpretation and faithful execution of them; that every man may, at all times, find his security in them." Using the three-part separation of powers he had explained in his *Thoughts on Government*, Adams outlined a framework of basic rights and structure of government that would at once protect what was inalienable, permit the commonwealth to "secure its existence," and ensure "the blessings of life" to its citizens.[18]

In an address to the people offering the constitution for ratification, the convention declared that the delegates, acting in a way becoming to "the representatives of a wise, understanding, and free people," had deliberated and compromised, seeking to answer "the great inquiry . . . wherein the common interest consists." To them, this common interest rested upon a conception of virtue long hallowed in Western thought: "That the honor and happiness of a people depend upon morality, . . . that the public worship of God had a tendency to inculcate the principles thereof," and that therefore towns were authorized and might be required "to make suitable provision . . . for the institution of the public worship of God, and for the support and maintenance of public Protestant teachers of piety, religion, and morality." Nevertheless, and with little sense of contradiction, the convention proclaimed that "the free exercise of *the rights of conscience*" prohibited interference with any form of public worship and permitted each denomination to direct religious taxes gathered from its members to its own "teachers." The delegates were unwilling, however, to abandon what they regarded as essential links between virtue, religion, and state support.

To these conventional religious avowals they added John Adams' effusive secularized plans to create a "higher civilization" in Massachusetts. Harvard College, a separate section of the constitution declared, founded by "wise and pious ancestors," had graduated "many persons of great eminence . . . both in church and state," and should therefore be confirmed in all its "powers, authorities, rights, liberties, privileges, immunities, and franchises." Furthermore, seeking to fix before the people and their governors the highest humane ideals and noting that "the preservation of . . . rights and liberties" depended on "wisdom and knowledge, as well as virtue, diffused generally among the body of the people," the constitution set forth three broad duties for legislatures and magistrates:

To cherish the interests of literature and the sciences, and all seminaries of them, [and] public schools and grammar schools in the towns: to encourage private societies and public institutions, rewards and immunities, for the promotion of agriculture, arts, sciences, commerce, trades, manufactures, and a natural history of the country; [and] to countenance and inculcate the principles of humanity and general benevolence, public and private charity, industry and frugality, honesty and punctuality in their dealings; sincerity, good humor, and all social affections, and generous sentiments, among the people.

Like Aristotle, John Adams clearly believed that "a state exists for the sake of the good life, and not for the sake of life only."

In explaining the proposed machinery of government the convention tacitly acknowledged a growing fear that the new American states had so much neglected "energy" in government that they seemed likely to "sink into anarchy." Nonetheless, since "power without *any* restraint is tyranny, . . . the powers of government [have to] be balanced, a task requiring the highest skill in political architecture." To find this delicate counterpoise between energy and restraint, the convention went even further in the separation of powers than John Adams had outlined in his *Thoughts on Government*. Most critical was the need to prevent all power from being drawn into the "vortex" of the lower house of the legislature, as state constitutions of 1776 had tended to induce. This not only eliminated effective checks, but also, by infusing the legislature with Blackstonian notions of supremacy, negated the idea of a fundamental law which even the legislature was forbidden to abridge. Thus the last clause of the Declaration of Rights affirmed that the departments of government had to be separate, the legislative, executive, and judicial branches each forbearing to infringe on the other, "to the end that it may be a government of laws and not of men."

The principle of consent underlay the choice of both houses of the legislature as well as of the governor: each would be elected annually by an electorate limited by a small-property qualification intended to exclude only the idle and the profligate. (Careful study of voting patterns in Massachusetts both before and after adoption of the 1780 constitution has shown that few adult males were excluded from town elections, and that such property qualifications as existed seldom narrowed the franchise in state elections.) With *three* parts of the government thus resting on a broad base, the constitution was radically republican by the standards of its day. But to provide a check on this power and to afford an explicit protection for property rights, office-holders had substantially higher qualifications: members of the lower house had to possess a freehold of one hundred pounds; senators, three hundred pounds; and the governor the considerable freehold of one thousand pounds. Further checks against hasty, factious legislation were that the houses would vote separately, each would have a negative on the other, and the governor would have an absolute veto. Though he was to have a council, his veto power was final regardless of their concurrence. This power, much greater than that given to executives in Virginia and Pennsylvania, was thought to be safe because the governor was "emphatically the representative of the whole people, being chosen, not by one town or county, but by the people at large." It was further agreed that his unitary character would make him clearly accountable for his actions, and that his legislative power would "preserve the laws from being unsystematical and inaccurate." Judges, with "fixed and ample salaries" and appointed to serve during good behavior, would "at all times feel themselves independent and free." In this framework the convention thought the commonwealth would "long enjoy the blessings of a well-ordered and free government."

IV

Though often viewed as a reaction against the mild, simpler, legislature-dominated governments devised by other states earlier in the Revolution, the Massachusetts constitution of 1780 more importantly revealed the *continuing* efforts of Americans to work out the implications of self-government as their experience with it and speculation about it went on. They did, of course, benefit from the lessons of the preceding few years, but the basic intention was to further, not hinder, the growth of *viable* republican institutions. By 1787, according to Jefferson's famous calculation designed to ease fears over Shays' Rebellion, there had been thirteen times eleven or nearly 150 years of experience under governments by consent in the American states. From his European vantage point, Jefferson thought republicanism had been overwhelmingly vindicated, despite such trifles as the Shays affair, which he regarded as the most "honorably conducted" rebellion in history and on the whole a sign of the vigilance of the Massachusetts citizenry. Jefferson's deep concern was for change and improvement that would continue to exploit the opportunities opened up in 1776. Though many Americans differed with him in diagnosis and prescription, and though some even had grave doubts that republican government could work, a constructively critical mood prevailed.[19]

Many, responding to the long debate leading to the Declaration of Independence, focused on representation. How could it be made to reflect the will of the people with the least possible distortion or corruption? Devices intended to achieve this included small districts, annual elections, rotation in office, versions of referendum and recall, and a unicameral legislature, the object being to create a legislature that would somehow embody the people: their interests, their will, their spirit. What meaning did government by consent have, if not that? With the corruptions of the British Parliament, the sophistries of "virtual representation," and the many infringements of English authority on colonial government fresh in their minds, Americans thought they knew very well where they had been and where they should be going. The most alluring proposition, then—suggested by Tom Paine in *Common Sense* and tried most earnestly by Pennsylvania in 1776—was direct, unicameral, legislative government.

This arrangement, it soon appeared, resulted not in a prevailing unity guiding the government of the commonwealth, but in a clash of interests reflecting the diversity of the people of Pennsylvania. Even the conduct of the Revolution itself, in which the fight against a common enemy most demanded unity, aroused bitter dissension. Raising money, recruiting soldiers, responding to the needs of the Continental Congress, and dealing with shades of Toryism all evoked bitter disputes. Moreover, animosities decades old in the province—Presbyterians versus Quakers, British settlers versus German settlers, Westerners versus Easterners, and so on—had from the very beginning injected partisanship into the new government adopted in 1776. The most simple, direct model of representative government, far from eliminating factions and selfishness, seemed almost to encourage them. Since hardly anyone in the eighteenth century thought a government acting merely as a broker among conflicting interests had any virtue at all, it seemed important to rethink assumptions and perhaps design new structures.

In most states bicameralism, with real separation of the houses and real power granted to the upper chamber, seemed a good way to modulate factious tendencies. The aim was both moral and practical. Requiring legislation to pass two houses would entail more delibera- tion and more considered judgment, and thus would heighten the chance that justice and wisdom, not passion and impulse, would pre- vail. Furthermore, the wealth and social continuity represented in the higher chamber (senate) would furnish a stability and a sense of the enduring interests of the state unlikely to be heard amid the *vox populi*. This view of the senate was, of course, frankly conservative, but entirely within the range of respectable eighteenth-century repub- licanism.

Though republican theorists increasingly saw that factions or parties were inevitable in a free society, and some, like Madison, advanced a dynamic view that the ill effects of factions could be substantially dampened, none advocated or foresaw that an organized opposition party might be a useful, loyal watchdog on the group in power. Trans- fixed by the corruptions of English party politics and raised on the ideas of Bolingbroke and others that a good ruler was one who rose above partisan concerns, neither those who wanted to change the Ar- ticles of Confederation nor the defenders of the Articles entertained the possibility that permanent parties might be a constructive component in republican government. As Richard Hofstadter has observed, "The fathers hoped to create not a system of party government under a con- stitution but rather a constitutional government that would check and control parties."[20]

As experience with state governments accumulated, the executive and judicial branches received fuller consideration than they had in 1776. If simple government by consent through a single representative assembly seemed insufficient, then one had to take seriously the inclu- sion and structure of the other branches. The main deficiencies of the executive in such states as Virginia were a general lack of power to do anything, a dilution of responsibility because consent of the council was required to act, and a debilitating entanglement in legislative cabals during the annual elections by that branch. Thus beginning with New York in 1777 and especially in Massachusetts in 1780, a powerful, independent executive began to reemerge. It was increasingly argued that the election of the governor by the people made his powers to veto legislation, appoint officers of government, and command the militia a proper *fulfillment* of the republican principle, rather than a subversion of it, as theories of legislative dominance had assumed.

The need in the judiciary was to ensure independence. Either election by the people or appointment by the legislature, especially if for a limited term, left judges subject to precisely those political pressures that would prevent the impartiality implicit in the idea of "equal justice." Experience with assembly-appointed judges was so bad in Virginia by 1785 that James Madison declared the British system preferable. Under it, he noted, executive appointment, fixed salaries, and life tenure enabled judges to maintain "private Rights against all the corruptions of the two other departments." Though these strategies to preserve judicial independence seemed unrepublican to some, it was widely agreed that a steady protection of personal and property rights was essential to good government, and that an impartial judiciary seemed the best way to achieve this.[21]

Equally important for the protection of natural rights was some device to exalt their standing above that of mere statute law. A similar need for immutability required that the structure and process of government also have a foundation firmer than statute law. Inalienable rights and mode of government had somehow to be made "fundamental law." Thus the idea of constitutionalism—written law enacted by grand conventions of the people to be altered only by similarly explicit and solemn action of the people—acquired an increasingly strong hold in the United States during the 1780s, and for a time there seemed little difficulty in reconciling this implicit restraint on popular legislatures with the *sine qua non* of rule by the people.

But as Americans debated and tested various modes and devices of republican government in the years after 1776, they confronted again and again the basic tension implanted in the Declaration of Independence: that certain rights were "unalienable" and that governments were instituted among men to secure these rights, but also that governments derived "their just powers from the consent of the governed." Under these propositions, governments resting on consent

might agree to, even insist upon, a violation of an "unalienable" right.
Which principle then had priority? The vogue of legislative supremacy implied that the first concern was for government by consent—
and rather facilely to assume that such government by its very nature
would cherish natural rights. Yet, Madison, Jefferson, and many others
thought that state legislatures and even the Continental Congress itself,
often responding directly and obviously to the demands of the people,
passed outrageously unjust laws. Madison had no difficulty deciding
which side to take when that happened:

There is no maxim in my opinion which is more liable to be misapplied, and
which therefore more needs elucidation than the current one that the interest of the majority is the political standard of right and wrong. Taking the
word "interest" as synonymous with "ultimate happiness" in which sense it
is qualified with every necessary moral ingredient, the proposition is no
doubt true. But taking it in the popular sense, as referring to immediate
augmentation of property and wealth, nothing can be more false. In the
latter sense it would be the interest of the majority in every community to
despoil and enslave the minority of individuals. . . . In fact it is only re-
establishing under another name and a more specious form, force as the
measure of right.

Jefferson made the same point more pithily in *Notes on Virginia*
(1782): "One hundred and seventy-three despots would surely be as
oppressive as one."[22]

The vital dynamic of political thought in the United States during
the 1780s, then, was not substantial shifts to the left or right, but
rather a dawning sense of the difficulty and intricacy of establishing a
republican government that both rested on popular consent and protected inalienable rights of individuals.

7. The Convention of 1787

I

IN THIS MOOD THE FEDERAL CONVENTION GATHERED IN MAY 1787. ITS LEADING SPIRIT, JAMES MADISON, HAD SPENT THE PRECEDING MONTHS STUDYING THE PROBLEMS "OF ANCIENT AND MODERN CONFEDERACIES" AND THE "VICES OF THE POLITICAL SYSTEM OF THE UNITED STATES." Handling the tension between rights and majority rule, as well as attending to the conduct of government as he had observed and experienced it for fifteen years, left Madison preoccupied with structure and mechanism. He catalogued the modes of financial support, diplomatic representation, wartime cooperation, regulation of commerce, and coercion of delinquent members used by the various confederacies, noting especially the bonds of union more or less effective in practice and the particular causes of enfeeblement or dissolution of confederacies in history. He discovered that the Greek confederacies had proved too weak, first to resist Philip of Macedon and later to confound "the vast projects of Rome." Another kind of difficulty arose in the United Provinces of the Netherlands, where, though the confederation appeared strong on paper, "the jealousy in each province of its sovereignty renders the practice very different from the theory." Vulnerability to attack from without, intrigue by foreign governments within, and the debilitating effect of internal quarreling, all circumstances experienced by the United States during Madison's service in the Continental Congress, convinced him that however idyllic small or loosely organized states might seem, reality required a strong union.[1]

Studying the "vices" of American governments, Madison was appalled at the selfishness, provincialism, and inconstancy of the thirteen autonomous states. "Is it to be imagined," he asked, "that an ordinary citizen or even an Assemblyman from Rhode Island in estimating the policy of paper money, ever considered or cared, in what light the measure would be viewed in France or Holland; or even in Massachusetts or Connecticut? It was a sufficient temptation to both [citizen and assemblyman] that it was for their interest; it was a sufficient sanction to the latter that it was popular in the state; to the former that it was so in the neighbourhood." In Congress, courting popularity, whining about imagined as well as real hardships, and defaulting on commitments because of suspicion of the defaults of others so undermined authority that Madison pronounced the Articles of Confederation "a mere treaty of friendship," devoid of the uniformity and compulsion essential to law and government. The great need was for some structure, some mechanism, that could overcome pettiness and give effect to "the general and permanent good of the community."[2]

In letters to Washington and to Governor Edmund Randolph of Virginia on the eve of the Convention Madison explained a frame of union that he thought might overcome these glaring flaws and yet remain faithful to the republican principle. He "sought for a middle ground," he wrote, between "an individual independence of the states . . . irreconcileable with their aggregate sovereignty" and a consolidated nation both unacceptable to the states and dangerous to the liberties of the people. The need was for "a due supremacy of the national authority [that did not] exclude the local authorities wherever they can be subordinately useful." Madison argued that a legislature elected by the people and proportioned according to population was the vital need. Then the general government could in justice claim enlarged power over commerce, war, diplomacy, currency, and, generally, "all cases to which the separate states are incompetent," as well as possess a veto over acts of the state legislatures. A national executive and judiciary would give the necessary force and uniformity to national measures, while a bicameral legislature would lift deliberation above impulse in enacting laws. Finally, to give the new constitution the sanction of higher, fundamental law, Madison proposed that it be ratified by the people of the various states in conventions called especially for that purpose. These propositions, laid before the Constitutional Convention by Randolph in what has since been known as the

Virginia Plan, formed the practical point of departure for the delegates in Philadelphia during the summer of 1787.[3]

In Madison's study before the Convention he had in the back of his mind basic questions of political philosophy, but his attention centered on specific needs and devices. Debate in the Convention had generally the same focus, but in explaining themselves to each other, and in rising to challenges, the delegates also continued the intense and occasionally creative consideration of first principles that had characterized both the controversy with Great Britain before 1776 and the formation of state governments after that. In addition to the primary need to devise a proper union (the delegates were well aware that it probably fell to them to decide whether the former colonies were to be one nation or many), the theory and practice of government in the United States as it had evolved in the dozen years before 1787 bequeathed substantial and intricate questions: How could the flaws manifest in legislative supremacy be avoided and government by consent still be retained? Could an energetic executive and a firm judiciary be separated from their long connection with monarchical despotism? Could the new constitution receive special legitimization as "supreme law" in a way that would shield it from manipulation by special interests and abuse by impassioned majorities? Could a central government that ruled over more than a half-million square miles of territory meaningfully rest on the consent of the governed? These questions showed that Americans had come a long way from the simple agenda of Revolutionary idealism in 1776. It was not that the goals of the Revolution were to be repudiated or even retrenched, but rather that two decades of debate had at once clarified and complicated the meaning of these goals.

All the questions, in fact, received answers in terms of a proposition that had evolved out of the Revolutionary debates. Rather than conceiving of government as self-existing, sovereign, and separate from the people, and therefore defining good government as a matter of a just "contract" between it and the people that guaranteed rights to the people, it was supposed that in a new nation without a primordial division between rulers and ruled the people themselves were sovereign. Locke, John Wise, and others had theorized the existence of a people before the existence of a government, but in fact, as Locke's endorsement of monarchy showed, they more or less accepted traditional institutions not, strictly speaking, emanating from the people. The classic divisions between monarchy, aristocracy, and democracy, and the much-admired "separation" of these components under the British Constitution, required a monarch and an aristocracy separate from society at large and, ordinarily, self-perpetuating. To these elements "the people" were then added, presumably in a separate chamber like the British House of Commons. Within such a structure some element had to be sovereign, that is, authorized to have final power. Following Blackstone's interpretation of the Settlement of 1688 in Great Britain, Parliament was this sovereign body.

When, however, the American Revolution swept royal authority away and substituted for it "we the people," the hallowed argument over balance among ancient orders, to say nothing of the debate over which element was sovereign, became irrelevant: the people and the people alone were sovereign under the republican doctrine developed in the decade after the Declaration of Independence. Thus the governors and judges were conceived as "of the people," rather than as separately existing authorities with whom the people's representatives had to negotiate in order to govern. "The executive and judicial powers," lectured James Wilson, "are now drawn from the same source, are now animated by the same principles, and are now directed to the same ends, with the legislative authority; they who execute, and they who administer the laws, are as much the servants, and therefore as much the friends of the people, as those who make them." Radical Whig and Revolutionary suspicions of executive and judicial power, as well as the concomitant exaltation of the legislature, were therefore not necessary when the people were sovereign. In a new nation the people could entirely structure and empower the government. They could distribute power as they saw fit, among the three branches as well as between national and state governments. This transformed the traditional view of balance of powers, which had supposed that the government essentially reproduced preexisting orders in the society. Now, properly speaking, there were no more *orders*, but simply the people—with all their diverse and multifarious *interests*. Thus the need in a constitution was to devise sufficiently different embodiments of the people's sovereignty to provide real balances of power (experience under the state constitutions seemed to make such balance still of prime importance), but the structure and mechanism had to be much more intricate and skillfully arranged than in a society where there were distinct classes which formed obvious sources of power capable of being set against one another.[4]

Now the need was not to design a government to reflect preexisting orders in society, and thus ideally to embody in the government both the useful qualities of each order and checks against their harmful tendencies, but rather to find means to capitalize on the good qualities of man in general and to guard against his depravities. Without, for example, first, second, and third estates, or bishops, lords, and commons, there was no way in the United States to gather the elements of society into countervailing assemblies. American society did not even contain such elements in the traditional sense. Clashing interests, social distinctions, diverse ethnic and religious groups, disparities in wealth, and other inequities it had in abundance, but these did not at all resemble the divisions of a formally, legally hierarchical society. The only such division in the United States—the status of black slaves—was adroitly handled by simply not regarding slaves as being "in society" and hence denying entirely their rights as citizens. But apart from this exclusion, Americans generally recognized by 1787 that the Declaration of Independence required them to devise a government containing only one order, the people, and to rest it entirely on them. There simply was no other foundation or legitimate source of power after the Revolution. On the other hand, between 1776 and 1787 preoccupation with the sobering facts of human weakness and greed had heightened. The need, therefore, as Madison expressed it in *The Federalist* No. 51, to "first enable the government to control the governed; and in the next place, to oblige it to control itself," remained as strong as under classical conceptions of balance of power. But without social orders the entire burden fell on a structure and mechanism that would somehow—almost miraculously, it must have seemed to men raised on Montesquieu and Blackstone—afford the checks and balances made necessary by the limitations of human nature.[5]

II

The Convention of 1787, as its members fully recognized and as scholars ever since have emphasized, was an arena for reconciling and compromising clashing interests as well as a deliberative body. On almost every issue delegates acted as they did in part because of some tangible or provincial bias. Differences over geography, commerce, wealth, religion, customs, social attitudes, land speculation, and credit were often behind disputes over proposals for this or that structure of government. Yet, except for some quickly tabled suggestions, notably by Alexander Hamilton, Gouverneur Morris, and Charles Pinckney, the delegates accepted the political imperative of a government resting on the people. Disqualifications, privileges, and segregation by class, wealth, or religion (excepting, again, the total exclusion of slaves) are absent from the finished Constitution, and, in fact, were not even seriously considered. The indirect acceptance of *state* qualifications for voting (ordinarily a small freehold or other relatively modest property holding, and, not even discussed at this time, excluding women) recognized prevailing practices and, more important in the long run, erected no barriers to the removal of such qualifications by the states. That the Convention easily bypassed what had hitherto been considered a vital question is evidence of how fully accepted, by 1787, was the sovereignty of the people.

With Madison's Virginia Plan before them, the delegates accepted at once a resolution that "a national Government ought to be established consisting of a supreme Legislative, Executive, and Judiciary." Thus the Convention committed itself, with only Connecticut dissenting, to a new frame of government, not merely an alteration of the Articles of Confederation. Though such a course violated the instructions of many of the delegates (a point often raised in the ratification debates), it seemed justified by the natural right of a people (through their representatives) to decide upon their own government—merely another manifestation of their sovereignty, it was often noted.

In considering limitations on legislative power the delegates had especially in mind the turbulent, shortsighted actions of so many state legislatures since 1776. Noting the "popular clamour in Massachusetts [and] . . . the danger of the levelling spirit," Elbridge Gerry proclaimed that "the evils we experience flow from the excess of democracy." Such a conviction made delegates take seriously Madison's proposal for a federal veto power over state laws, led eventually to substitution of the supreme law clause for the direct veto, and lay behind excluding the state legislatures from a role in electing the House of Representatives and the President. Concerning the national legislature, however, many delegates agreed with George Mason of Virginia that the lower house ought to be "the grand depository of the democratic principle." Wilson of Pennsylvania added that the national government ought to have "as broad a basis as possible" since a republic "could not long subsist without the confidence of the people."[6]

After the Convention accepted this argument by providing for direct proportional election of the House of Representatives, discussion of the Senate hinged on how to make it reflect a different constituency and be a more detached, deliberative body than the lower house. Some delegates pointed out that if there was but one sovereign (the people), a genuinely different base for the upper house was ultimately impossible. The Great Compromise embodied the novel theory that sheer structural ingenuity could assure checks and balances: the states were to be equal in the Senate, which would have special powers over treaties and appointments; Senators were to be elected by their legislatures and have longer terms and be fewer in number than Representatives. Madison bitterly opposed the compromise giving tiny Delaware and huge Virginia the same representation in the Senate ("the rotten borough" system all over again, he thought), but he nonetheless argued that it could become a useful part of the new government. The Senate would check "the propensity of all single and numerous assemblies, to yield to the impulse of sudden and violent passions, and to be seduced by factious leaders, into intemperate and pernicious resolutions." Furthermore, "no small share of the present embarrassments of America is to be charged on the blunders of our governments . . . [whose acts were often] but so many monuments to deficient wisdom." Madison hoped the more select, more deliberative Senators would discover "the comprehensive interests of their country." Thus the Senate was conceived as a mechanical check on the power of the lower house, and also as a source of wisdom that might improve the quality of legislation. Furthermore, this design for the legislature, by complicating the process of lawmaking, was thought to embody a restraint on the legislature's tendency to dominate the other branches of government.[7]

Constructing the executive was the Convention's most perplexing task, because before 1776 Americans had had very little experience with republican (elected) governors. Moreover, they tended to equate their bad experience with *arbitrary* executive power under royal rule with executive power in general. Scrutinizing history proved of little use either, because more often than not even republics and confederacies had depended on some hereditary device for the executive authority. The Virginia Plan failed to specify even whether there should be a single or a plural executive, perhaps because Madison knew the Virginia spokesman, Edmund Randolph, believed "a unity in the Executive [was] the foetus of monarchy." Equally unformed were notions about the powers and election of the executive. In two weeks of intermittent debate Wilson and others secured approval for a single executive largely because the universally trusted Washington sat before the delegates—living proof that one man could wield power responsibly—and since all assumed he would be the first national leader, it was thought safe to construct the executive office at least in part according to his qualifications. Though disagreement remained over the powers of the executive, delegates tentatively granted the right to appoint subordinates to carry out the laws, special powers over diplomacy and national defense, and a veto the legislature might override by a two-thirds vote.

Roger Sherman of Connecticut urged election of the executive by the state legislatures, while others wanted the national legislature to choose him. Wilson, who among the delegates best understood the dawning idea of the sovereignty of the people, urged direct election by the people. Sherman, preoccupied with legislative supremacy and haunted by the Whiggish specter of Tudor-Stuart alliances with the people against the authority of Parliament, declared Wilson's proposal "the very essence of tyranny." Brushing aside Wilson's compromise suggestion of an electoral college scheme, the Convention accepted instead, but with little conviction, election by the national legislature.[8]

After a month of contentious debate about issues surrounding the Great Compromise, Madison, characteristically, offered the telling analysis of the executive question. The alternatives, he argued, were four: election by state legislatures, by the national legislature, by the people, or by some especially chosen intermediate group, i.e., an electoral college. The first two modes were inadmissible not only because they made the executive subordinate to legislative bodies, but also because election by any "standing body" would find its members being "courted and intrigued with by the Candidates, by their partizans, and by the Ministers of foreign powers." Choice by the people, though theoretically sound as Wilson had argued, was impractical: small states would object as would the less populous South because of "a disproportion of qualified voters" in the larger and Northern states.

The only recourse left, though Madison shrewdly did not press the point, was some variety of electoral college. Major unresolved questions about the executive were referred in late August to a committee on unfinished parts which reported the plan finally adopted: a President chosen by an electoral college for a term of four years (with reeligibility) and empowered to appoint judges as well as executive officers, and to make treaties, all with the advice and consent of the Senate. Though these provisions reflected clauses drawn variously from the Massachusetts, New York, and Maryland constitutions, overall the executive office was novel. Its design revealed, too, how deeply committed the delegates were to the sovereignty of the people. The executive was viewed increasingly not as a remote, irresponsible officer whose powers had to be restrained by the representatives of the people, but rather as one who could speak and act for all the people. His perspective and his election would be more on a "continental scale," as Wilson put it, than any other officer in the government.[9]

The formation of the judiciary, though it occasioned much less debate, was guided by the same growing awareness of what it means to rest a government entirely on popular authority. The Convention readily accepted the idea that there be a national court system and gave the legislature power to establish federal district and circuit courts, but questions of appointment, jurisdiction, and relation to state courts were more troublesome. The supreme law clause satisfied nationalists like Madison and Wilson that the state courts could be made sufficiently subordinate, while the growing confidence in the unprecedented executive office, plus the impracticality of other plans, in the end threw the appointing power into the President's hands. Satisfactory experience, under English rule and in the new states, with judges serving during good behavior led to quick adoption of that tenure, but the delegates were aware nonetheless that this insulation from popular control needed special justification in a republic. Hamilton later explained the Convention's view in *The Federalist* No. 78. Life tenure for judges, under a constitution ratified by the people and guaranteeing their prerogatives, he argued, would guard "the rights of individuals from those ill humours" that often afflicted legislatures. Courts independent of the other branches of government, in other words, would *preserve* the declaration of the general will represented by the act of adopting a constitution as fundamental law. This fundamental law, then, was not so much a means of *resisting* the voice of the people expressed by the legislature, as a means of *sustaining* the more considered view of the people set forth in the solemn, uniquely important state ratifying conventions.

In fact, concern over the careless ad hoc institution of the first state constitutions and of the Articles of Confederation had long troubled thoughtful republicans—approval of these constitutions by existing legislatures amounted merely to a self-interested assumption of "higher" authority. Madison and Jefferson had concluded in the mid-1780s that the Virginia constitution of 1776 was seriously flawed because it rested on mere legislative promulgation. During the Federal Convention Madison declared that "the true difference . . . between a *league* or *treaty*, and a *Constitution*" was the difference between "a system founded on the Legislatures only, and one founded on the people." Gouverneur Morris pointed out that if judges were to be permitted to declare statute law contravening the Constitution "null and void," the Constitution would have to be "ratified in the most unexceptional form, and by the supreme authority of the people themselves." The federalists, then, saw state ratifying conventions as a device for having the people discern, declare, and establish "fundamental law," something few thought could be done by legislatures even if chosen by the people. The special election for a purpose clearly designated in advance, the aura of momentousness, the gathering of "the first characters" of each state, the elevated debate, and the single, solemn vote "yes" or "no" of the delegates combined to give a ratifying convention an authority superior to state legislatures and constitutions and to Congress. It was thus capable in a unique way of expressing both supreme law and the will of the people. Somehow, for a brief period, the tension between natural law and the consent of the people was reduced enough to permit the two concepts to combine in the same body and hence virtually to consecrate a basic frame of government. Though this "solution" had theoretical and practical deficiencies, it seemed a sufficiently pure embodiment of Lockean verities to confer on law thus sanctified the requisite "higher" quality. The ratifying convention seemed, at any rate, the only way the newly enshrined sovereignty of the people could be reconciled with a devotion to inalienable rights.[10]

Though this device took care of the knottiest theoretical problem facing the Convention, it left unresolved the practical difficulty of uniting so many states spread over such a huge area under one government. Hallowed authorities from Aristotle to Montesquieu had declared that democratic and even republican government could work only over a small area on the model of a Greek city-state, or at best in a tiny country such as Holland or Switzerland. Indeed, many people had worried considerably whether some of the thirteen states were not too big for successful republican government. The people in a republic, under this view, had to know their representatives intimately and even know each other in some real sense for the deliberations of government to reflect their needs and their concerns. Obviously, then, only a small province, on the order of a German *Heimat*, could be a republic. On the other hand, large nations or empires were thought to need strong, energetic leadership that could be provided only by a monarch like Alexander, Julius Caesar, or Louis XIV. Such a monarchy, of course, was synonymous with tyranny and therefore incompatible with what all agreed was the purpose of the American Revolution. Attempts to exercise free republican government over extensive areas had always led to the fatal cycle of misunderstanding, clashing interests, chaos, and tyranny. The argument, then, that the tumultuous tendency of republics made that form suitable only for small areas seemed to forbid stretching such government over a nation a thousand miles long.

Madison, in a now familiar conception, reversed the argument: a large republic, by encompassing many interests, far from being more unstable and factious than a small republic, would in fact be less tumultuous because the various factions would check each other. Tiny Rhode Island, Madison noted, had been, as nearly all the delegates acknowledged, the most narrow-minded, faction-ridden, and unstable of the states during the Confederation period. The extended sphere of government, and the "refinements" achieved in electing representatives, would prevent factions from coalescing and thus neutralize their danger. As Madison explained at a crucial point in the Convention debates, an *enlarged* republic "was the only defense against the inconveniences of democracy consistent with the democratic form of government; ... thereby [dividing] the community into so great a number of interests and parties, that in the first place a majority [faction] will not be likely at the same moment to have a common interest separate from that of the whole or of a minority, and in the second place, that in case they should have such an interest, they might not be apt to unite in the pursuit of it." In persuading the Convention to this view, Madison both undercut the arguments against a large republic and rested the federal government on a realistic recognition of the variety of interests sure to be spawned by a free society.[11]

With the major structural problems resolved, and armed with an ingenious argument validating "an extended republic," delegates of all the states present at the Convention on September 17, 1787, approved its work. The Constitution was, they hoped, a republican solution to the intricacies of human government revealed in twenty years of Revolutionary experience and in a summer of intense debate. The delegates noted, in making public their labors, that "in all our deliberations . . . we kept steadily in our view . . . the consolidation of our Union, in which is involved our prosperity, felicity, safety, perhaps our national existence." Impressed with the threatened demise of Revolutionary hopes (Washington had written in November 1786 that "no morn ever dawned more favorably than ours did; and no day was ever more clouded than the present"), the Convention sought to find a framework capable of sustaining them.[12]

8. The Ratification Debate

I

AS THE NATION BEGAN THE GREAT DEBATE OVER RATIFICATION, THE AD-
VOCATES OF THE NEW CONSTITUTION TOOK FOR THEMSELVES THE
NAME "FEDERALISTS." THIS WAS ADVANTAGEOUS BECAUSE NEARLY
ALL AMERICANS LOOKED UPON THEIR COUNTRY AS A FEDERATION (OR CON-
federation—the terms were synonymous in 1787) of states rather than
a consolidated nation. No group could campaign under a "nationalist"
banner with any hope of success. As Madison explained in *The Federalist* No. 39, however, the Constitution was actually a "composite" of
federal and national parts. It was federal in that the states as political
units participated in the general government. The method of electing
Senators and the definition of *state* powers in the Constitution, for example, were federal features. On the other hand, the method of electing
Representatives and the enforcement of laws of Congress directly on the
people by officers of the general government were national features.
Since this composite was championed by people calling themselves
federalists, in time the composite itself came to define what was meant
by "federal government."

The ratification debates sustained another long-standing usage in
Western political thought. The general term "government by consent" encompassed several forms: (1) constitutional monarchy, where
the monarch's powers were limited and where the government included some form of house of commons; (2) republic, meaning a
representative form of government; (3) democracy, generally referring to a direct manifestation of the voice of the people within a

[121]

government, but also meaning a small-scale direct democracy such as might exist in a town meeting. Nearly all shades of American opinion (at least that received public expression) regarded "government by consent" as the only acceptable foundation for the United States. Within that agreement, some public leaders, including at times Hamilton, John Adams, and Gouverneur Morris, and perhaps a substantial number of less vocal people, thought a constitutional monarchy would provide *better* government for the country, but that the recent unhappy experiences under George III made this form anathema to Americans. At the other extreme, there was nearly unanimous agreement that "democracy" was unsuitable, both because the country was too large to make it practical and because as a pure form it too often resulted in injustice, turmoil, and chaos. The convergence of opinion, then, was that republicanism peculiarly suited the American people; they needed some kind of representative system protecting their rights, yet also providing executive and judicial officers capable of enforcing the laws made by the legislature. Thus federalists and antifederalists alike were generally hostile to both monarchy and democracy as they debated which of a variety of republican forms would be best.

Nonetheless, it soon became apparent that embodied in the new Constitution and indeed crystallizing objections to it were quite different conceptions of national direction and purpose. Within every contest over such issues as the division of functions between state and federal authority, the powers of Congress, the election of Senators and Representatives, and the nature of the executive lurked presumptions that this or that device would help or hinder in reaching a certain kind of nationhood. Also related to these differing conceptions were the severe sectional, economic, and self-interested disputes that had an important effect on the contours and outcome of the struggle.

Hamilton had stated the basic federalist outlook ten years earlier in urging the Governor of New York to send the state's best men to Congress. "However important it is to give form and efficiency to [state governments], it is infinitely more important to have a wise general council; otherwise a failure of the measures of the Union will overwhelm all your labors for the advancement of your particular good, and ruin the common cause. . . . Realize to yourself the consequence of having a Congress despised at home and abroad. How can the common force be exerted if the power of collecting it be put in weak, foolish, and unsteady hands?" To Hamilton's cogent mind, the

linkages were clear: a worthy nationhood required wisdom in its definition, efficiency in its execution, and power to gather the force and
energy of all the people. Though he and other federalists recognized
the hold of the states on the affections of the people and were honestly
willing for them to have a role in government, their stronger allegiance was to what the general government might, indeed must, accomplish. They saw the United States growing, expanding, respected
among the nations, and soon assuming a leading role in the world.
Many of them were young men fully committed to independence for
the nation but frustrated during the war and under the Articles of
Confederation by weak, ill-organized, quarreling governments. Over
and over they found themselves unable to *do* anything.[1]

The federalists, then, supported almost every provision of the new
Constitution that would relieve this frustration, reverse the trend toward provincialism, and realize the goals of the Revolution. The issue,
Hamilton declared in the first paragraph of *The Federalist* No. 1, was
"whether societies of men are really capable or not, of establishing
good government from reflection or choice, or whether they are forever destined to depend, for their political constitutions, on accident
and force." He stated the fundamental federalist faith and view of
history in the same essay, declaring that "the vigour of government is
essential to the security of liberty, . . . that a dangerous ambition more
often lurks behind the specious mask of zeal for the rights of the
people, than under the forbidding appearance of zeal for the firmness
and efficiency of government, . . . and that of those men who have
overturned the liberties of republics the greatest number have begun
their career, by paying an obsequious court to the people, commenc-
ing Demagogues and ending Tyrants."[2]

To elaborate this view of government, the three authors of *The
Federalist*—Hamilton, Madison, and John Jay—writing under the
pseudonym "Publius" and addressing the people of the state of New
York, began by describing the ills of American government under the
Articles of Confederation. Then, principally using Hamilton's pen,
"Publius" argued that the provisions of the new Constitution would
provide the requisite "energy" in the federal government. Finally,
most of Madison's contributions sought to show that these "energiz-
ing" provisions were both entirely republican and unlikely to overawe
the state governments. Jay pointed out that "Union and a good national government" instead of inviting war, as weakness was inclined

to do, would "repress and discourage it" by allowing the entire force
of the country to be gathered in its defense. Hamilton noted that only
"a firm union [could insure] . . . the peace and liberty of the States"
by being able to discourage "domestic faction and insurrection." Madison made the point more general in three long essays detailing how
the weak confederacies of ancient Greece, the Holy Roman Empire,
and the Netherlands had produced growing anarchy followed by
either tyranny or foreign domination. Surely, "Publius" argued, unless
the United States strengthened its union, it would find itself on the
same fatal path.[3]

Hamilton asserted that "under a vigorous national government, the
natural strength and resources of the country, directed toward a common interest, would baffle all the combinations of European jealousy
to restrain our growth." Effective commercial regulations depended
on *national* laws. Furthermore, agricultural prosperity and the impending industrial growth would become stagnant without consistent,
harmonizing national support. Hamilton also argued that only "one
national government" could efficiently and with relatively little force
and expense collect revenue to support the common needs of the
country. To antifederalist charges that the power to raise armies and
declare war would lead to military dictatorship and that therefore
national defense should be left to the state militias, Hamilton, remembering the desperate, often defeated campaigns when he served as aide
to Washington, responded that "the steady operations of war against a
regular and disciplined army, can only be successfully conducted by a
force of the same kind. Considerations of economy, not less of stability and vigor, confirm this position." It was, on the contrary, he
asserted, the existence of many small, quarreling principalities, unregu-
lated by the peaceful rule of law, that compelled the maintenance of
large military forces so burdensome to the common people. "Every
view we take of the subject," Hamilton concluded, "will serve to
convince us, that it is both unwise and dangerous to deny the Federal
Government an unconfined authority, as to all those objects which are
entrusted to its management." "*It is impossible to foresee or define,*"
he emphasized, "*the extent and variety of national exigencies, or the
correspondent extent and variety of the means which may be necessary to satisfy them.*"[4]

In describing the executive and judicial branches, Hamilton similarly
sought to demonstrate the virtues of firm government. Defending the

executive was especially difficult, he noted, because antifederalists played upon the well-known "aversion of the people to monarchy," picturing the President as "seated on a throne surrounded with minions and mistresses; giving audience to the envoys of foreign potentates, in all the supercilious pomp of majesty." For one thing, Hamilton argued, "talents for low intrigue and the little arts of popularity may alone suffice to elevate a man to the first honors in a single state; but it will require other talents and a different order of merit to establish him in the esteem and confidence of the whole union. . . . There will be a constant probability of seeing the [Presidency] filled by characters pre-eminent for ability and virtue." Confident that the President would usually be a man well-qualified for the office (Hamilton was not always contemptuous of the judgment of the people), he then defended expanded executive powers because "energy in the executive is a leading character in the definition of good government." It was necessary to protect the community against foreign attacks, to achieve a "steady administration of the laws," to protect property against "irregular and high-handed combinations," and to secure personal liberty against the "assaults of ambition, affection, and of anarchy." Hamilton summed up his whole administrative theory: "A feeble executive implies a feeble execution of the government. A feeble execution is but another phrase for a bad execution. and a government ill executed, whatever it may be in theory, must be in practice a bad government." The growing awareness of how the idea of the sovereignty of the people subordinated all branches of government to them, and the consequent unprecedented prospect that governors could themselves be made *instruments* of the people, allowed Hamilton, following James Wilson, to "republicanize" the argument for an energetic executive. Thus understood, such an executive did not subvert a revolution fought against the tyranny of a British king. An elected President exercising carefully defined powers, and a hereditary monarch surrounded by the prerogatives of his crown, though structurally each "executives," were in vital respects quite differently related to government by consent.[5]

Hamilton defended a powerful, independent judiciary with equal enthusiasm and a similar thrust. Quoting Montesquieu, he declared that "there is no liberty, if the power of judging be not separated from the legislative and executive powers." Like the executive, in a republic the judiciary was vulnerable, hardly able to defend itself from legislative encroachments and domination. But this was especially unfortunate under a written constitution because its interpretation was both vitally important and, in the nature of the case, a judicial function. Only judges independent and firm in their authority could ascertain and declare the meaning of the fundamental law and the subservience of statute law to it. Hamilton also made the key connection with the emerging view of sovereignty: "Nor does this conclusion by any means suppose a superiority of the judicial to the legislative power. It only supposes that the power of the people is superior to both; and that where the will of the legislature declared in its statutes, stands in opposition to that of the people declared in the constitution, the judges . . . ought to regulate their decisions by the fundamental laws [the constitution], rather than those which are not fundamental." In this view, the rights of the people, as contained and defined by them in the Constitution, far from being threatened by a strong judiciary, received their only firm protection from it. Otherwise, "those ill humours which the arts of designing men, or the influence of particular conjunctures, sometimes disseminate among the people themselves" would subvert justice and oppress minorities.[6]

Madison more persistently and more explicitly upheld the entirely republican character of the new Constitution, that is, its compatibility with both the continued vitality of the states and the principle of government by consent. "The powers delegated by the proposed Constitution to the Federal Government are few and defined," Madison reminded the people of New York in *The Federalist* No. 45, while "those which are to remain in the State Governments are numerous and indefinite. . . . The powers reserved to the several States will extend to all the objects, which, in the ordinary course of affairs, concern the lives, liberties, and properties of the people; and the internal order, improvement, and prosperity of the State." There was no reason to heed the alarms of antifederalists that the new Constitution would undermine local government and thus destroy self-government at its most meaningful level.[7]

Madison's strongest insistence on the republican character of the new Constitution, however, came in his response to antifederalist charges that the House of Representatives would "be most likely to aim at an ambitious sacrifice of the many to the aggrandizement of the few." Such a charge, he wrote scornfully, was "most extraordinary" because, by imputing every corruption and mischievous tendency to the elected representatives of the people, "it strikes at the very root of republican government." After explaining patiently and realistically why the people could be expected for the most part to choose able Representatives and why they would be inclined to remain faithful to their trust while in office, Madison raised the key question: "What are we to say to the men who profess the most flaming zeal for Republican Government, yet boldly impeach the fundamental principle of it; who pretend to be champions for the right and the capacity of the people to choose their own rulers, yet maintain that they will prefer those only who will immediately and infallibly betray the trust committed to them?" It was not the federalists, defending a Constitution that over and over again *conferred power* on agents of the people, who were antirepublican, Madison explained unanswerably. Rather, the antifederalists, in sniffing out some real and a host of imaginary abuses of power, undercut every possibility of the people governing themselves and thus proved themselves disbelievers in republican government.[8]

This focus on a government that could *do things*, on organizing the sovereignty of the people so that it could have some force and effect, was the vital dynamic of the federalist persuasion. Furthermore, though Hamilton and Madison had differing emphases in *The Federalist*, "Publius" was entirely, and creatively, consistent: he expounded a Constitution at once energetic and republican, the very combination needed to fulfill, not betray, the Revolution. Hamilton and Madison accepted the double verdict of twenty years of political debate and republican experiment: that firm government apart from the republican principle was tyranny, and that self-rule without authority was anarchy. Their contribution was to see how the dangers could be neutralized and the virtues constructively wedded.

II

Beneath their radical Whig rhetoric of doubt and suspicion, the antifederalists, too, had a compelling sense of national purpose, less dynamic than that of the federalists, but no less thoroughly republican and perhaps more sensitive to the day-to-day needs of self-government. On the surface the debate over the Constitution comprised hundreds of pages of antifederalist carping about specific provisions, inflated fears of "monarchy," and bickering over the meaning of various clauses—to which the federalists responded in kind, in what are now tedious and irrelevant polemics. The antifederalists bespoke as well, though, an ideal of simple, virtuous republicanism. George Mason alluded to it, as the Convention completed its work, in protesting that "in the House of Representatives there is not the substance, but the shadow only of representation." It could "never inspire the confidence of the people," and therefore the laws would be made "by men little concerned in, and little acquainted with their effects and consequences." Within a month of the publication of the new Constitution an unknown writer questioned whether it offered "a full and equal representation of the people in the legislature" and whether "the extreme parts of the [nation]" were as fully represented as the central parts. He wondered further whether under the national laws "each citizen [would] find a court of justice within a reasonable distance, perhaps, within a day's travel of his home." He feared that federal laws, made by a Congress elected only every two years and "far removed from the people," would be disregarded "unless a multitude of officers and military force be continually kept in view." "Neglected laws, or a military execution of them," he warned, "must first lead to anarchy and confusion, . . . [and then to] despotic government." A Pennsylvania antifederalist wrote that "the form of government which holds those entrusted with power in the greatest responsibility to their constituents [is] best calculated for freemen." Only then could the people really be sovereign and "their sense or opinion [be] the criterion of every public measure." He added further that since under a complicated plan of government, however allegedly ingenious, "the people will be perplexed and divided in their sentiments about the source of abuses or misconduct, . . . the highest responsibility is to be attained in a simple structure of government."[9]

Obviously these writers had fears, assumptions, and hopes far different from those expressed by "Publius." Their ideal was an intimate, grass-roots relationship between the people and their government that was not so much denied as passed over lightly by the federalists. They had quite different ideas of the character of virtuous, republican government. When it was charged that the proposed Constitution came from "young visionary men and the consolidating aristocracy," the essence of antifederalism was stated: a fear that consolidated nationhood would make a farce of self-rule by again gathering, as human society had almost always done, the force of government to some far-off, alien court from whence it would be imposed, irresponsibly and unfeelingly, on the people in the course of their daily lives. This, plain and simple, was tyranny, the subversion of all that the American Revolution stood for.

An eloquent Massachusetts antifederalist, writing under the pseudonym "John DeWitt" and addressing people long used to the intimacy of New England town meetings, asked "who is there among you" who would trade the system of the Massachusetts House of Representatives, where each of the two hundred towns had a delegate, for a House of ten members based on large, arbitrarily drawn districts? Yet this was precisely what the people were being asked to do under the new Constitution. In Massachusetts, "DeWitt" noted, "the elections were annual, the persons elected resided in the center of you, their interests were yours, they were subject to your immediate control," and they were not prey to conniving deliberations at some distant capital. Under the new Constitution, however, "DeWitt" warned that Representatives "chosen for double the time" would, however well disposed, "become strangers to the very people choosing them," they would lose touch with and be uncontrollable by their constituents, and instead "consult and finally be guided by" equally alienated Representatives from other states having a variety of conflicting interests. In a few years, he declared, such a government would "degenerate to a compleat Aristocracy, armed with powers unnecessary in any case to bestow, and which in its vortex swallows up every other Government on the Continent. In short, my fellow citizens, it can be said to be nothing less than a hasty stride to Universal Empire in this Western World, flattering, very flattering to young ambitious minds, but fatal to the liberties of the people." Though "DeWitt's" charges are not entirely fair, the tendency he saw in the new Constitution and in federalist arguments on its behalf reveals clearly what the antifederalists valued—and what they feared.[10]

It was left to Patrick Henry, however, at the Virginia ratifying convention of June 1788, to proclaim most grandiloquently the antifederalist vision. Consider the situation of the poor man under the existing state governments, Henry implored: "He enjoys the fruits of his labor, under his own fig tree, with his wife and children around him in peace and security." Tranquillity, ease, and contentment, freedom from alarms or disturbances, were his blessings. "Why, then,"

Henry thundered, "tell us of danger, to terrify us into adoption of this new form of government? . . . I dread the operation of it on the middling and lower classes of people. . . . In this scheme of energetic government the people will find two sets of tax-gatherers, . . . unfeeling blood-suckers [who would] commit the most horrid and barbarous ravages on our people." The American spirit, he feared, had surrendered its ancient devotion to liberty, and instead had gone "in search of a splendid government—a strong, energetic government. Shall we imitate the example of those nations who have gone from a simple to a splendid government?" He warned, "If we admit this consolidated government, it will be because we like a great, splendid one. Some way or another we must be a great and mighty empire; we must have an army, and a navy, and a number of things. The ropes and chains of consolidation," Henry admitted, could convert the "country into a powerful and mighty empire," and might "make nations tremble," but, he asked pointedly, "would this constitute happiness, or secure liberty?" Was this "compatible with the genius of republicanism?" Like Richard Henry Lee and "John DeWitt," Henry saw an immensely important contrast between the mild, grass-roots, unaggrandizing, small-scale state governments (idealized, to be sure, but susceptible of improvement in that direction), and the splendid edifice and overweaning ambitions implicit in the new federal Constitution. The first left citizens free to live their own lives and to cultivate the private virtue vital to republicanism, while the second soon entailed taxes and drafts and offices and campaigns that harnessed the people to an engine at first oblivious to and then destructive of their human dignity and thus fatal to self-government.[11]

In New York, where antifederalism emerged even before the Constitutional Convention adjourned, the critical voices found their greatest range and depth. Seeking to fasten on federalist pretensions the image of Caesarism (or Cromwellism, in the other notorious example of the day), the antifederalists, following Addison, Franklin, and many other admired neoclassical essayists, assumed the pose of Cato, the simple, incorruptible, freedom-loving patriot of the Roman republic, and chose for their *noms de plume* Roman heroes, to remind their readers of the tragedy that ensued when an empire was raised on the ruins of a virtuous republic. "Your posterity," George Clinton ("Cato") warned, "will find that great power connected with ambition, luxury, and flattery will as readily produce a Caesar, Caligula, Nero and Domitian in America, as the same causes did in the Roman Empire."[12]

Robert Yates ("Brutus"), applying antifederalist standards of republicanism to specific provisions of the Constitution, found apostasy on all sides. Under the power to tax, Congress could "annex any penalties they please to the breach of the revenue laws; and appoint as many officers as they think proper to collect the taxes and [federal] courts of law will have cognizance of every case arising under the revenue laws, and the officers of these courts will execute their judgments." The state governments would soon be impotent and even the people themselves helpless before the force thus accumulated:

Power, exercised without limitation, will introduce itself into every corner of the city, and country— It will wait upon the ladies at their toilett; . . . it will accompany them to the ball, the play, and the assembly; . . . it will enter the house of every gentleman, watch over his cellar; . . . preside over the table, and note down all he eats or drinks; it will attend him to his bedchamber, and watch him while he sleeps; it will be the constant companion of the industrious farmer in all his labour; it will be with him in the house, and in the field, observe the toil of his hands, and the sweat of brow; it will light upon the head of every person in the United States; [and] the language in which it will address them will be GIVE, GIVE!

Antifederalists again and again pointed out that this awful picture was the logical end of "Publius'" doctrine that "it is impossible to foresee the extent and variety of national exigencies, or the means which may be necessary to satisfy them."

Turning to the vaunted independence of the Supreme Court and its supposed authority to judge the constitutionality of acts of the legislature, "Brutus" pointed out that "men placed in this situation will soon feel themselves independent of heaven itself." Better than this profoundly unrepublican independence, he declared, would be to leave

the construction of the constitution to the legislature. They would have explained it at their peril; if they exceed their powers, the people from whom they derived their power could remove them. A constitution is a compact of the people with their rulers; if the rulers break the compact, the people have a right and ought to remove them, and do themselves justice: those whom the people choose at stated periods should have the power in the last resort to determine the sense of the compact. When this power is lodged in the hands of men independent of the people and of their representatives, and who are not, constitutionally, accountable for their opinions, no way is left to control them but *with a high hand and an outstretched arm.*

Taking direct issue with "Publius'" defense of executive vigor and judicial independence, "Brutus" saw lawlessness and then tyranny resulting not from too little authority, but rather from a power too heavy and too remote, against which the people would have no recourse except their natural right of revolution.[13]

Fittingly, it seems in retrospect, antifederalism found its best expression in speeches made in the presence of Alexander Hamilton himself, at the New York ratifying convention of July 1788. The technical clause-by-clause arguments had by this time become hackneyed. Melancton Smith reflected on "the real issues" as he heard Hamilton, Robert R. Livingston, John Jay, and other federalists extoll the benefits of strong central government and proclaim the need for talented leadership. They headed entirely in the wrong direction, Smith concluded, moving further and further away from meaningful self-government. In speaking of Representatives, for example, instead of the high-toned Burkean concepts praised by the federalists, Smith insisted:

Representatives [should] resemble those they represent. They should be a true picture of the people, possess a knowledge of their circumstances and their wants, sympathize in all their distresses, and be disposed to seek their true interests. The knowledge necessary for the representative of a free people not only comprehends extensive political and commercial information, such as is acquired by men of refined education, but it should also comprehend the common concerns and occupations of the people, which men of the middling class of life are, in general, more competent to than those of a superior class. To exercise the power of laying taxes with discretion requires something more than an acquaintance with the abstruse parts of the system of finance. It calls for a discernment how the burdens imposed will bear upon the different classes.

Smith was not so much expounding a class-interest theory of government as emphasizing that the "middling sort" of people had distinctive virtues vital to good government, and that government, by relying too much on refined knowledge and a natural aristocracy, could very easily lose touch with the people. In every society, Smith pointed out, those of "greater capacities, [advantages in] birth, education, talents, and wealth commanded influence and respect among the common people." Smith had no objection to this and was even willing for these qualities to have their due influence in society, but the difficulty was that "if the government is so constituted as to admit only a few to exercise the powers of it," *only* the natural aristocracy would ever gain office. "Frame your election laws as you please," he warned, in a district of thirty-thousand inhabitants "the influence of the great; [those of] conspicuous military, popular, civil, or legal talents" would carry all elections. Under the proposed Constitution, offices would be "highly elevated and distinguished, [and] the style in which the members live will probably be high." "Sensible, substantial men, who have been used to walk in the plain, frugal paths of life" would seldom be chosen or would find the high-toned society of a remote capital so uncomfortable (or corrupted) that they would be disinclined even to seek office.

I do not mean [Smith said] to declaim against the great and charge them indiscriminately with want of principles and honesty. The same passions and prejudices govern all men. The circumstances in which men are placed in a great measure give a cast to human character. Those in middling circumstances have less temptations; they are inclined by habit, and the company with whom they associate, to set bounds to their passions and appetites. They are obliged to employ their time in their respective callings; hence the substantial yeomanry of the country are more temperate, of better morals, and less ambition, than the great.

Temperateness, morality, and restrained ambition: these were the qualities Smith admired in men, and constitutions were to be judged by their likelihood of producing rulers possessed of those qualities. Any other government, whatever its checks and balances, energy, splendor, or ingenuity, would reestablish the hoary system under which the bulk of mankind would be overawed, intimidated, dominated, and ultimately degraded by those who felt they had "a right of preeminence," even though they were not a hereditary nobility of "titles, stars, and garters."[14]

Though often obscured by the bickering over particular clauses of the Constitution and distrustful, doom-laden rhetoric, antifederalism implied a compelling, even beautiful conception of what human life might be like. Its central concern was to abolish the ancient equation of power whereby the arrogance, oppressiveness, and depravity of the rulers on one side produced subservience and a gradual erosion of self-respect, capacities, and virtues of the people on the other side. (This was exactly what had happened in Great Britain since 1688, according to a legion of radical Whig writers.) The result was an increasing corruption and degeneracy in both rulers and ruled. Only a change in "the circumstances in which men are placed," that is, a new system of government and eventually a new social dynamic that would remove the tendencies toward degeneracy on both sides, would result in fulfillment of the Revolutionary ideals. Though the picture came through blurred during the ratification debates, the antifederalists had a clear notion of the good society: virtuous, hard-working, honest men and women living simply in their own communities, enjoying their families and their neighbors, devoted to the common welfare, and possessed of such churches, schools, trade associations, and local government as they needed to sustain the values and fulfill the purposes of society. To achieve this they saw little need for "energetic" government (a euphemism for harsh rule, many felt instinctively), a splendid empire (an excuse for burdensome taxes and press gangs), or, in Henry's apt phrase, "an army, and a navy, and a number of things." How in the world were these things useful to the common man intent on enjoying the fruits of his own labor? To the antifederalists the question answered itself: They were *not* useful; rather, they always ground fond hopes in the dust.

Sophisticated opponents charged over and over that antifederalist political theory was too simple—pathetically, even tragically primitive. With eyes fixed on the grass roots, the antifederalists offered largely town-meeting nostrums and representative simplicity. For commercial growth, for settling and expanding Western lands, for building a national capital, for increasing national revenues, for raising and leading armies and navies, and for partaking in world diplomacy— all of which required a powerful new constitution and multiplying officers of government—they cared very little. They were, as their foes alleged, *provincial*, and gladly so, brandishing instructive, horrendous images of imperial grandeur: the Children of Israel drenched in blood after their kings had led them outward from their godly, judge-guided community; the people of Rome enthralled by free bread and obscene circuses while the Caesars and their legions despoiled and enslaved the known world from Jerusalem to the Celtic fringes of Britain. What price glory, Mason and Henry and "DeWitt" and "Cato" and "Brutus" and Smith asked. Another New Yorker expressed the deep disdain of the antifederalists when he called the

Constitution "this Goliath, this uncircumcized Philistine." These spokesmen offered contradictory and perhaps insufficient alternatives to the new Constitution and thus were defeated in the debate over a frame of government, but they were considerable thinkers who imagined a better day in terms poignantly relevant to the lives of the common people.[15]

The dispute, then, between federalists and antifederalists was over the *meaning* of republicanism and the *ways* it could achieve practical effect in the lives of men in the New World—and in the real world. Each side, therefore, as each generally recognized in the other, was honestly and legitimately heir to the ideals of the Revolution. Each responded to and grew out of the decade of shifting loyalty and movement toward independence, and the decade of search for new national purpose and experimentation with republican government that followed.

III

A remarkable exchange of letters in 1790 between George III's detested "brace of Adamses" revealed where the nation was as it began life under its new Constitution. Samuel and John Adams agreed that "it is a fixed principle . . . that all good government is and must be republican," but in pondering that vital foundation, John began to fret. Aware of the convulsions beginning in France (from which he expected only chaos followed by tyranny), he feared that under the republican banner "everything will be pulled down . . . [and nothing] built up." The French revolutionaries had learned from Locke the "principles of liberty; but I doubt whether they have not yet to learn the principles of government," John noted. He doubted further whether they *could* learn them from such mentors as Voltaire and Rousseau. Samuel Adams responded by agreeing that history had, as John argued, been a record of depravity, bloodshed, and oppression, but the older man denied the implication that republicanism needed more firmness and order in government to survive. "What, then, is to be done?" Samuel asked. "Divines and philosophers, statesmen and patriots" should unite, should educate everyone, including *little boys and girls*, in "universal philanthropy, . . . in the art of self-government, . . . and in the study and practice of the exalted virtues of the Christian system . . . which [would] introduce that golden age beautifully described in figurative language, when the wolf shall dwell with the lamb." This might commence the millennium, Samuel thought, when improved republican forms, if any, would be the only civil government necessary.[16]

John, of course, approved the abstractions, but complained in reply that "instead of particularizing any of them, you seem to place all your hopes in the universal, or at least more general, prevalence of knowledge and benevolence." John despaired of ever seeing the principles "sufficiently general for the security of society, [so he was] for seeking institutions which may supply in some degree the defect." This was the basic thrust of those who supported the new Constitution: to devise mechanisms of government that would sustain the republican principle in the face of its avowed opponents, its simpleminded friends, and, most important, the weaknesses of human nature that imperiled all attempts at improvement. To accomplish this difficult task John insisted men would always need "assistance from the principles and system of government," that is, they needed proper discipline, institutions, and leadership. He then defended the system of checks and balances, against "the people" as well as against wealth, nobility, and the government itself, as essential to free government. To him demagogues were as dangerous as hereditary monarchs. He believed, too, that in the few places in Europe where liberty had existed, a nobility had been its essential prop, hereditary in most cases, but in any event, a "natural and actual aristocracy among mankind" would be needed to balance the alliance of "kings and people" that had so often resulted in "hideous despotism, as horrid as that of Turkey." The aristocracy, including both "natural" aristocrats distinguished by merit alone and men of wealth and family whose interests and pride could be sources of stability and public spirit, John argued, should have its own branch in the legislature where it could make its own special contribution as well as check the passions and factionalism of the popular branch. John regarded devices such as "an upper house" and an executive armed with a veto and other substantial powers as the only way to make self-government work. Though many federalists did not favor his particular devices, they agreed that some mechanisms, refinements, or restraints were needed to build the institutions and sustain the habits without which self-government was impossible.

In reply Samuel spotted at once John's apostasy:

A republic, you tell me, is a government in which "the people have an essential *share* in the sovereignty." Is not the *whole* sovereignty, my friend, essentially in the people? . . . *We the people*, is the style of the Federal Constitution: they adopted it; and conformably to it, they delegate the exercise of the powers of government to particular persons, who, after short intervals, resign their powers to the people; and they will re-elect them, or appoint others, as they think fit.

This was the plain meaning of self-government—the only "check" needed in "the system" was that which the people themselves furnished at frequent elections, and the only legitimate authority was that specifically delegated by the people. To Samuel, as to many antifederalists before 1790 and to many Jeffersonians afterward, everything else was pretty much sophistry. To them, to accept the reservations and "realism" of John Adams was to admit defeat at the outset. Government by consent, Samuel admitted, depended on "the expectation of the further progress and *extraordinary* degrees of virtue," but wasn't such a prospect justified? "The present age," he said, was "more enlightened than former ones. Freedom of inquiry is certainly more encouraged; the feeling of humanity have softened the heart; the true principles of civil and religious liberty are better understood; tyranny, in all its shapes, is more detested; and bigotry, if not still blind, must be mortified to see that she is despised." Such faith, Samuel observed, offered mankind its only hope because all other reliances had been found inadequate—including dependence on an aristocratic upper house, as the connivance of the British House of Lords in the plunder and oppression of the colonies proved. Thus discouraged about traditional aristocracy, Samuel asked, "Where is the natural and actual aristocracy to be found?" "Among men of all ranks and conditions," he answered:

The cottager may beget a wise son; the noble, a fool. The one is capable of great improvement; the other is not. Education is within the power of men and societies of men; . . . it will cultivate the natural genius, elevate the soul, excite laudable emulation to excel in knowledge, piety, and benevolence; and finally it will reward its patrons and benefactors by shedding its benign influence on the public mind. . . . The man of good understanding, who has been well educated, and improves these advantages as far as his circumstances allow, in promoting the happiness of mankind, in my opinion, . . . is indeed "well born."

To Samuel, then, the problem was straightforward and down-to-earth: successful republican government depended on virtuous citizens insisting upon virtue in their rulers. This required care, vigilance, and hope, especially at the local level, but these were the privileges and responsibilities of those who would govern themselves. John's fear of the *demos* that led him to his sophisticated political theory were to Samuel self-defeating in advance because such elaborate ideas of government were sure to result in the people being subjected, sooner or later, to the spurs and burdens of rule they had always known. In a sense John Adams sought to devise a republican frame of government that would *work within* traditional conceptions of human nature and the orders of society—an immense advance for the dignity and happiness of man and a perfectly honest effort to fulfill the goals of the Revolution. Samuel Adams, on the other hand, discerned a broader need: to be willing to hope that human nature itself, and with it the basic values and relationships of human society, could be slowly but surely altered in fundamental ways. A republican nation without such change was a chimera. These positions, in a way polar but in another way urging different paths to a viable republicanism, defined the contours of American political thinking as government under the new Constitution began.

9. The Political Thought of James Madison

JAMES MADISON WAS THE LEADING THEORETICIAN, AND INDEED THE PRIME MOVER OF EVENTS, DURING THE FORMATIVE PERIOD FROM THE CALLING OF THE CONSTITUTIONAL CONVENTION THROUGH THE RATIFICATION DEBATES TO THE ESTABLISHMENT OF THE NEW GOVERNMENT DURING the first session of the First Congress, which adjourned in September 1789. During 1789 he was President Washington's most trusted advisor and also floor leader in the House of Representatives for generally nonpartisan measures to set the new government in motion. He proposed an addition of a bill of rights to the Constitution not only to reconcile antifederalists whose only objection was the absence of guarantees of personal liberty, but more fundamentally because he had come to see, in light of the arguments of Jefferson and others, that a *written* bill of rights would formalize what he and other federalists thought was implicit in the document completed at the 1787 Convention. A codified bill of rights would both mobilize public opinion in its support and provide a ready resort for the courts in turning aside executive or legislative invasions of individual rights.[1]

In considering the President's power to remove his appointed officers Madison laid foundations for executive responsibility. The President, he argued, ought to have the power to remove his appointees to preserve "the chain of dependence" vital to republican government: "the lowest officers, the middle grade, and the highest will depend . . . on the President, and the President on the community." Far from creating a dangerous power in the executive branch, the removal authority was, in Madison's opinion, essential to republican govern-

[139]

ment. It at once put the means of effective administration into the President's hands and made clear to the people his accountability to them for the conduct of the executive departments.

I

In working out these and other proposals and arguments in the years 1787–1789 Madison developed a public philosophy that has long been basic to American government. Like Jefferson and Franklin, he began with the moral standards of John Locke's *Second Treatise on Civil Government*, primarily that reason required all men be esteemed free and equal. By this Madison meant that to regard man, or any group of men, *a priori*, as "unfree" was immoral, that is, could not be defended rationally. There was nothing about the "nature" of any men that could be grounds for depriving them of freedom or that could entitle one man to rule another. Likewise, there was nothing in the nature of men that conferred upon some of them special privileges. Considered rationally, men were equal in rights and in the esteem to which they were entitled on earth and in Heaven. When Madison spoke of man in a state of nature he meant simply to express a moral requirement that men ought to be free and equal. He meant to deny the immemorial traditions of government that some men were "by nature" slaves or subjects, that classification of men into unequal orders was both just and inevitable, that obedience was the only duty in government of the mass of men, and that social order required the subjugation of man to authoritarian control. A man could become fully human only insofar as he was free.

Madison did not need to suppose that in some primeval age, before the rise of unjust social institutions or tyrannical governments, a society had once existed where all men had enjoyed the full freedom and equality of the state of nature. The concept "state of nature" was moral or normative, describing a condition that ought to be, rather than historical, having reference to a society which might once have existed. Nor did Madison use the terms "free" and "equal" in any absolute or literal sense. He knew perfectly well that any society, especially a complex, civilized one, imposed many legitimate, unavoidable limitations on the right of a man to do as he pleased. Furthermore, since men obviously were unequal in talents and abilities, they would necessarily differ in their achievements in life. The moral imperative of equality did not require, according to a popular eighteenth-century example, that Isaac Newton and his stable keeper be equal in fame or wisdom or wealth, but rather that one could not justly rule the other and that each had the same "natural" right to his life, liberty, and the pursuit of happiness. When Madison spoke of the natural rights of freedom and equality he had in mind ideals, or standards, in terms of which societies and governments could be judged and toward which men should aspire.

In applying these moral imperatives, Madison and other men of reason on both sides of the Atlantic insisted, to begin with, that the state existed to protect and expand freedom and equality of opportunity, and that the surest way to realize this purpose was to rest the powers of government on the consent of the governed. This concept did not always mean in Madison's day, as it might seem to in the twentieth century, universal suffrage or the elimination of such unrepublican features as a House of Lords or a hereditary monarch. Rather, it meant, in the English Whig formulation following Locke (which Madison knew by heart), that a powerful *portion* of the government had to be responsive to the people, ordinarily through a legislative body composed of their elected representatives. The antiroyalist sentiment of the American Revolution, and the absence of a hereditary nobility in the United States, caused American theorists to lay aside Lockean formulations that the people might consent to hereditary forms, but Madison and most of his colleagues in nationbuilding continued to accept Whiggish limitations on the "one man-one vote" dictum, and to work earnestly at "refinements" in government capable of restraining the majority. The essence of consent for Madison was to insure that the government could not ignore or oppose ultimately the will and interests of the people being governed; this was his hallowed "republican principle" to which all just governments had to conform. Madison's preoccupation as a political theorist and statesman was to find the mechanisms that would provide such insurance while maintaining order and virtue in government.

Also implied in the doctrine of consent was the right of national independence. Locke had scored the injustice of domination by conquest, the clearest and most complete denial of freedom and equality.

The harsh rule of alien armies, wherein some were absolute masters and others abject slaves, was in the political literature of the Age of Reason always the prime example of injustice and denial of the rights of man. When the resistance to British oppression in North America became a movement for independence and a war to expel occupying armies, the sense of connection between natural rights and nationhood increased immensely. Then, as a means to realize both national independence and the principle of consent, the natural rights theorists insisted on the right of revolution. They reasoned that since government existed to nourish and insure freedom and equality, and indeed had no other purpose, when it betrayed those obligations it lost its legitimate authority and in a sense annulled itself, leaving the people obliged to replace it. The right of revolution, in fact, was inseparable from the insistence that government, far from being an absolute or divine institution recognizing no superior authority, was subordinate to certain purposes or principles, which those being governed could discern and judge for themselves. A gap between the acts of government and rationally discoverable natural rights required that the government be changed or abolished.

To give effect to "the republican principle" within a nation, Madison asserted that the clearest meaning of freedom, that least subject to social restraint, was freedom of expression, including the right to believe, speak, and write according to one's own lights. Without these rights, so often denied by allegedly legitimate governments, freedom meant very little. Put positively, man could not be the kind of being Enlightenment philosophers insisted he should or might be without these opportunities of expression. To give further reality to freedom, Madison also considered certain personal immunities sanctioned in English law to be natural rights—trial by jury, confrontation of witnesses, freedom from general warrants, seizures, excessive bail, and cruel punishments, a guarantee of habeas corpus, and subjugation of armies to civil control. Freedom meant more than these things, but considering the arbitrary, oppressive acts of the Stuarts, Bourbons, and other mighty rulers around the globe, it seemed clear to Madison that substantial success in achieving them would bring mankind immeasurably closer to the moral imperatives.

Madison and other theorists of the American republic generally assumed or implied these fundamentals. They seldom thought it necessary to argue for them as opposed to other basic principles. They were the sentiments John Adams said were "hackneyed in Congress" in 1774–1776 and which Jefferson said, explaining his objective in drafting the Declaration of Independence, were "an expression of the American mind" at that time.[2]

Next, Madison and his colleagues sought to give meaning to the moral requirements of the natural rights doctrine in a way relevant to the actual character of man and the society in which he lived. In discerning the nature of man Madison followed John Locke's *Essay Concerning Human Understanding* which, by insisting that sensory impressions were the sole source of human knowledge, emphasized the diversity of mankind. Each human being was the product of a unique pattern of sense impressions, and therefore was in some measure different from other humans. Since this limitless variety resulted from the very nature of the human mind, the life of man had to be organized in ways permitting expression of this diversity. To do otherwise would impose unjust constraints on human potential. Hence the emphasis on freedom in the thought of Locke and all those who followed him. Furthermore, since, as Locke had put it after describing the inclination of men to cherish or value different things, "men may choose differently, and yet all choose right," a good society had to be tolerant, flexible, receptive to change, open. Privilege and hierarchy arbitrarily restraining the choices, opportunities, and inclinations of any person were inadmissible. In accepting Lockean epistemology and its understanding of the diversity of mankind, Madison in fact accepted the essential foundation of an open society and the burden, as a theorist of government, of blending variety, change, and diversity with such fixed concepts as "unalienable rights" and natural law.

Madison's political experience confirmed this diversity, the good and bad sides of human nature, and all the infinite gradations that could exist between the extremes. The contrast between the benign religious freedom of Pennsylvania and the persecuting bigotry of Virginia had led him to favor liberty of conscience. During the Revolution he had experience with both patriots and knaves. In seeking to correct the weaknesses in the Union, he had suffered the opposition of such perversely selfish men as those who dominated the Rhode Island legislature, and he had enjoyed the support of the men gathered in

Philadelphia in the summer of 1787 whom he thought "pure in their Motives, . . . [and] devoted to the object committed to them." Near the end of his life, reflecting on over half a century of experience with public affairs, Madison observed

Some gentlemen, consulting the purity and generosity of their own minds, without averting to the lessons of experience, would find a security against [tyranny and malice] in our social feelings; in a respect for character; in the dictates of the monitor within. . . . But man is known to be a selfish as well as a social being. Respect for character, though often a salutary restraint, is but too often overruled by other motives. . . . We all know that conscience is not a sufficient safeguard; and besides that conscience itself may be deluded; may be misled . . . into acts which an enlightened conscience would forbid.[3]

Madison insisted, as he remarked during the Federal Convention, that in framing governments "we must not shut our eyes to the nature of man, nor to the light of experience." Following Locke's empirical method, he studied as fully and carefully as he could the experience of mankind recorded in the histories of his day. From these books, and from the generalizations of philosophers from Aristotle to David Hume, he absorbed a sober view of human history. The record was generally one of war, tyranny, violence, stupidity, and corruption with distressingly few instances of peace, prosperity, and enlighten- ment. Madison and his colleagues rejected the systematic thought of Machiavelli, Calvin, and Hobbes, but they kept in mind their cogent reminders of human depravity. On the other hand, they did not fol- low Enlightenment thinkers who emphasized human goodness to the point of blaming all evil on social conditions. Rather, they sought realistically to recognize and take into account the limitations of human nature. "If men were angels," Madison pointed out in *The Federalist* No. 51, "no government was necessary." Yet, if men were absolutely evil, as he told the Virginia convention of 1788, "we are in a wretched condition . . . [where] no form of government can render us secure." The real and difficult problems of government existed precisely because of the mixed character of men. There was sufficient reason, virtue, and charity among them to afford some prospect that good government might result from the principle of consent, but there was also sufficient greed, corruption, and ignorance to require the lawful restraints traditionally associated with government. Madison took seriously both modest hopes and grave dangers. The problem was to devise a government that would give maximum scope to the former and raise the surest barriers against the latter—to find what Aristotle called "the mean between two extremes." "We may add," Aristotle had observed, "that it is a good criterion of a proper mixture of democracy and oligarchy that a mixed constitution should be able to be described indifferently as either. When this can be said, it must obviously be due to the excellence of the mixture. It is a thing which can generally be said of the mean between two extremes; both of the extremes can be traced to the mean, (and it can thus be described by the name of either)." When some critics called the Constitution too "aristocratical" and others labeled it too "democratic," students of Aristotle were inclined to think they had found "the golden mean."[4]

Madison had both reservations about democracy and confidence that republican government was far better suited to the nature of man than any other form. He wrote Jefferson in 1787:

Those who contend for a simple Democracy, or a pure republic, actuated by the sense of the majority . . . assume or suppose a case which is altogether fictitious. They found their reasoning on the idea that the people composing the Society, enjoy not only an equality of political rights, but that they have all precisely the same interests, and the same feelings in every respect. . . . We know however that no Society ever did or can consist of so homogeneous a mass of Citizens. . . . in all civilized societies, distinctions are various and unavoidable. A distinction of property results from that very protection which a free Government gives to unequal faculties for acquiring it. . . . [There are also] differences in political, religious, or other opinions, or an attachment to the persons of leading individuals. However erroneous or ridiculous these grounds of dissention and faction may appear to the enlightened Statesmen, or the benevolent philosopher, the bulk of mankind, who are neither Statesmen nor Philosophers, will continue to view them in a different light.

It was delusive, in Madison's view, to suppose that simple majoritarian democracy would overcome all the contentions and difficulties of civil society. He saw with special clarity that appeals for unity of feeling (he probably had in mind repudiating Rousseau's "general will" in the letter to Jefferson) neglected, and even often tended to suppress, the vital diversities born of freedom.[5]

In 1833, after sixty years' experience with republican government,

Madison applied the same understanding of human nature to refute more dogmatic theorists:

It has been said that all government is evil. It would be more proper to say that the necessity of any government is a misfortune [a thrust at Paine and Rousseau]. This necessity however exists; and the problem to be solved is, not what form of government is perfect [a thrust at Plato], but which of the forms is least imperfect; and here the general question must be between a republican government in which the majority rule the minority, and a government in which a lesser number or the least number rule the majority. If the republican form is, as all of us agree, to be preferred [because of the moral requirements of natural rights], the final question must be, what is the structure of it that will best guard against precipitate counsels and factious combinations for unjust purposes, without a sacrifice of the fundamental principles of republicanism [the task of the federal Constitution]? Those who denounce majority governments altogether because they may have an interest in abusing their power, denounce at the same time all republican government and must maintain that minority government would feel less of the bias of interest or the seductions of power [a thrust at Hobbes and apologists for monarchy].[6]

Madison would have agreed with Reinhold Neibuhr's dictum that "man's capacity for justice makes democracy possible; but man's inclination to injustice makes democracy necessary." (Madison, of course, would have used "republican government" to indicate what Neibuhr meant by "democracy.") The very flaws in human nature pointed to by authoritarians to confound theories of government by consent provided for Madison the surest defense of republicanism. He turned against the authoritarian theorists their often effective claim that the weaknesses of human nature made government by consent impractical and absurd. By pointing out that absolute power wielded by tyrants not exempt from human failings would be far more dangerous than a republican *dispersal* of power into the hands of the people, Madison made government by consent seem the most realistic and prudent, as well as morally preferable, form.[7]

II

Using the recognition of human diversity and tendency toward faction ("sown in the nature of man," he had asserted in *The Federalist* No. 10), Madison explained the dynamics of the forces he supposed would be at work in the enlarged republican government created by the Constitution of 1787. The existence of many interests and factions would in the United States prevent the domination of any one. This was the proposition he advanced to diminish the argument that unjust and selfish interests would control the state. His key contribution to the political dialogue of his day was to show that in a large territory a republican government, by dispersing power, provided the surest guard against the corruptions and abuses of power feared by federalists and antifederalists alike.

The realism of this position—its ironic reliance on selfish interests to sustain freedom and government by consent, and its failure to emphasize the need for virtue in the people or noble purposes for the nation as a whole—does not mean that Madison had no concern for "the good life." The realistic doctrine of selfish interests restraining one another was but part of his political theory. The often unstated but assumed moral requirements of the Lockean natural rights theory, founded as they were on human dignity and fulfillment, embodied his concept of "the good life." To insist on freedom and equality excluded practices that had for centuries in all parts of the world denied most of mankind any hope of fulfillment. Madison argued repeatedly that the future of republican government was hopeless without *some* confidence in human virtue, and, despite his inattention to the need for virtue in free government in the famous *Federalist* No. 10, his interest in education (to produce *good* rulers and citizens), his concern that the national economy provide virtue-sustaining occupations, and his attention to the virtue-demanding processes of local government, all testify to his moral approach. Perhaps even more basic, though, was his acceptance in part, if not in its full meaning, of the classical dictum that "a state exists for the sake of the good life, and not for the sake of life only." Aristotle insisted that the state nourish the primary ethical principle, "the golden mean," and argued that fortitude, temperance, justice, and prudence were the qualities that made a man happy. A man "afraid of every insect which flutters past him," a man who would "sacrifice his dearest friend for the sake of half-a-farthing," or who had no more understanding than "a child or a madman," would, thus lacking virtue, be miserable. "It is evident," Aristotle declared, "that the form of government is best in which every man, whoever he is, can act best and live happily." In a country where both the classical tradition and the Puritan Ethic were strong, Madison's stratagems for balancing power were not regarded as a means of *defining* the public interest (as his twentieth-century admirers of the "conflict of interest" school of political science supposed), but rather as a way of *neutralizing* selfish factions so that a disinterested, virtuous public philosophy could be formulated and carried out.[8]

These axioms, though seldom stated explicitly by Madison, nevertheless constituted the underlying *purpose* beneath his diligence in devising mechanisms of government. His admiration for George Washington, for example, rested squarely upon the first President's embodiment of the Aristotelean (or Addisonian) virtues. A clever structure of government or a shrewd notion of political dynamics, in Madison's view, meant nothing separated from the intention that they protect and provide ways to enlarge the private virtues and public blessings associated with a traditional understanding of "the good life." The first without the second was mere cynical opportunism, while the second alone was mere idle dreaming. Like many antifederalists, Madison's ideal was the virtuous republic, a concept he thought compatible with a large nation, though not, as his subsequent break with Hamilton showed, with one dominated by selfish commercialism. Madison's quarrel with an antifederalist such as George Mason was over means, not ends. They would have agreed readily on the goal of a virtuous republic, but then differed on whether this was compatible with a centralized government including the commercial Northern states, whether such a government would too much vitiate virtue-producing local responsibility, whether a strong executive would dominate and debauch the representatives of the people, and so on. Madison stood between a Mason and a Hamilton and displayed the central insight of American political thinking precisely in supposing that with sufficient ingenuity, the ideals of a virtuous republic and an enlarged, energetic government were not only compatible but mutually reinforcing.

To Madison, then, separation of powers did not mean *paralysis* of powers. He ridiculed the impotent office of governor created by the Virginia constitution, and he scorned the incapacity of the Continental Congress under the Articles of Confederation. His zeal for efficient governments at all levels arose from the frustration he felt in seeking to *do* the things necessary to fulfill the Revolution. The domestic chaos and internal quarreling among the states was to him at least as great a threat to freedom and progress as the "spectre of tyranny" antifederalists saw haunting every move to strengthen government. Even more fatal was the weakness of the country in the face of formidable threats from abroad. The intrigues of Spain, England, and France, to say nothing of hints of direct aggression, could only be met by a strong, united nation. Madison discerned, as Jefferson was to proclaim in his first inaugural address, that an enlarged republican government "where every man, at the call of the laws, would fly to the standard of the law, and would meet invasions of the public order as his own personal concern, [was] . . . the strongest government on earth."

In seeking separation of powers Madison meant not only to prevent simple tyranny, but also to tap more fully the latent increment to power for constructive action afforded by the republican principle. In this insight he transcended the traditional dogma, so strong in English radical Whig rhetoric reacting against royal prerogative, that freedom meant *release* from the authority of government. Under a government of consent, properly constructed to prevent domination by faction, freedom could mean the *use* of power in the public interest. The antifederalist assumption that the powers of republican government were equally oppressive as those of monarchy utterly missed the new dimension, which was the freedom-extending basis of Madison's vigorous nationalism. More fully than any of his colleagues in nation-building, Madison came to understand that powers exercised by governments resting on the consent of the governed were not necessarily tyrannical, as were those exercised by arbitrary government. A large republic could, under a properly constructed constitution, combine inherent strength with inherent protection against faction and tyranny to realize the fulfillment under self-control implicit in Jefferson's phrase "an empire of liberty."

III

Almost as revealing as Madison's unchanging opinions are three vital matters on which he revised or enlarged his views. First, he abandoned his insistence that the federal government have explicit power to void state legislation and accepted instead James Wilson's argument that a clause declaring federal acts supreme law would be more consistent with free government and in the long run fully as effective. Aware of the repeated, flagrant contempt of various states for the acts and requisitions of the Continental Congress and sure that state power and ingenuity would thwart or evade anything other than a perfectly clear coercive authority vested in the federal government, Madison had gone to Philadelphia in May 1787 determined to place such coercive power at the heart of the new constitution. He came to see, though, that efforts to enforce a federal veto of a state law would result in "a scene resembling much more a civil war than the administration of a regular government." More subtly effective and more consistent with the national principle would be a constitutional statement of the supremacy of federal laws throughout the nation. Hamilton's understanding of the use and efficacy of federal judges, marshals, collectors, and other officials in upholding federal law against state encroachment or defiance, evident in *The Federalist*, further reconciled Madison to the omission of the coercive clause. Making federal law supreme within its defined sphere and directly applicable to the people established a mixed government with limited sovereignty at the federal level rather than a crude league of states empowered to punish recalcitrant members. Furthermore, creating direct bonds of consent and obedience between the people and the federal government enhanced the republicanism of that government itself rather than allowing it to be merely reflective of republican states.

Second, Madison switched during the Federal Convention from support of a broad power of the federal government to act and legislate in the public interest to a belief that its powers ought to be enumerated. He first supported enumerated powers after the Convention had adopted the Great Compromise assuring state equality in the Senate. At first regarding the compromise as unjust and unwise, Madison thought it imprudent to invest such a poorly devised Congress with undefined powers. As a large-state delegate he also had an aversion to placing his state's interests at the mercy of small-state power in the Senate. Madison's nationalism, in fact, began to recede the moment the nation committed itself to what he considered an unrepublican state equality. The principle of consent in his view forbade granting unlimited power to a flawed government. Soon, though, and especially during the fight against Federalist party programs in the 1790s, Madison came to see that the enumeration of the powers of Congress reinforced the concept of the rule of law, and was therefore useful, perhaps even necessary, in a republic. In fact, a Senate based on state equality (and thus dependent on a basically different constituency from that of the House of Representatives), coupled with enumerated powers, expanded substantially the checks and balances implanted in the Constitution. Madison's eventual support of the Senate and of enumeration demonstrated the depth of his distrust of "the idea of a government in one center, as expressed and espoused by [Condorcet], . . . a concentration of . . . power universally acknowledged to be fatal to public liberty." Madison thus displayed a sensitivity to what would become a persistent dilemma in American politics: how to give government the power to act in the public interest and how at the same time to prevent it from acting in oppressive or factious ways.[9]

His final shift, to support of an explicit bill of rights in the federal Constitution, was at first tactical but finally principled as well. Reading Jefferson's persuasive arguments, he came to believe a bill of rights would make the Constitution a better instrument of free republican government. The clear statement of important liberties would help engraft them in the public consciousness and provide a ready defense against future assaults on them. Madison, of course, had never opposed the rights themselves, but rather changed his mind about the surest means of their protection. Again the effect was a deeper understanding of the devices of government most likely to preserve the moral imperatives of the good society he had learned from Aristotle, John Locke, "Cato," and Joseph Addison.

Edmund Burke wrote at about the time of the Constitutional Convention that "to make a government requires no great prudence; settle the seat of power, teach obedience, and the work is done. To give freedom is still more easy. It is not necessary to guide; it only requires to let go the rein. But to form a free government, that is, to temper together the opposite elements of liberty and restraint in one conscious work, requires much thought; deep reflection; a sagacious, powerful, and combining mind." Resolving this paradox had become the central concern of the generation that sought to frame a government embodying the purposes of the new nation as defined in the Declaration of Independence. Increasingly, attention focused on what it meant for the people to be sovereign—how they could *really* be represented, how far *any* government could be trusted to act on their behalf, how the power to do things could be reconciled with protection of inalienable rights, how a written "perpetual" constitution could coexist with the right of each generation to legislate for itself, and so on. Furthermore, it became increasingly clear that for the people to be meaningfully sovereign, they themselves would have to embody virtuous qualities, to have the character capable of sustaining the demands of self-government. This fulfillment, this addition of flesh and blood to the skeleton of statements and constitutions, became the task of the last and most complex phase of the American Revolution.

IV

The Revolution in Character

THOUGH AMERICANS in the 1780s would have understood John Adams' observation that by 1776 the American Revolution was over, meaning that by then self-conscious loyalty to Britain had largely disappeared, they were nonetheless excited by a sense of unfulfillment and fateful opportunity. While much depended on a disciplined, even Spartan beginning, as American armies fought desperately at Camden and King's Mountain and American diplomats scoured Europe for money and supplies to keep the Revolution alive, thoughtful men looked ahead to more sophisticated stages. "The science of government is my duty to study," wrote Adams to his wife in 1780. "I must study politics and war, that my sons may have liberty to study mathematics and philosophy. My sons ought to study mathematics and philosophy, geography, natural history, and naval architecture, navigation, commerce, and agriculture, in order to give their children a right to study painting, poetry, music, architecture, statuary, tapestry, and porcelain." Jeremy Belknap asked the same year, "Why may not *a Republic of Letters* be realized in America as well as a Republican Government? Why may there not be a Congress of Philosophers as well as of Statesmen? . . . I am so far an enthusiast in the cause of America as to wish she may shine Mistress of the Sciences, as well as the Asylum of Liberty."[1]

In 1785 Richard Price, an Englishman who had long supported the American Revolution, saw oppositely awesome prospects in its failure:

The consequence will be, that the fairest experiment ever tried in human affairs will miscarry, and that a REVOLUTION which had revived the hopes of good men and promised an opening to better times, will become a discouragement to all future efforts in favour of liberty, and prove only an opening to a new scene of human degeneracy and misery.

But one of his correspondents, Benjamin Rush, a Philadelphia physician, philanthropist, politician, and signer of the Declaration of Independence, after reading Price's words asserted:

Most of the *distresses* of our country, and of the *mistakes* which Europeans have formed of us, have arisen from a belief that the American Revolution is *over*. This is so far from being the case that we have only finished the first act of the great drama. We have changed our forms of government, but it remains yet to effect a revolution in our principles, opinions, and manners, so as to accommodate them to the forms of government we have adopted. This is the most difficult part of the business. . . . It requires more wisdom and fortitude than to expel or to reduce armies into captivity.[2]

At a quite different level an aspiring young teacher and author from Connecticut, Noah Webster, noted the difficulties of using a long-popular English spelling book by Thomas Dilworth in American schools. "The proper names for places which belong to Great Britain" included in it, Webster complained, "are totally useless in America." He found American children "incapable and unwilling to learn" words so remote from their experience. The fact that Dilworth "was universally esteemed in Great Britain half a century ago," Webster added, was no sign that he was fit for American use in 1783; he was "out of date . . . [and] really faulty and defective in every part of his work." "America," Webster proclaimed, "must be as independent in *literature* as she is in *politics*, as famous for *arts* as for *arms*." To encourage such independence at an early age, Webster left out English examples from his book *The American Instructor*, including instead "a short account of the discovery of America, the time of the settlement of each state, with an epitome of their respective constitutions as established since the revolution—which is designed to diffuse a political knowledge of this grand confederation of republics among that class of people who have not access to more expensive means of information." Thus, while "a folio upon some abstruse philosophical subject, . . . like a taper gives light only in the chamber of study, . . . a little fifteen-penny volume . . . may convey much useful knowledge to the remote, obscure recesses of honest poverty." Twenty-five years later, considering "the connection between language and knowledge, and the influence of a national language on national opinions," Webster declared it necessary "to detach this country as much as possible from its dependence on the parent country. . . . Our people look to English books as the standard of truth on all subjects and this confidence in English opinions puts *an end to inquiry*." For sixty years he labored to adapt the very quality of language itself to what he hoped would be a somehow unique, worthy American culture growing in the new nation.[3]

10. John Adams, Franklin, Jefferson, and the Puritan Ethic

I

THIS SENSE OF CULTURAL DISTINCTIVENESS SHOWED ITSELF IN HUN-
DREDS OF WAYS IN THE YEARS AFTER 1776, BUT NOWHERE MORE
VIVIDLY THAN DURING TRAVELS TO STRANGE PLACES BY SELF-
CONSCIOUS EX-COLONIALS, FIRST IN AMERICA AND THEN IN EUROPE. FOR
someone like John Adams, a fifth-generation New Englander keenly
aware of how the values, habits, institutions, and community government of a Massachusetts town had shaped his life, the curiosity about his
own character began as soon as he first reached the Hudson River. After
a few days of socializing in New York on his way to the First Continental Congress (1774), Adams complained that amid "the Opulence
and Splendor of this City, there is very little good Breeding to be
found." People entertained so much that there was no time for improving one's mind—and people talked "very loud, very fast, and all
together." Somehow society lacked the dignity, seriousness, and human
touch he enjoyed in New England. In Philadelphia Adams was fascinated, and sometimes horrified, by the cultural differences. He found a
Roman Catholic service (probably his first) "most awfull and affecting." Though he admired the "sweet and exquisite" chanting, the rich
vestments of the priest and altar, and the "good, short, moral Essay"
delivered from the pulpit, he pitied the parishioners, "poor Wretches,
fingering their Beads, chanting Latin, not a Word of which they understood." "Here is every Thing which can lay hold of the Ear, Eye, and
Imagination," Adams concluded to his wife, "every Thing which can
charm and bewitch the simple and ignorant. I wonder how Luther ever

broke the spell." Even the Presbyterians and Episcopalians were so much "Slaves to the Domination of the Priesthood" that he declared "the Congregational Way best."[1]

Philadelphia society, too, had many displeasing aspects. After observing a doctor who "used Wine and Women very freely," he pronounced "Epicurism and Debauchery more common in [Philadelphia] than in Boston" and insisted to Abigail that "Truth, Sobriety, [and] Industry should be perpetually inculcated upon" their children. By 1777 Adams was so disgusted with Philadelphia that he thought "America will lose nothing, by [General] Howe's gaining this town" —the Quakers were "dull as Beetles, . . . a kind of neutral Tribe, . . . [a] Race of the insipids," while the rest of the people were "a pack of sordid Scoundrels Male and female, [who] seem to have prepared their Minds and Bodies, Houses and Cellars" to receive the British army. Furthermore, though Adams often admired the oratory and patriotic zeal of the Southern delegates to Congress, he had little use for their aristocratic airs, their love of gaming, liquor, and whoring, and their slothful, immoral dependence on slaves. Altogether, he reflected increasingly on the grounds of his preference for New England. Eight months before the Declaration of Independence he wrote Abigail of his "overweening Prejudice in favour of New England," founded in part, he knew, on the natural sentiment to love one's home province, but also resting on solid advantages: "the Institutions . . . for the Support of Religion, Morals, and Decency; . . . the public Institutions . . . for the Education of Youth; . . . [town government that] makes Knowledge and Dexterity at public Business common; . . . [and] a frequent Division of landed Property [that] prevents Monopolies of Land." Ten years later, in London, Adams explained to a visiting Virginian that "The Towns, Militia, Schools, and Churches" formed the "Virtues and Talents" of the people of New England, producing the "Temperance, Patience, Fortitude, Prudence, . . . Justice, . . . Sagacity, Knowledge, Judgment, Taste, Skill, Ingenuity, Dexterity and Industry" for which they were famous. A complex array of institutions, values, and habits, not easily acquired or maintained, were of critical importance in forming national character.[2]

When Adams went to France as one of the American Commissioners in 1778, he was awed by the strange world he found—and acutely conscious of how momentous it was that he, born and raised in a provincial town in the New World and the representative of a self-proclaimed republic, should be traveling as a distinguished personage amid the ancient nations of Europe. On his first voyage he landed at Bordeaux, where the neatly cultivated countryside charmed him: "The Fields of Grain, the Vineyards, the Castles, the Cities, the Parks, the Gardens, must be seen to be known. . . . Yet . . . every place swarms with beggars . . . because the Poor depend upon private Charity for Support, instead of being provided for by Parishes as in England or Towns in America." The customs were similarly incongruous and startling. At a welcoming dinner characterized by lavish furnishings, court dress, and food, a lady, remarking on Adams' name, asked if his family might therefore know how the first man and woman "found out the Art of lying together." Shocked at such conversation in mixed company, Adams "determined not to be disconcerted" but later concluded that "if such are the manners of Women of Rank, Fashion and Reputation in France, they can never support a Republican Government. . . . We must therefore take great care not to import them into America." Alternately amazed and appalled, Adams reflected again and again on the refinement and elegance of European civilization on the one hand—and how his country might attain them —and on the degradation and corruption that followed when a nation lacked the republican institutions and Puritan habits he knew in America. At another dinner he talked geopolitics with a Dutch merchant who complained that the colonies supported despotism by fighting England and making an alliance with France. Adams answered that he "had been educated from [his] cradle in the same opinion," but that nevertheless the colonies would not tolerate the bloody tyranny England sought to impose on them. "Precarious Speculations about the Protestant Interest and the balance of Power in Europe," he declared, would not deter America from defending her liberty. "Our Plan," he concluded, "was to have no Interest, Connection or Embarrassment in the Politicks or Wars of Europe, if we could avoid it." New nations, it seemed, had also to reconsider the ancient staples of international politics and decide anew what connections and principles were congruent with their stated purposes—and with the new character they sought.[3]

After another Atlantic crossing, Adams and his two young sons were driven into an isolated harbor near Caronna, Spain, by a leaky vessel and British warships. Then, traveling overland to Paris, the journey through unfamiliar country evoked a thousand comparisons of national character. The Spanish officers he found grave and silent, while the French were gay, vivacious, and loquacious. Living arrangements in Spain were unbelievably primitive and dirty—no chimneys for the fires, stone floors that "had never been washed nor swept for a hundred Years," animals and people living in the same rooms, and straw mats to sleep on:

I see nothing but Signs of Poverty and Misery, among the People. A fertile Country, not half cultivated, People ragged and dirty, and the Houses universally nothing but Mire, Smoke, Fleas and Lice. Nothing appears rich but the Churches, nobody fat, but the Clergy. The Roads, the worst without Exception that ever were passed, in a Country where it would be easy to make them very good. No Symptoms of Commerce, or even of internal Traffic, no Appearance of Manufactures or Industry.

To a practical Yankee, used to applying ingenuity to everyday problems and to having such energy yield benefits to himself and to his family, the torpor, ennui, and injustice of an exploitative society were horrendous. After another week of uncomfortable travel through the Spanish countryside, Adams concluded that "Church, State, and Nobility exhaust the People to such a degree, I have no Idea of the Possibility of deeper Wretchedness." Though he appreciated Spanish politeness, the fresh mountain air, and the skill of the farmers in raising crops and herds in the rugged land, he was overwhelmed by the misery of the people.[4]

Crossing the Pyrenees into France, it seemed to Adams, was like coming into paradise: "The numerous Groves, Parks and Forrests in this Country form a striking Contrast with Spain." Again John Adams had observed the stark differences between peoples and the critical effect on them of their institutions, habits, and cultural heritage. Obviously a new nation's vision would have to range wider and deeper than winning a revolutionary war and organizing a new system of law. Thinking about what they wanted their new nation to become pushed Americans into novel speculations and new approaches in every aspect of thought, manners, and culture. The opportunities Adams, Rush, and Webster foresaw in the 1780s became the absorbing task of Jefferson, Hamilton, Barlow, Stiles, Ames, Randolph of Roanoke, Marshall, Gallatin, Peale, Trumbull, Freneau, Brackenridge, Irving, Tyler, Channing, and a host of others in the first generation or two of government under the Constitution. Though these men had widely different concerns and did not share a common ideology, their thought was dominated by a consciousness that they possessed a new nationality and that their lives would be profoundly affected by it. The United States would remain for a time an appendage of European culture, but the spreading effect of the new national feeling began gradually to furnish a fuller definition of a peculiarly "American character."

II

The search for the broad meaning of new nationhood impinged on many aspects of the Revolution itself. Edmund Morgan has pointed out, for example, that to many people in the colonies the American Revolution was an attempt to rest national character on the "Puritan Ethic" of devotion to a "calling," diligence, productivity, frugality, charity, support of church and commonwealth, stewardship of one's talent and wealth, and a belief that nations must serve the Kingdom of God. The Puritan Ethic thus fleshed out the skeleton of political arrangements with habits and attitudes and values that could guide daily life, and if made widespread among the people, could mark them with a distinctive national character. There was, of course, nothing new or particularly American about the Puritan Ethic—it had been given classic formulation by William Perkins and other English writers early in the seventeenth century, and its secularized version had been promulgated on both sides of the Atlantic by Daniel Defoe, Benjamin Franklin, and others. But in the pre-Revolutionary decade those protesting British rule in the thirteen colonies more and more insisted that the purpose of the resistance was to ensure that the virtues of the Puritan Ethic would not be destroyed. Congregational Puritan Samuel Adams warned Anglican Puritan Arthur Lee in 1771 that "the Conspirators against our Liberties are employing all their Influence to divide the people, . . . introducing Levity, Luxury, and Indolence," while a Rhode Island town objected in 1774 that "so many unnecessary officers are supported by the earnings of honest industry, in a life of dissipation and ease; who, by being *properly* employed, might be useful members of society." The basic trouble with British rule, that is, was its subversion of a way of life.[5]

A Rhode Island traveler in England saw the threat graphically when he reported often hearing arrogant Britons saying of rebellious Americans, "We shall never do any Thing with Them till we root out that cursed puritanick Spirit, . . . debauch their Morals—Toss off to them all the Toies and Baubles that genius can invent to weaken their Minds, fill them with Pride and Vanity, and beget in them all possible Extravagance in Dress and Living." Franklin made the vital connection between personal habits and government in comparing American and British ways:

Every man in America is employed; the greatest number in cultivating their own Lands, the rest in Handicrafts, Navigation, and Commerce. An idle man there is a rarity; Idleness and Inutility is a character of Disgrace. In England the Quantity of that Character is immense. Fashion has spread it far and wide. Hence the Embarassment of private Fortunes, and the daily Bankruptcies, arising from the universal fondness for Appearance and expensive Pleasures; and hence, in some Degree, the Mismanagement of their publick Business: For Habits of Business, and Ability in it, are acquired only by Practice; and, where universal Dissipation and the perpetual Pursuit of Amusement are the Mode, the Youths who are educated in it can rarely afterwards acquire that patient Attention and close Application to Affairs, which are so necessary to a statesman charged with the Care of national Welfare.[6]

To Americans imbued with the Puritan Ethic, then, the Revolution had its deepest root in a concern for habits and values that had to be protected against English corruption and, after independence, sustained by the new nation. This view touched Americans far removed from the Puritan churches of New England. Jefferson's letters to his daughter while he supervised her education in France, for example, resemble a Puritan catechism:

Of all the cankers of human happiness, none corrodes with so silent, yet so baneful a tooth, as indolence. Body and mind both unemployed, our being becomes a burden, and every object about us loathsome, even the dearest. . . . If at any moment, my dear, you catch yourself in idleness, start from it as you would from the precipice of a gulf. . . . No person will have occasion to complain of the want of time, who never loses any. It is wonderful how much may be done, if we are always doing.

Henry Laurens, a South Carolina merchant and a zealous Anglican, became a revolutionist after British officials fraudulently seized one of his ships and then asked a bribe for its return. Industrious, successful, and wealthy, like Henry Fielding's Squire Allworthy, Laurens denounced the "sacreligious Robberies of public Money" by "pitiful Rogues" during the Revolution. He disapproved of gambling and card-playing, and when he did win a social game in Charleston, he "uniformly refused" his gains, "esteeming it wrong to take any man's money without giving an equivalent." This ethic was an ideal respected (though not always practiced) throughout the colonies and to a remarkable degree became a goal of the Revolution. At the very least the recurrent moral comparisons between English society and American indicated a widespread recognition that for the Revolution to be really significant it had to affect the ways and values of everyday life. The verbal omnipresence of the Puritan Ethic in the colonies, and the relative absence of the jaded, corrupt, debauched hedonism characteristic of aristocracies all over Europe, was further evidence, too, of the cumulative screening effect of the Atlantic Ocean—the vigorous Puritan Ethic, surging forth from the world view of Milton, Bunyan, and Defoe, made the journey much more often and much more robustly than the "values" of English society represented by Fielding's Parson Thwackum or Lady Bellaston.[7]

Projected onto the public stage, the ethic played a key role in the disputes between the "Lee-Adams faction" of the Continental Congress that first coalesced in opposition to Silas Deane in 1778, and Deane's supporters and others zealous for the French Alliance. The anti-Deane people, led by the Adamses, the Lees, and Henry Laurens, prided themselves on their incorruptibility, their sturdy self-reliance, and their faith that diligence, sacrifice, courage, and common effort could win the war against Great Britain. They were, in short, sure that their virtues, nourished and lived up to by the people, could both win independence and be the foundation for the character of the new nation. As for Deane, they agreed with John Adams that he was "a person of plausible readiness and Volubility with his Tongue and his Pen, much addicted to Ostentation and Expence in Dress and Living, but without any deliberate forecast or reflection or solidity of Judgment or real Information." His wheeling-and-dealing contracts in France for supplies for American armies were to the Lee-Adams faction suspiciously negotiated and resulted in appalling, speculative profits. Also, the lavishly sustained French legation in Philadelphia, presided over by suave French aristocrats given to manipulating American politics, seemed a veritable den of iniquity from whence all the arts and intrigues fatal to a virtuous republic spread out like poison. The Lee-Adams faction was exceedingly sensitive to the qualities of the Puritan Ethic, judged persons and nations by its standards, and saw the success of the Revolution almost entirely in terms of its capacity to implant Puritan virtues in the life of the new nation. The faction was generally provincial and isolationist, reflecting the conviction that virtue needed to be protected from outside corruption and that self-government depended on an intimacy in politics that allowed citizens to judge the personal character of public officials.[8]

Their opponents, who included both Franklin and Jefferson, were not hostile to the Puritan Ethic, but were more sophisticated, less rigid about it. Thus Franklin regarded Deane's activities, though perhaps devious and speculative, as justified since they did dispatch arms across the Atlantic. Franklin not only enjoyed French elegance and civility, but also thought French aid vital to the Revolution and in no serious way subversive of its purposes. A kind of cosmopolitan and pragmatic internationalism infused his view of American foreign relations. He thought the need for French friendship as a counterweight to English hostility more important than the "taint" of alliance with a despotic king, because he was sure "a few years of Peace" would so increase American strength that she could then safely depend solely "on our union and our virtue." In Philadelphia Franklin's supporters sought increased national powers, welcomed the aid of French ministers, and even thought the financial measures of Robert Morris were "safe" and useful to the Revolution. Young nationalists such as Madison, Hamilton, and James Wilson easily identified with this view because it seemed to them the only practical way to gain the power and international esteem a respectable nationhood required. As for John Adams, Franklin considered him "always an honest Man, often a wise one, but sometimes . . . absolutely out of his senses"; James Madison found him vain, prejudiced against France, and venomous about Franklin, and Deane thought Adams retained nothing of his education except "law, knowledge, and the fierce and haughty manners of the Lacedemonians [Spartans] and first Romans." Had Adams seen Deane's characterization, he would have taken pride in it, for to him and to many other Americans from Charleston to Boston the Puritan Ethic received strong reinforcement because its virtues were shared by such stern, incorruptible heroes of the ancient world as Lycurgus of Sparta and Cato of Rome. Clearly, the nationalist group had different personal emphases as well as quite different ideas of what the posture of the new nation should be in the world.[9]

This division, in a general way, paralleled the disputes between federalists and antifederalists in 1788 and between Federalists (Hamiltonian variety) and Republicans in the 1790s.* The federalists accepted the emphasis on greater national power and the more "realistic" approach to international relations that characterized the friends of the French Alliance during the Revolution, while the antifederalists reflected more strongly the localism and the focus on personal virtues so important to the Lee-Adams faction. The same predispositions applied to the party divisions of the 1790s. Though there were many personal crossovers (Madison and Robert R. Livingston, for example, were nationalists and federalists but then Jeffersonian Republicans, while John Adams was Lee-Adams but then federalist and of the Federalist party), and there was no continuity of organization, nevertheless significant sentiments survived. These continuities, moreover, reflected the basic concern for the *character* of the new nation that increasingly dominated American thought from the 1780s on. A Samuel Adams, incorruptible, deeply Puritan, and sustained by town meeting values, would naturally have a different conception of what the new nation should be like from that held by Robert Morris, energetic, eager for national development, and attuned to a world of international trade. Both rank as patriots in that each fought hard for independence, but they had different ideals in mind for the national future.

III

It seemed sometimes that almost any topic thoughtful Americans considered could trigger speculation about the national future. Asked to describe the plants and animals of North America, Jefferson told of huge bones found in the Mississippi Valley and quickly used this evidence to refute Buffon's thesis that nature being "less active, less energetic" in the New World than in the Old, plants and animals were on a lesser scale in America than in Europe. Buffon extended the "slur" to

* In this book "federalist" refers to those who in 1787–1788 and afterward supported the new Constitution, while "Federalist" refers to the political party founded by Hamilton and others after 1789.

argue that domesticated animals "degenerated" when brought to the New World and that American Indians were less fecund, less intelligent, and less courageous than men raised in the Old World. Jefferson compiled detailed measurements to demonstrate the impressive stature of American animals and refuted Buffon's generalizations with examples of Indian prowess. Way of life, nourishment, education, and government, all changeable by human effort, were to Jefferson the important variables that controlled the stature and accomplishments of men. Even worse to Jefferson was the Abbé Raynal's projection of Buffon's theory of degeneracy to "Whites transplanted from Europe" —Raynal having declared that "one must be astonished that America has not yet produced a good poet, an able mathematician, a man of genius in a single art or single science." After citing Washington, Franklin, and David Rittenhouse as Americans of genius, Jefferson observed that "as in philosophy and war, so in government, in oratory, in painting, in the plastic art, so we might show that America, though but a child of yesterday, has already given hopeful proofs of genius, as well of the nobler kinds, which arouse the best feelings of man, which call him to action, which substantiate his freedom, and conduct him to happiness, as of the subordinate, which serves to amuse him only."[10]

When Franklin's daughter noted that the bald eagle on the American Seal looked like a turkey, he answered that he wished the turkey, not the bald eagle, "had been chosen as the Representative of our country." The eagle, he said, "does not get his living honestly. . . . He watches the Labour of the Fishing-Hawk; and, when that diligent Bird has at length taken a Fish . . . the Bald Eagle pursues him, and takes it from him. . . . Like those among Men who live by Sharping and Robbing, he is generally poor, and often very lousy." "The Turkey is in comparison a much more respectable Bird," not only native to America, but as well useful, industrious, and courageous. In the same letter he objected to titles descending in a family because "Honour, worthily obtained . . . is in its Nature a *personal* Thing, and incommunicable to any but those who had some share in obtaining it." Thus though *ascending* honor for the parents of worthy persons, because they provided "a good and virtuous Education," made some sense, *descending* honor was "not only groundless and absurd, but often hurtful to that Posterity, since it is apt to make them proud, disdaining to be employed in useful Arts, and thence falling into Poverty, and all the Meannesses, Servility, and Wretchedness attending it, which is the present case with much of what is called the *Noblesse* in Europe." Custom, and hence character, he hoped, would take a different course in the New World.[11]

In 1782 Franklin wrote on the unique features of the new nation in a widely distributed pamphlet offering *Information to Those Who Would Remove to America.* Among other misconceptions, he noted that many Europeans supposed that in America "there are . . . an abundance of profitable offices to be disposed of, which the Natives are not qualified to fill; and that, having few Persons of Family among them, Strangers of Birth must be greatly respected, and easily obtain the best of those Offices, which will make all their Fortunes." It was not advisable for a person to go to America, Franklin warned, "who has no other quality to recommend him but his Birth. In Europe it has indeed its Value; but it is a Commodity that cannot be carried to a worse market than that of America." There, he said, remembering his own runaway arrival in Philadelphia without friends or money, "people do not inquire concerning a Stranger, *What is he?* but, *What can he do?* If he has any useful Art, he is welcome, and if he exercises it, and behaves well, he will be respected by all that know him, but a mere Man of Quality, who, on that Account, wants to live upon the Public, by some Office or Salary, will be despised and disregarded." Who should come to America, then? "Hearty young Labouring Men" willing to carve a farm from the wilderness, "tolerably good workmen in any of [the] Mechanic Arts," and even "Persons of Moderate Fortunes and Capitals" who sought a country where their children would have abundant opportunity. "Multitudes of poor People from England, Ireland, Scotland, and Germany," Franklin pointed out, had "in a few years become wealthy Farmers, who, in their own countries . . . could never have emerged from the poor Condition wherein they were born." Apprenticeships where masters trained young men in a trade and taught them to "read, write, and cast accounts" were readily obtainable even by ignorant immigrants just off the ship. "If they are poor," Franklin noted in summing up what he hoped would become the "meaning" of America in the world, "they begin first as Servants or Journeymen; and if they are sober, industrious, and frugal, they soon become Masters, establish themselves in Business, marry, raise Families, and become respectable Citizens."

Franklin recognized that this concentration on prosperity and the well-being of the common people, though of prime importance, had its short-run limitations. There were in America "very few rich enough . . . to pay the high Prices given in Europe for Paintings, Statues, Architecture, and other Works of Art, that are more curious than useful." Aware of the careers of Benjamin West, John Singleton Copley, Gilbert Stuart, and others, Franklin observed that Americans with artistic genius "have uniformily quitted that Country for Europe, where they can be more suitably rewarded." He was sure that given some years of peace and growth, learning and the arts would flourish in America as they did in Europe, but he was unwilling to purchase these, as had been the case in every known high civilization, at the expense of the poverty and enslavement of the people.[12]

Jefferson made the same point when he admitted that though he enjoyed Parisian "architecture, sculpture, painting, [and] music," and that Europe did indeed far outshine America in these arts, the cost was that "the people are ground to powder by the vices of the form of government. Of twenty millions of people supposed to be in France, I am of the opinion there are nineteen millions more wretched, more accursed in every circumstance of human existence than the most conspicuously wretched individual of the whole United States." Both Franklin and Jefferson were enough attracted to European culture to consider living there for much of their lives, and both left Europe hoping to return soon, but upon reflection the ways of the New World, highlighted for each by a residence in Europe, seemed of more fundamental virtue. "In science," Jefferson concluded, the mass of the people in Europe were "two centuries behind ours; their literati, half a dozen years before us."[13]

IV

They saw similar forces at work in the effect of a European sojourn and a European education on young Americans. Franklin became poignantly aware of the danger with his own children and grandchildren. His son William lived with him in England for five years (1757–1762), undertook law studies there, enjoyed London society, married an English gentlewoman, and, as a favor from the Court, received an appointment as Royal Governor of New Jersey. Thenceforth he accomplished almost nothing, remained rigidly Loyalist during the Revolution, and spent his last thirty years in lonely, bitter exile in England. William's son, William Temple Franklin, who was raised in England, in 1776 at the age of sixteen went to France where he worked intermittently as his grandfather's secretary, but generally reveled in French society as an idle gallant. Thereafter, despite his grandfather's earnest urging, indulgent care, and assiduous sponsorship, he drifted aimlessly about the Western world, almost a man without a country. He even managed to waste the legacy of his grandfather's papers—it took him thirty years to get the priceless *Autobiography* and some letters and essays published. Franklin put his younger grandson, Benjamin Bache, aged seven when he went to France in 1776, into school in Geneva where he hoped a republican government and a less rigidly clerical education than that available in Paris might save the lad from becoming a foppish courtier. This precaution, plus Bennie's youth and the wise vigilance of the twice-burned old diplomat, seem largely to have preserved his character, but the force of the lesson remained undiminished: American society had become so distinct from European that an education in the latter unsuited a person for a life in the former.

Jefferson elaborated the reasons for the difference after considerable experience in supervising the education of young men and women in both the Old and the New World and after long talks with Franklin about the problem:

Let us view the disadvantages of sending a youth to Europe [for his education]. . . . If he goes to England he learns drinking, horse-racing, and boxing. . . . He acquires [anywhere] a fondness for European luxury and dissipation, and a contempt for the simplicity of his own country; he is fascinated with the privileges of the European aristocats, and sees, with abhorrence, the lovely equality which the poor enjoy with the rich in his own country; he contracts a partiality for aristocracy or monarchy; . . . he is led, by the strongest of all human passions, into a spirit for female intrigue, destructive of his own and others' happiness, or a passion for whores, destructive of his health; . . . he recollects the voluptuary dress and arts of the European women, and pities and despises the chaste affections and simplicity of those of his own country; . . . he returns to his own country, a foreigner, unacquainted with the practices of domestic economy necessary to preserve him from ruin, speaking and writing his native tongue as a foreigner. . . . It appears to me, then, that an American, coming to Europe for an education, loses in his knowledge, in his morals, in his health, in his habits, and in his happiness.[14]

The dramatist Royall Tyler made the same point in deploring the effect of the English novel on American girls: "It . . . impresses on the young mind an erroneous idea of the world in which she is to live. It paints the manners, customs, and habits of a strange country; excites a fondness for false splendor; and renders the homespun habits of her country disgusting." Jefferson and Tyler shared an intense concern for particular virtues maturing in the life of the new nation. It forced them to conclude that European ways of forming young minds were certainly unsuitable and probably dangerous.[15]

11. Republicanizing American Character

I

THE FULLEST AND EVENTUALLY MOST FAMOUS REFLECTIONS DUR-
ING THE 1780S ON THE NATURE AND MEANING OF THE NEW
AMERICAN CHARACTER WERE IN LETTERS FROM AN AMERICAN
FARMER BY A FRENCH IMMIGRANT, J. HECTOR ST. JOHN CRÈVECOEUR. HE
asked, and answered, the question that dominated both American thinking about itself and European curiosity about the strange republic across
the Atlantic: "What is the American, this new man?" Crèvecoeur, a
lesser French nobleman who lived in America for a generation before
the American Revolution, answered that an American was a "strange
mixture of blood, . . . [for] here individuals of all nations are melted
into a new race of men, whose labours and posterity will one day
cause great changes in the world." He was a man who:

leaving behind him all his ancient prejudices and manners, receives new
ones from the new mode of life he has embraced, the new government he
obeys, and the new rank he holds. . . . The American is a new man, who
acts upon new principles; he must therefore entertain new ideas, and form
new opinions. From involuntary idleness, servile dependence, penury, and
useless labour, he has passed to toils of a very different nature, rewarded
by ample subsistence—This is an American.[1]

Crèvecoeur's sense of American distinctiveness owes as much to
physiocratic, romanticized ideals as to his experience of life in America—
but this romantic thinking was itself powerfully stimulated by the
prospects of the American wilderness. Crèvecoeur noted, for example,
that in America one "might contemplate the very beginning and out-
lines of human society," free from the "misguided religion, tyranny,

and absurd laws [that] everywhere depress and afflict mankind." He noted further that one could "compose many a good sermon . . . [following] a plough," and that no one supposed in America that a people could become prosperous and happy, as some English economists seemed to think, by "sending epistles to and fro" and by trading in bank notes. Crèvecoeur idealized the Indians and condemned "politics" as a vice-prone distraction from productive life, but he glorified the *cultivated* frontier, not the "ferocious, gloomy, and unsociable" wilderness where men, "no better than carnivorous animals," lived in a state of "lawless profligacy." He hoped further that in America men would "not fear God according to the tenets of any one seminary," nor worship a Supreme Being who resided "in peculiar churches or communities . . . [or had a] peculiar political tendency," but rather that they would learn to worship God "upon the broad scale of nature, . . . the great Manitou of the woods and of the plains."[2]

Thus conceptions formed in France salons and arising from European imagination and aspiration found in the New World an otherwise unattainable relevance and immediacy. Just as Franklin was able to apply easily in Philadelphia Daniel Defoe's schemes for civic improvement that fell stillborn in London, and Locke's idea of a state of nature achieved unique vividness in America, Crèvecoeur found that the physiocratic vision (as old as Virgil and Horace) became flesh in Pennsylvania. He told, for example, of Andrew the Hebridean, a wretched peasant from a barren Scottish island who in a few years became "independent and easy" on a New World farm. It was the story of "a poor man, advancing from indigence to ease; from oppression to freedom; from obscurity and contumely to some degree of consequence—not by virtue of any breaks of fortune, but by the gradual operation of sobriety, honesty, and emigration." There was in Andrew's story, Crèvecoeur observed with some sarcasm, "not a single remarkable event to amaze the reader, no tragical scene to convulse the heart, no pathetic narrative to draw tears from sympathetic eyes" —just a plain man who made a new life for himself. Like the deliberately down-to-earth account in Franklin's *Autobiography*, Andrew's saga was actually far more marvelous than the lurid tales of soldiers and sea captains and paramours that were the best-sellers of the day.[3]

Crèvecoeur returned to Europe, however, rather than take part in the warfare of the American Revolution, a curious move, perhaps, for one so preoccupied with the newness of America, but less so in light of what he conceived that newness to be. To a simple farmer, the rancor and the tumult and the bloodshed of revolution were baffling, unwelcome distractions. "The innocent classes are always the victim of the few. . . . It is for the sake of the great leaders on both sides, that so much blood must be spilt; that of the people so counted as nothing. Great events are not achieved for us, though it is *by* us that they are principally accomplished; by the arms, the sweat, and the lives of the people. . . . Sophistry, the bane of freemen, launches forth in all her deceiving attire." The loyalty of a free man, Crèvecoeur declared, was not to dynasties or national honor or grandeur, but to his farm and his family and his industrious, self-reliant way of life, the only real sources of human happiness. Though it may have been naïve of Crève-coeur to suppose that such an idyll was unthreatened by British rule or did not need the power of revolutionary arms for its long-run security, it was nonetheless true, as Franklin, Jefferson, and many others said often, that war and all related exertions and inhumanities were antithetical to the virtues they came more and more to associate with the new nation. "There never was a good war or a bad peace," Franklin wrote many times. If this view could become characteristic in a nation, then its values, and the demands it made upon the people, would indeed be transformed.[4]

II

The omnipresent question was: What was the potentiality, the destiny of the United States of America? Franklin and Jefferson, John Adams and Noah Webster, Royall Tyler and Crèvecoeur, awed at the opportunity to discover the full range of human creativity, reflected endlessly on the implications of new nationhood. During the first thirty years or so of government under the Constitution, policy formulations, laws, financial plans, political party platforms, State of the Union messages, and patriotic orations all reflected a concern for national identity. Institutions and habits of life seemed somehow to be different from their Old World antecedents—or should be made different. Moreover, as poets, painters, writers, preachers, teachers, and historians practiced their arts, they, too, faced the fact of new nation-hood.

In public life the official response, guided by George Washington and John Adams, was cautious. Unwilling to trust themselves entirely to novelty and uncertain whether people could be governed without some reverence for the old forms, the Federalist Presidents generally accepted usages familiar from England and from a century or more of colonial experience. Formal relations among the branches of government, reception of foreign ministers, and official hospitality all so closely followed British practices that charges of "apeing monarchy" were widespread. The mode of addressing the President provoked the most revealing debate. Senator Richard Henry Lee urged an exalted title for the President since "all the world, civilized and savage," resorted to that custom. Vice President Adams took the floor with his sword at his side to argue earnestly for "the efficacy of pageantry," which, he wrote a friend, was "indispensably necessary to give dignity and energy to government." Though Senator William Maclay of Pennsylvania and others scoffed at these high-toned ideas, Adams had considerable support—ladies toasted Washington as "His Highness" at a ball given in his honor, and the Senate voted to address him as "His Highness, the President of the United States of America, and Protector of the Rights of the Same."[5]

Representative James Madison, however, upheld the plain title "President of the United States," for pompous titles only made insignificant princes seem absurd, and being contrary to "the nature of our Government [and] the genius of the People, . . . [they would] diminish the true dignity and importance of a Republic." "Splendid tinsel or [a] gorgeous robe," Madison continued, "would disgrace the manly shoulders of [Washington]. . . . The more simple, the more republican we are in our manners, the more rational dignity we shall acquire." The Republicans made the same point more emphatically after 1801 when they deliberately set aside Federalist formality. President Jefferson received visitors in slippers while Secretary of State Madison permitted a mere clerk to announce calls from foreign ministers.[6]

The notorious "Merry Affair" in 1803–1804 revealed the intent of the new social atmosphere. Mrs. Anthony Merry, the wife of the new

British minister in Washington, had a snobbish sense of precedence that left her disgusted at social life in the United States. During one banquet at the President's House, Jefferson conducted Dolley Madison to the dinner table instead of Mrs. Merry, who, according to European court custom, was "the ranking lady" present. Other Americans present also merely turned to the nearest lady and went informally to the table. The Merrys tagged along as best they could. Four days later, at the Madisons', the Merrys again found the head of the table occupied. Mr. Merry nonetheless conducted his wife to the chair next to the host where, it happened, Mrs. Gallatin was sitting. She offered her place to Mrs. Merry, "who took it without prudency or apology." Thus unnerved and feeling insulted, the Merrys accepted no more invitations from the Republican leaders. For a month or two Washington society was in an uproar. Things reached such proportions that Madison thought it necessary to explain to the American minister in London about "this display of diplomatic superstition, truly extraordinary in this age and in this country." There was, of course, a certain amount of calculation in Jefferson's etiquette. He intended, he said, to change the practices of his predecessors "which savoured of anti-republicanism" and to demonstrate that "the principle of society with us, as well as of our political constitution, is the equal rights of all; and if there be an occasion where this equality ought to prevail preeminently, it is in social circles collected for conviviality." Republican resentment at the "high tone" of the Federalist administrations, their charges of "monarchy," and their disgust at the pompous titles suggested for federal officials arose from a conviction that genuine republicanism required a revolution in manners and customs as well as in government. Far from being neglectful of customs, the Republican leaders set out most deliberately to reform them. To do so was an essential task of their administration. Writing anonymously in the press in 1804, Jefferson said:

There is no "Court of the U.S." since the 4th of March 1801. That day buried levees, birthdays, royal parades, and the arrogation of precedence in society by certain self-stiled friends of order, but truly stiled friends of privileged orders. . . . No precedence . . . of anyone over another, exists in right or practice, at dinners, assemblies, or any other occasions. "Pell-mell" and "next the door" form the basis of etiquette in the societies of this country.[7]

Jefferson and his colleagues were as certain as Washington and Adams had been that the social life practiced by government officials was of considerable importance. For centuries a nation's "image" had been set by life at the court of its monarch, and its international posture had been symbolized by the treatment accorded its representatives in foreign countries. Insofar as a nation had meaning, purpose, or character, it was customary to find that meaning in court customs, whether in Peking, Constantinople, Madrid, or St. Petersburg. As the Federalist administrations' obsession with precedence gave way to Jefferson's comfortable, self-confident informality, it became clear that the new nation was indeed discovering important things about its character. Its founding principles, it seemed, as much required rejection of the etiquette of St. James and Versailles as rejection of quitrents and the monarch's throne.

Basic differences that appeared early in Jefferson's Presidency over the nature of law and the place of the judicial system in a republic further revealed that issues of self-government implicit in the Revolution remained on the national agenda—and they also led to sharp controversy within the Republican party. Some Jeffersonians, apprehensive that the victory of 1801 would lead to "a mere change of *men*," called upon the President to destroy Federalism root and branch. Longstanding fears of high-handed aristocratic courts and lawyers, heightened by the determined Federalist efforts of 1800–1801 to pack the judiciary, caused Republicans to question the whole nature of the federal court system. The best-known manifesto, Edmund Pendleton's *The Danger Not Over*, called for the appointment of judges by the legislature rather than the President, the removal of judges by "a concurring vote of both houses of Congress," a declaration "that the Common Law of England . . . in criminal cases, shall not be considered as a law of the United States," and, "to defy the wiles of construction," the explicit exclusion of the concept of sedition from treason prosecutions. These measures were necessary, Pendleton insisted, in order to "seize the opportunity to erect new barriers against folly, fraud, and ambition." More radically, others saw the whole ethos of the legal profession as antithetical to the spirit of the new republic. A New Hampshire farmer who had become a judge, for example, charged a jury to listen to the lawyers if they wished, but to remember that "it is not law we want, but justice. They [lawyers] want to govern us by the common law of England; trust me for it, common sense is a much safer guide for us." Law, like all institutions, would have to purge itself of Old World pretensions and adjust to the principles of republican government.[8]

Moderate Jeffersonians, including the President himself and all his chief advisors, accepted no such simple view of justice, though, and despite their continuing battle with Chief Justice John Marshall, left the federal judiciary intact. In state after state these moderates formed generally successful alliances with Federalists to resist radicals who sought to "democratize" the judicial system by disconnecting it from English precedents and by subjecting it more immediately to legislative or popular control. Nonetheless, the struggles reveal a continuity between Revolutionary and antifederalist suspicion of lawyers and Jacksonian legal reforms. Many Americans in the early 1800s felt that a pettifogging tradition-bound legal system would have to be replaced by one more consistent with the republican character of the new nation.[9]

III

Another American, Joel Barlow, after some years' residence abroad, came to see that an entirely new character for man might be implicit in the American and French revolutions. In the preface to an epic attempted in 1787, *The Vision of Columbus*, Barlow observed that the usual material for a national epic, legends of the past, was somehow unfitting for the United States. "The most brilliant subjects incident to" an American epic, Barlow declared, "arise from *consequences . . .* and must be represented in vision." The epic, then, was "the train of events that might be presented" to Columbus as he envisioned the prospects for mankind in the New World. It was not the storied past but the glorious future that most excited Americans thinking about the "epic" dimensions of their experience.[10]

In 1792 Barlow wrote some *Advice to the Privileged Orders in the several States of Europe*: Cast aside ancient, irrational oppressions and superstitions, and instead attune yourselves to the inevitable progress of mankind toward freedom. Two very powerful weapons in the hands of "political reformers," Barlow thought, "the force of reason and the force of numbers," would soon accomplish all over the world the same revolution already undergone in the United States and in

France. (Note Barlow here identified the two dicta of the Declaration
of Independence, natural rights and majority government, but instead
of regarding them as often in tension, he assumed they were substantially the same.) Barlow considered it possible, moreover, "to induce
the men who now govern the world to adopt these ideas" and thus
prevent the tumult and bloodshed that would result from futile resistance to the new order. In language reminiscent of *Common Sense* and
indebted to the French *philosophes*, Barlow scorned the absurdity and
tyranny of feudalism and the Established Church as they existed in
Europe. Always he saw the meaning of the new order most evident in
astonishingly novel practices in the United States. In religion, for
example, he noted that "there is, strictly speaking, no such thing as a
Church, and yet in no country are the people more religious. All sorts
of religious opinions are entertained there, and yet no *heresy* among
them at all; all modes of worship are practised, and yet there is no
schism; men frequently change their creed and their worship, and yet
there is no *apostasy*; they have ministers of religion, but no *priests*. In
short, religion is there a *personal* and not a *corporate* concern." Barlow also thought that war itself would cease when men understood
that "the people belong not to the government but the government
belongs to the people. . . . The consequence of this will be such a total
renovation of society, as to banish standing armies, overturn the military system, and exclude the possibility of war," which in the past was
always engendered by the ambitions and quarrels of kings, churches,
and nobles, not by the interests of the people. Barlow found as well
that the systems of justice and the demands of the tax collector were
in privileged societies actually means of oppression and theft. In 1806
he urged the establishment of a national university in Washington, D.C.,
to "give a uniformity to the moral sentiment, a republican energy to
the character, a liberal cast to the mind and manners, of the rising and
following generations." "The liberal sciences," he believed, "are in their
nature republican; they delight in reciprocal communication; they
cherish fraternal feelings, and lead to a freedom of intercourse." To
him, the history of the United States offered an inescapable lesson to
the old order in Europe: the day of liberation, of a profound reorienta-
tion of human energy and human society, was at hand.[11]

Barlow's teacher, and the president of Yale College, Ezra Stiles
(1727–1795), viewed the future of republican government from a

rich background. The descendant of long lines of Puritan clergymen, himself a minister for half a century, a learned scholar fully abreast of Enlightenment thought, and an early, earnest friend of the American Revolution, Stiles heard in 1793 of the beheading of Louis XVI while writing a history of three of the judges who had ordered the execution of Charles I. From this perspective, he thought the horror so many New Englanders expressed at a king's death unwarranted. It was proper, even necessary, he declared "in the spirit of prophecy," that the people of England and all others groaning under tyranny in Europe "resume the work which Oliver [Cromwell] and the Judges [of Charles I] once achieved before them" by enlisting again under the banner "rebellion to tyrants is obedience to God." Stirred by the events of 1789–1793 in France, Stiles declared that "the Jacobin societies have proved the salvation of France," as would similar popular, "self-erected societies" in any nation in the world. Where the policy was tyrannical, such assemblies were necessary to deal with an oligarchy that would never willingly or even peaceably reform itself. "Almost all the civil politics on earth," Stiles thought, "are become so corrupt and oppressive, as they cannot stand before a well-formed system of revolutionary societies." On the other hand, republics such as "the United States and France will sustain [self-erected societies] without injury or eversion." The need was to abolish not only acknowledged despotisms but also hypocritical, halfway republics so that the powers of government everywhere would rest in *"annual parliaments and universal suffrage."* The English Parliament, for example, was "such a mockery on representation that the nation will never rest in its present state." The few plebeians who managed to get into the House of Commons were so soon "assimilated to the aristocracy [that] the two hundred and fifty nobles and five hundred and fifty commons, or their venal majorities, became a combined Phalanx against the people, set out firmly united against any real alteration or reform of the polity." Thus Stiles went far beyond the technical charges against Parliament characteristic of the earlier Revolutionary era, and even rejected the whole notion of balanced powers in society implicit in the republican models favored by James Madison and John Adams. For the excited clergyman, the answers were "self-erected societies," education of the people, and grand national assemblies. "If well-informed, it is impossible the community at large can be inimical to the public good," Stiles declared. Far from introducing chaos and perpetual tumult, he argued that even an "endless progression" of such popular assemblies would, by discovering and carrying out "the general sense of the community, . . . thus strengthen the whole community into a firm and united bulwark for its support and defence."[12]

Though Stiles was obviously caught up in the doctrines and rhetoric of Rousseau, Condorcet, Paine, and other heralds of the French Revolution, he nonetheless found these ideas logical projections of Puritan concepts of obedience to a higher law and American Revolutionary ideals of self-government. The impressive thing to him was not that the deeds of the French revolutionary assemblies were unprecedented, but that they merely fulfilled the implications of what English Puritans had said and done in the 1640s and what Americans of the generation just past had accomplished in throwing off the rule of George III. Edmund S. Morgan has observed that Stiles' essay "marks the final adjustment of Puritan political thought to the needs of a democratic republic." Considerable adjustment was indeed necessary to reconcile the ideas of John Winthrop, for example, with "the needs of a democratic republic"—but in Stiles' mind this was not only possible, it was inevitable. Viewed in this light, Puritan thought, pervasive in the United States during the eighteenth century, and the natural rights philosophy of Jefferson and others, entailed basically compatible political theories useful not only in freeing America from Britain but also in furnishing conceptions of the future national character. When Jefferson stopped to see Stiles on his way to France in June 1784, they toured Yale College, discussed educational philosophy and land distribution in Virginia, examined electrical apparatus, and speculated on the bones of the mammoth. Stiles found his guest "a most ingenious Naturalist and Philosopher—a truly scientific and learned Man—and every way Excellent." The Puritan educator and the Enlightenment statesman were kindred spirits, impelled by their common citizenship in a new nation to find enlarged meaning in patterns of thought and receptive to the idea that men and society could be transformed.[13]

IV

A Massachusetts farmer, able to read the newspapers but otherwise not a man of learning, in his own unsophisticated way expressed similar hopes for a new society during the 1790s. William Manning, a fourth-generation New England Puritan who had marched to the

"Concord fite" with his militia company on April 19, 1775, was a staunch Jeffersonian Republican disgusted with the Federalism of Hamilton and John Adams. Accepting the assumptions of Barlow and Stiles that the force of reason and the power of the people required the reconstruction of society and would someday achieve it, Manning wrote earnestly of "the Causes that Ruen Republicks . . . [and] the means by which the few Destroy it." The basic trouble, he observed, was that the only people who could stand vindicated before God, those who performed honest labor, had always been victimized and oppressed by "all ordirs of men who get a living without labour." How did this happen? "It is the universal custom and practis of monorcal and dispotick government to train up their subjects as much in ignorance as they can in matters of government, and to teach them reverance and worship of grate men in office, and to take for truth what ever they say without examining for themselves." Furthermore, "The few . . . write their plans and scheems by asotiations, conventions, and correspondances with each other. . . . Their professions are often called together and know each others minds, and all letirary men and the over grown rich, that can live without labouring, can spare time for consultation." Thus merchants, physicians, ministers, lawyers, and government officers could "counter act the interests of the many and pick their pockets, which is efected ondly for want of the means of knowledge amongue them."[14]

For the same purpose, Manning charged, "the few are always crying up the advantages of costly colleges, national acadimys and grammer schools, in ordir to make places for men to live without work, and so strengthen their party. But are always opposed to cheep schools and woman schools, the ondly or prinsaple means by which learning is spred amongue the Many." Similarly doctors established medical societies that "have so nearly emelated Quacary of all kinds, that a poor man cant git so grate cures of them now for a ginna, as he could 50 years ago of an old Squaw for halfe a pint of Rhum." Lawyers, an "ordir of men [who] git their living intirely from the quarrils, follys, disputes and destreses of the Many, and the intricacy of our Laws," not only established bar associations but colluded with "Juditial and Executive officers" to keep government beyond the understanding of "the Many." Most diabolical, "the prinsaple knowledge nesecary for a free man," that obtained from an unrestricted press, "is almost ruened of late by the doings of the few." Until recently, Manning observed, "we could have the hole news by one paper in a week, and could put some dependence on what was printed. But the few, being closely combined . . . imploy no printers but those that will adhear strictly to their vuies and interests, . . . and strive to make the peopel believe falsehood for truts and truts for falsehood, and as they have money and lasure they have their papers every day in the week." This forced republican papers to come out more often, increasing the expense, and, even worse, made "a labouring man . . . read and studdy halfe his time, and then be at a loss to know what is true and what not—thus the few have almost ruened the Libberty of the press."

True to his principles, Manning said he was not "against the asotiations of any ordirs of men, for to hinder it would hinder their improvements in their professions, and hinder them from being servisable to the Many. Their need ondly one Society more being established," he urged, a "proper meens of information amongue the Many," to prevent the associations of "the few" from "being daingerous politicks." A nationwide "Labouring Society" would "establish as cheep, easy, and sure conveyance of knowledge and learning necessary for a free man to have as posable, and promote a similaraty of sentiments and manners, Industry and Economy, agraculture and Manifactoryes, etc." If the many had a knowledge of human nature, of government under the Constitution, of the laws related to their interests, and of "the true prinsaples, caritor and abilityes of all those they vote for in any kind of office," they would be able to maintain their rights at election time. Thus organized and thus informed, Manning was sure that the common people would be more than a match for the machinations of the rich and that the officers of government would respond to their needs. The Labouring Society would publish a weekly magazine that would go to every town in the country where "librarians" would make them available even to people who couldn't afford them. The magazine would be free of the triviality and biases that filled the existing "ruened Press," thus for the first time furnishing the *useful* knowledge vital in a republic. The government should support the magazine on behalf of the public welfare, Manning thought, and could do so at much less expense than Shays' Rebellion, the Whiskey Rebellion, or the Quasi-War with France had entailed, all events that would not have happened if the public had been well enough informed to have properly influenced their government. In fact, if the insights and interests of an enlightened public were the basis of public policy,

Manning foresaw millennial prospects: "I have often had it impressed on my mind that in some such way as this Society might be organized throughout the world, . . . and by sotial corraspondance and mutual consestions all diffirences might be settled, so that wars might be banished from the Earth. For it is from the pride and ambition of rulers and the ignorance of the peopel that wars arise, and no nation as a nation ever got anything by making war on others, for what ever their conquests may have bin the plunder goes to a few individuals, and always increases the misiryes of more than it helps."

One might dismiss Manning's performance as a potpourri of opinions gathered from his favorite Boston newspaper, the fervently Jeffersonian *Independent Chronicle* (almost all his formulations reflected articles that had appeared in the *Chronicle*). But from his farm kitchen in North Billerica, Massachusetts, Manning gave voice to the specific ills a plain man saw in the society of the new nation, the specific measures he thought would correct them, and the kind of world he hoped for as a result. He shared Barlow's faith in the beneficence of reason and Stiles' trust in the voice of the people, but he shows us more clearly than they exactly what these meant in the daily life of a workingman. His troubles arose from the difficulty of getting dependable information, the sway well-organized professionals had in the community, the selfish power of the rich, the irrelevance, harmfulness, and absurdity of so much national policy, and the chasm he felt between the ideals of the harmonious, benign world view of the Enlightenment and the reality of the hierarchical, grasping society he lived in. His mind was possessed by the hopes of new nationhood and the chance it offered to transform the cycle of life. Thus such things as relations between physician and patient, "elitism" in the colleges, the incongruity of the Society of the Cincinnati in a republic, the dangers of a politicized ministry, and "the management of news by the establishment" troubled him deeply. If new nationhood were to mean anything beyond a reshuffle in the palace, if basic changes in habits and attitudes and character were to be achieved, then basic changes in the ways and institutions of everyday life would be needed.

12. Conservative Reactions

I

MANY MEN CONCERNED AROUT THE PROSPECTS AND CHARACTER OF THE NEW NATION WERE APPALLED AT WHAT THEY REGARDED AS THE FANTASIES OF DELUDED VISIONARIES. THOUGH JUST AS INTENT AS JOEL BARLOW ON DISCERNING THE CONTOURS OF THE FUTURE, more prudent men wanted the nation kept on familiar paths. As the debate over titles showed, many Americans fond of British habits were convinced that human beings, even in the New World and with the benefit of a new government, needed the comfort and security of customary ways. Indeed, many argued that the often perilous environment of the New World heightened the need for the familiar, the tried and the tested symbols and forms of civilized society. "If all decorum, discipline, and subordination are to be destroyed and universal Pyrrhonism, anarchy, and insecurity of poverty are to be introduced," John Adams wrote in 1790, "nations will soon wish their books in ashes, seek for darkness and ignorance, superstition and fanatacism as blessings, and follow the standard of the first mad despot who . . . will endeavor to obtain them." After fifteen more years dominated by tumultuous events in France, another Bostonian urged a "steady, sober, and religious application . . . to the first principles in morality and politicks [taught by] . . . Locke, Montesquieu, Vattel, [and] Burlamaqui" as a way of resisting the pernicious doctrines of "Voltaire, Priestley, Condorcet, and the bloody band of atheists." John Adams believed that civilized society depended on preserving the useful forms and practices of the past at least as much as upon discerning grand

[186]

hopes for the future. He insisted on American political independence and was a fervent nationalist, but his conception of what the new nation might realistically hope to become bore little resemblance to the projections of Ezra Stiles or William Manning. Many deeply conservative Americans shared Adams' concern to retain time-tested practices.[1]

Fisher Ames (1758–1808), a zealous Federalist Congressman during the 1790s and after that a caustic critic of Jeffersonian democracy, rested his distaste for "government of the people" on a profound conviction that such government led not to a good society but to a dreadful one. "We are sliding down into the mire of a democracy," Ames wrote in a Boston magazine in 1805, "which pollutes the morals of the citizens before it swallows up their liberties." He explicitly repudiated all the fond hopes of Barlow and Manning that in a new day "the will of the people" could be the foundation of a new society. Ames insisted:

The people as a body cannot deliberate. Nevertheless, they will feel an irresistible impulse to act, and their resolutions will be dictated to them by their demagogues. The consciousness or the opinion, that they possess the supreme power, will inspire inordinate passions, and the violent men, who are the most forward to gratify those passions, will be their favourites. What is called the government of the people is in fact too often the arbitrary power of such men. Here, then, we have the faithful portrait of democracy. . . . Of what value is the will of the majority, if that will is dictated by a committee of demagogues, and law and right are in fact at the mercy of a victorious faction? To make a nation free, the crafty must be kept in awe, and the violent in restraint. The weak and the simple find their liberty arise not from their own individual sovereignty, but from the power of law and justice over all.

In thus bespeaking an attitude toward democracy as old as Aristotle, and in upholding a theory of the orderly society restraining human excesses similar to that of Edmund Burke (whose view of the French Revolution Ames so much admired), he espoused notions of human nature and of national character poles apart from those accepted by fervent Jeffersonians. He was, however, as much concerned as they were to set guidelines for the nation's future.[2]

Ames expressed his idea of a good "temperate" society, and of the dangers of a democratic one, in a metaphor:

Temperate liberty is like the dew, as it falls unseen from its own heaven; constant without excess, it finds vegetation thirsting for its refreshment, and imparts to it the vigour to take more. All nature, moistened with blessings, sparkles in the morning ray. But democracy is a water spout, that bursts from the clouds, and lays the ravaged earth bare to its rocky foundations. The labours of man lie whelmed with his hopes beneath masses of ruin, that bury not only the dead, but their monuments.

In a free, stable government based on a rule of law, he continued, there would of course be "differences of opinion and [even enough] pride of opinion . . . to generate contests, and to inflame them with bitterness and rancour," but there would not be the pervasive spirit of faction that in democracies consumed or poisoned every good thing. Who, he asked rhetorically, would in a democracy "combine, intrigue, lie and fight" for power? His answer:

Certainly not the virtuous, who do not wish to control society, but quietly to enjoy its protection. The enterprising merchant, the thriving tradesman, the careful farmer will be engrossed by the toils of their business, and will have little time or inclination for the unprofitable and disquieting pursuits of politicks. It is not the industrious, sober husbandman, who will plough in that barren field; it is the lazy and dissolute bankrupt, who has no other to plough. The idle, the ambitious, and the needy will band together to break the hold that law has upon them, and then to get hold of law. Faction is a Hercules, whose first labour is to strangle this lion, and then to make armour of his skin.

Though Ames thus accepted much of the *moral* ideal of the pastoral society, he regarded as visionary and misguided any effort to unite this ideal with the increasingly democratic emphases of the American and French revolutions. To him the temperate, orderly, basically apolitical society of sober industrious farmers and artisans needed for its government the attitudes, skills, authority, and responsibilities for two thousand years associated with an Aristotelian view of aristocracy: rule by the good. In retrospect it seems clear that Ames upheld a way of life already anachronistic in the United States, but in his lifetime his conception offered an "alternative society" taken seriously by many Americans.[3]

Ames was similarly unwilling to abandon traditional standards of taste and literary excellence. Beside the great lights of Western civilization, American efforts seemed dim indeed—the new nation, then, should be careful of departing too far from valued models. "Shall we match Joel Barlow against Homer or Hesiod? Can Thomas Paine contend against Plato?" Ames asked contemptuously. With a similar scorn for republican educational reforms, the *New England Quarterly Magazine* in 1802 noted that "the best ages of Rome afford the purest models of virtue that are anywhere to be met with. Mankind are too apt to lose sight of all that is heroic, magnanimous and public spirited. . . . Left to ourselves, we are apt to sink into effeminacy and apathy." In the same mood Joseph Dennie, a deeply conservative Philadelphia literary critic, warned American lexicographers not to make a "record of our imbecility" by including in their volumes the corruptions Americans had imposed on the language of Shakespeare and Milton. Native humor, frontier tales, and Fourth of July orations Dennie dubbed "the militia style," fit only for provincial, uncivilized people.[4]

The web of culture, an author in the *New England Palladium* argued in 1802, was seamless. "There is a strong connexion," he intoned, "between literature, morality, politics and religion. It is usually true, that he, whose mind is filled with visionary theories, on any of these subjects, either is at present, or will soon become equally visionary concerning the rest." Jefferson was, of course, the perfect target for such allegations. His scientific speculations pushed him to absurd raptures about the future of Louisiana as well as to a hypocritical racism, his educational ideas seemed sure to unhinge discipline in the schools, his deism loosened institutional and doctrinal restraints essential to a well-ordered society, and his assault on the federal judiciary linked him to Daniel Shays, John Fries, and other foes of law and stability. New England Federalists, in fact, in the first decade of the nineteenth century, fashioned a comprehensive dissent from what they regarded as the intoxicating projections of Jeffersonian democracy. To them, the new nation could find meaning and respectability and long life only by measuring up to, if not imitating, the best standards of Western culture.[5]

In 1803 Dennie clarified his attitude toward "the new culture" he saw rising in the United States in a bitter attack on the life, writings, and reputation of Benjamin Franklin. Dennie noted that even in Franklin's lifetime everyone praised him, "read his precepts with rapture . . . [and] pronounced [him a] . . . wise, and good, . . . *patriotic* and . . . original writer." Americans, already quick to "eulogize extravagantly everything that is their own," declared that because Franklin had been born in Boston and worked in Philadelphia, "therefore he must be an

Addison in stile, and a Bacon in philosophy." Such strange opinions, Dennie declared, "never could have been entertained, except in a country, from its newness, paucity of literary information, and the imperfections of its systems of education" which had no sense of real literary or philosophic merit. After showing that many of the famous sayings, stories, and "discoveries" of "our Benjamin" had been "plundered" from others, Dennie proclaimed it time Franklin's life and writings were "diligently scrutinized." His style was far from comparable to Addison's, electricity was hardly his invention, "his string of proverbs [were far from] being wit, and his beggarly maxims humour." Franklin was merely a

pseudo philosopher [who had] been a great mischief to his country. He was the founder of that Grubstreet sect, who have professedly attempted to degrade literature to the level of vulgar capacities, and debase the polished and current language of books, by the vile alloy of provincial idioms, and colloquial barbarism, the shame of grammar and akin to any language, rather than English. . . . He was the author of that pitiful system of Economics, the adoption of which has degraded our national character. . . . [In it] there is a low and scoundrel appetite for small sums, acquired by base and pitiful means, and whoever planted or cherished it, is worthy of no better title than the foul disgrace of the country.

Instead of Franklin's "sordid economics," Dennie recommended a "liberal" variety "perfectly consistent with the habits and generosity of a gentleman and a cavalier."[6]

Dennie's critique of Franklin revealed the pervasiveness of his doubts about the celebrations of "new men," new character, and new life-style by Crèvecoeur and others. He found the new society so vulgar, shallow, and presumptuous as to be scarcely civilized—at least as he understood the meaning of that term as it had evolved through the centuries. Civilization, for Dennie, meant accepting the canons of taste set by the best writers and artists in the great centers of culture, not puffing up the pitiful, derivative productions of incompetent colonials; clinging to the wisdom of the ages, not depending precariously on the whims of an age; and taking pride in the customs of an ancient tradition of chivalry, not supposing that new habits and manners born in the wilderness could somehow replace them. Ames and Dennie knew exactly what sort of nation they wanted the United States to become and what sort of character they hoped their countrymen could attain—and it was nothing like what they regarded as the whimsies and fantasies of a Franklin or a Rush.

II

Two brilliant Southerners, John Taylor of Caroline and John Randolph of Roanoke, had agrarian rather than commercial predilections, which placed them far from Ames and Dennie politically, but they expressed a similar contempt for millennial enthusiasms. Both were exceedingly learned men, especially in the classics and in English history and literature. Their model was the Addisonian English country gentleman, happiest when tending his productive lands or reading in his library. They shared such Enlightenment ideals as a recognition of the immorality of slavery (especially the slave trade), a zeal for scientific agriculture, and a faith in republican government at the local level. The impelling aspect of their mentality, however, was an abhorrence of the "speculative capitalism" which they saw dominating the nation under Hamilton's leadership in the 1790s. "Solicitations and excitements to avarice and ambition," Taylor wrote, "will be offered to publick officers by the view of a rich nation, constituting temptations to vice, superior to any which can occur in private life." Despite Jefferson's promises and even after his election in 1801, Randolph and Taylor insisted that the linking of money and government continued to spread its corrupting poison across the land. Though their opposition to this thrusting capitalism was in part sectional defensiveness, it was also profoundly national, in that they sought to prevent the ascendancy of a rapacious, materialistic, unmannerly commercial spirit in the United States. To them such a nation would be unworthy of the American Revolution and a curse, not a promise, to mankind.[7]

In rejecting Hamiltonian capitalism, though, and in finding the lifestyle of a Virginia plantation so much more admirable than that of a cosmopolitan city or even a Yankee town, Taylor and Randolph fell back on what Jefferson called "quaint and mystical" notions of public life. Both upheld the slave-based society of Virginia, for example, as more humane and enlightened than the speculative, money-mad way of the North. Thus they defended the social effects of slavery and continued to own large numbers of slaves all their lives. Though emphatic Jeffersonians in 1801, they became disenchanted with the "nationalism" of Jefferson's administrations and regarded Madison as a villainous apostate who had betrayed the Republican party into the arms of the Federalists. Randolph broke formally with the Republicans over the Yazoo frauds—to him a perfect example of a nation gone mad over speculation and a crime not to be compromised with, as Jefferson and Madison felt was necessary. Taylor fulminated endlessly at Madison's "Federalism," meaning his willingness to strengthen national powers for republican purposes.[8]

Though they pictured themselves as "radical" or "true" Jeffersonians, Taylor and Randolph were in fact guided by ancient patterns. Their love of classical learning, their attachment to traditional English values, and their nostalgia for a Virginia pastoralism that perhaps never existed gave them the impetus to oppose rampant commercialism and its attendant view of national destiny, but prevented them from accepting or even understanding the egalitarian dynamism of Jefferson's "empire of liberty." Randolph, for example, saw only disgrace and folly in Madison's policy of steady resistance to British hostility and arrogance in the years before the War of 1812. Since this aligned the United States with France, he asked bitingly whether Madison wished to aid Napoleon, the successor to Attila, Tamerlane, and Kublai Khan, "malefactors of the human race who ground man down to a mere machine of their impious and bloody ambition." "Is war the true remedy" for American grievances? Randolph asked. "Who will profit by it? Speculators—a few lucky merchants, who draw prizes in the lottery—commissaries and contractors. Who will suffer by it? The people. It is their blood, their taxes that must flow to support it." Echoing the antifederalists of 1788, Randolph warned of following expansionist leaders who would "embark in a common cause with France and be dragged at the wheels of the car of some Burr or Bonaparte" in the mad, immoral project of conquering Canada. He urged instead sympathy for Great Britain, "from whom every valuable principle of our own institutions has been borrowed, . . . our fellow Protestants identified in blood, in language, and in religion with ourselves." Madison, on the other hand, despised Napoleon's career as a military conqueror but agreed with Gallatin's observation from Europe in 1815 that the French Revolution had not been "entirely useless. . . . A new generation [of peasants] freed from the petty despotisms of nobles and priests have acquired an independent spirit, and are far superior to their fathers in intellect and information. . . . No

monarch or ex-nobles can hereafter oppress them long with impunity."
Madison understood, too, the still urgent need of the United States to
escape the thralldom of Britain. To him the future should not be tied
to an old, familiar pattern—the United States, genuinely independent
of Britain, expanding republican government across the continent, and
allied with liberating forces in Europe, was part of a New World
where, as he wrote Lafayette in 1820, "too many lights of liberty had
been lighted in the political firmament, to permit [despotism] to remain anywhere, as it has heretofore done, almost everywhere."[9]

Randolph and Taylor, unable to escape ancient formulations of
basic political questions, became increasingly anomalous. "I am an
aristocrat," Randolph declared, "I love liberty, I hate equality." Thus
in resistance to the demands of western Virginians for political *equality*, Randolph defended the slave-based power of Tidewater Virginia
in the convention of 1829—but at the same time, to sustain *freedom*,
Randolph had provided in his will for the manumission of his nearly
four hundred slaves. Taylor upheld the ideals of the yeoman farmer
and with populist fury castigated bank monopolies and the manipulations of the stock-jobbers—but he fashioned defenses of provincialism
and apologies for slavery that found flower in the doctrines of John C.
Calhoun.[10]

The incongruity, and the essential timidity, of Taylor and Randolph
arose from their fright at the *new spirit*, which, especially in the
bustling North, they saw growing with national independence. They,
like Dennie and Ames, wanted the new nation to cling to older ways
and retain the deep attachment to the ancient values of Western civilization each of the four men knew so well. They feared, in short, the
United States would become the home of a new man on Crèvecoeur's
model—such a "new man" would be vulgar, uncivilized, materialistic,
strange. They wanted the United States to be an *independent* nation,
but really not a *new* one. Rather, they sought a transatlantic variety of
an ancient culture, anchored in values and habits derived from their
own cultured minds, not from the fulfillment of the new land and the
creativity of the "new men" they saw rising around them. Struggling
against the tide, they spent their lives viewing with alarm the course of
events. They were not political allies (in fact each was so profoundly
independent that public life was either a chore or a display of eccen-

tricity), but they agreed in having little use for the "new society" visions of Franklin or Hamilton or Jefferson—to say nothing of crackpots like Paine or Barlow. They represented a substantial segment of American opinion that wanted somehow to retain ancient moorings but yet be politically independent. The existence of this view, and its presentation by eloquent spokesmen, played an important role in the growth of American thought, for those who sought more profound changes had to explain how various originalities would be more worthy than the traditional ways. The dialectic also deepened understanding of how seamless the "new" culture might be—such questions as how much of the trappings of aristocracy could be rejected without losing the related sense of "the good life," and to what extent the dramatically new American environment could absorb the virtues of antiquity, had to be faced because of the criticisms of Dennie, Randolph, and their ilk.

13. Conceptions of New Nationhood: Jefferson and Hamilton

THE HOPES OF BARLOW AND STILES, AND THE FEARS OF TAYLOR AND AMES, WERE ON THE FRINGES OF THE AMERICAN EFFORT TO UNDERSTAND AND PROJECT A NATIONAL CHARACTER. THE CENTRAL DEBATE, AND THE CRUCIAL POLITICAL STRUGGLE, TOOK PLACE BETWEEN Alexander Hamilton and Thomas Jefferson, each an intellectual giant and a charismatic political leader. It was apparent early in the 1790s that President Washington had, by seeking to bring the finest talents in the nation into his cabinet, included in it supremely eloquent spokesmen for radically different conceptions of the nation's future. The split between Hamilton and Jefferson encompassed not only political philosophy, economic development, constitutional interpretation, and foreign policy, but differences in life-style, personality, social habits, and cultural affinity as well. It was no accident that the first political party division in the new nation polarized around these two men. In their brilliant arguments within the cabinet, in print, and in the drawing rooms of New York and Philadelphia during the four years they were cabinet "colleagues," they articulated for their followers rival conceptions of what kind of people they hoped Americans would become and, consequently, what kind of national programs and institutions would be appropriate for them.

I

The ideal of the pastoral yeoman republic colored Jefferson's vision for the new nation and infused his every word and deed in the fifty years between 1776 and his death. In Jefferson's context the word "pastoral" had far more than a merely agricultural or bucolic meaning.

It signified, much more importantly, the moral ideals and life-style of the long pastoral tradition in Western thought from Aristotle, Cicero, Virgil, and Horace, to Addison and the French physiocrats. Its basic concern was to characterize the good person and his appropriate relations with his environment and other human beings, rather than to focus on *public* purposes and programs as national leaders often did. Three years after retiring from the Presidency Jefferson expressed an apt analogy in a comment on gardening: "No occupation is so delightful to me as the culture of the earth and no culture comparable to that of the garden. Such a variety of subjects, some are always coming to perfection, the failures of one being repaired by the successes of another, and instead of one harvest a continuing one through the years." Jefferson wanted a similar pleasure and harmony to infuse all of life. The pastoral setting, though immensely significant, was only instrumental—one admired the shepherd or the farmer or the country gentleman not ultimately for his economic contribution or his aesthetic sensitivity, but for his moral integrity, his self-reliance, his personal style, his harmonious social life. Though most Americans doubtless had little knowledge of the Roman pastoralists and though Jefferson wrote no systematic pastoral treatise, his writings, and the productions of the American press at all levels, everywhere reflected pastoral values. Jefferson's critical contribution was to weave these values into virtually every law, every letter, every executive message, every manifesto for the new nation that he wrote. The persistence and profundity of these values, translated into public policy, raised Jefferson's political career from the level of mere dexterity to that of grand conception. This was the source both of his towering position in his own day and the sustained presence of a "Jeffersonian" tradition in our national life ever since.[1]

By the pastoral way, Jefferson had uppermost in his mind a clear, compelling idea of the admirable human being. Franklin, a classic moral pastoralist despite having lived always in cities, outlined this admirable character in creating a hypothetical "Cato"—and, of course, in using that name he recalled for his readers both the incorruptible Roman and Joseph Addison's popular re-creation of him for Augustan England. Franklin's "Cato"

appeared in the plainest Country Garb. His Great Coat was coarse and looked old and thread-bare; his Linnen was homespun; his Beard perhaps of Seven Day's Growth, his Shoes thick and heavy, and every Part of his Dress corresponding. Why was this Man received with such concurring Respect from every Person in the Room, even from those who had never known him or seen him before? It was not an exquisite Form of Person or Grandeur of Dress that struck us with Admiration. I believe long Habits of Virtue have a sensible Effect on the Countenance: There was something in the Air of his Face that manifested the true Greatness of his Mind, which likewise appeared in all he said, and in every Part of his Behaviour, obliging us to regard him with a Kind of Veneration. . . . The Consciousness of his own innate Worth and unshaken Integrity renders him calm and undaunted in the Presence of the most Great and Powerful. His strict Justice and known Impartiality make him the Arbitrator and Decider of all Differences that arise for many Miles around him. . . . His Moderation and his Loyalty to the Government, his Piety, his Temperance, his Love to Mankind, his Magnanimity, his Publick-spiritedness, and in fine, his *Consummate Virtue*, make him justly deserve to be esteemed the Glory of his Country.

The similarity of this "Cato" to Crèvecoeur's "Andrew the Hebridean," and the enthusiasm Jefferson would have had for both, suggest something of the pervasive appeal of this life-style in a neoclassical age.[2]

Jefferson's genius and opportunity were to move from this model to the government, the institutions, and the social structure that would nourish it. "Cato," obviously, was not a fit subject for tyranny, for he would be incapable of the servility required. Furthermore, he would be stunted and frustrated in developing his own self-reliant qualities, and a tyranny's focus on the grandeur of court and capital and its tendency to engage in war and conquest would repress and destroy his mode of life. "Cato," it seems, was conceived for self-government—his virtue, independence, sense of justice, and public spirit both required self-rule for their own fruition and offered exactly the qualities necessary to make such government work. Jefferson's political philosophy rested always on this compatibility. Injustice or perversion to him always meant a deficiency that destroyed the harmony: tyrannies that thwarted personal fulfillment, or personal weaknesses (ignorance, selfishness, submissiveness, vainglory) that made a tragedy or a farce of government by consent.

This sense of the close relationship between personal qualities and the government appropriate for them caused Jefferson to emphasize local government. Vitality at that level was needed to nourish the skills of judgment, the sense of charity, and the concern for public policy inherent in the good person, and to allow those qualities to have their due weight in the public councils. To a pastoralist, government was not grand, elegant, mysterious, or ambitious. It was close to the people, attuned to the needs of their daily lives. The whole was *not* greater than the sum of the parts, as might seem to be the case from Rome or Versailles or St. Petersburg or Constantinople or Peking; in fact, to resist that presumption was a cardinal reason for emphasizing towns, counties, and states rather than nations or empires. Under this conception, a national government might undertake rather large enterprises—found a national university, or construct internal improvements, or even purchase Louisiana, for example—but only upon impulses coming from the grass roots. Furthermore, the posture of the government had to be, in a favorite Jeffersonian word, *mild*. That is, it should not be heavy or high-handed; its officers were not to be arrogant or imperious nor its modes elegant and expensive. Its attitude was to be that of a servant of the people. Thus when Jefferson said "that government is best which governs least," he meant primarily that his good citizen, on the model of Franklin's "Cato," had qualities that make bureaus and proconsuls not only unnecessary but actually dangerous. The dictum applied principally to the federal level of government, farthest from the people, presumably least sensitive to their needs, and, in the eighteenth century at any rate, least capable of fulfilling legitimate public ends.

After Jefferson's return to Virginia in 1776 the whole direction of his career there in the next few years (described in Part III, Chapter 6), as well as the tone of his Presidency, outlined very well what he considered appropriate in governments. He revealed in a letter to Joseph Priestley in March 1801 his hope that his election as President might lead to happiness through tranquil self-government:

As the storm is now subsiding, and the horizon becoming serene, it is pleasant to consider the phenomenon with attention. We can no longer say there is nothing new under the sun. For this whole chapter in the history of man is new. The great experiment of our Republic is new. Its sparse habitation is new. The mighty wave of public opinion which has rolled over it is new ... The order and good sense displayed in this recovery from delusion [the Alien and Sedition Acts], and in the momentous crisis which lately arose [the votes in Congress between Jefferson and Burr], really bespeak a strength of character in our nation which augurs for the duration of our Republic.[3]

In thus defining the nature of government Jefferson did not at all intend to create a laissez-faire, atomistic, survival-of-the-fittest society like that espoused by Social Darwinists a century later. To him, social harmony and the value of human accord were supremely important. Franklin's career as a civic leader in Philadelphia—organizing clubs of tradesmen for their own improvement, founding libraries and hospitals, and extending government services such as street cleaning, night watches, the militia, and assistance to a college—was a Jeffersonian paradigm. Franklin and Jefferson were good friends and co-workers, and both nourished institutions, sought the benefits of cooperation, and supposed that human life, through sensible, well-organized, mutual endeavor, could be made better. Though Jefferson had contempt for many traditional institutions such as the remnants of feudalism, authoritarian churches, secret societies, and military brotherhoods, he was not, in either the Romantic or Darwinian modes, a rugged individualist who idolized Man Standing Alone; almost as much as Franklin, Jefferson epitomized Man Organizing. To achieve "Cato's" virtues, and to give proper scope to them, required a network of institutions— public, private, and mixed—where *philanthropy*, in its root meaning, could infuse society. Though the often lonely life of the yeoman farmer might be a vital source of the self-reliance Jefferson so much admired, the useful man thus brought into being found his fulfillment *in society*, contributing to the general welfare and discharging the obligations of citizenship—in the rich Athenian sense of that word which was always Jefferson's context for it.

The most important social institutions for Jefferson were educational. His concern for the discipline and courses of study suitable for young children, as well as for the reading and learning necessary for the potential leaders of a republic, was incessant and lifelong. Following Locke, Jefferson believed that human beings were liable to almost infinite influence by their experience of life; therefore, if they were to be *good* people, their education was supremely important. In addition to thus forming virtuous individuals, education would furnish ordinary citizens with the skills they needed to fulfill their responsibilities of self-government and to conduct their own affairs efficiently and prosperously. His plan to achieve this remained essentially the same throughout his life. He repeatedly recommended a national university in his Presidential messages, on the same grounds as those explained by President Madison in 1815:

A national seminary of learning claims the patronage of Congress as a monument of their solicitude for the advancement of knowledge, without which the blessings of liberty cannot be fully enjoyed or long preserved; as a model instructive in the formation of other seminaries; as a nursery of enlightened preceptors, and as a central resort of youth and genius from every part of the country, diffusing on their return examples of those national feelings, those liberal sentiments, and those congenial manners which contribute cement to our Union and strength to the great political fabric of which that is the foundation.[4]

Jefferson considered the University of Virginia to be in a way a substitute for the national university Congress showed little sign of patronizing, despite the urging of every President from Washington to John Quincy Adams. Resting on a system of primary and secondary schools, the university would educate Jefferson's cherished "aristocracy of talent and virtue" in a way different from the usual modes. Though the ancient languages and other traditional bases of education would be retained, Jefferson wanted modern languages and all the newest fields of science to be taught as equally important branches of knowledge, entirely freed from the superstitions, restraints, and degradations long imposed on them. "Everyone knows," he wrote in 1805, "that Oxford, Cambridge, the Sorbonne, etc., are a century or two behind the sciences of the age." Finally, the founder of the University of Virginia wanted his future statesmen trained in the theory and practice of republican government. Nothing less than this transforming process, supported by the public from primary school through the university, would sufficiently encourage the virtues, and the changes in character, necessary to make self-government work. In urging the state of Virginia to support the university, Jefferson scorned "the discouraging persuasion that a man is fixed, by the law of his nature, at a given point; that his improvement is a chimera, and the hope delusive of rendering ourselves wiser, happier, or better than our forefathers were." Rather, it was his faith that "each generation succeeding to the knowledge acquired by all those that preceded it, adding to it their own acquisitions and discoveries, and handing the mass down for successive and constant accumulation, must advance the knowledge and well-being of mankind . . . infinitely to a term which none can fix or foresee." In Jefferson's thought, more clearly than in that of any other American, the connection is firmly made between Enlightenment aspirations for man and the hoped-for character of the new nation—and the links were to be schools at every level.[5]

Jefferson also promoted an array of institutions for human enlightenment beyond those properly called schools. Following Franklin, appropriately, he served for nearly twenty years as president of the American Philosophical Society, which he conceived as an American version of the Royal Society or the French Academy, promoting and disseminating scientific and technical discoveries that would improve the life of mankind. He was a founder of the Albemarle Agricultural Society, which he hoped would be a model for such societies spreading useful information for farmers across the countryside. They would also further nourish the skills of self-help and neighborly cooperation Jefferson incessantly espoused. He encouraged state or national organizations to abolish slavery, improve life for the Indians, promote the arts, and stimulate trade. He approved, too, the growth of "rational" religious institutions he hoped would soon replace the bigoted, superstitious churches he thought degraded mankind. Franklin's "Cato," of course, would have turned readily to such organizations and possessed just the skills needed to make them effective.

The third foundation for good character, after vital local government and "improving institutions," Jefferson placed in a man's occupation. The habits and attitudes inculcated as one pursued his daily tasks, Jefferson knew, would have a decisive effect on character. A slave, beaten into submission, never allowed to think for himself, and accustomed to seeing the fruits of his labor enjoyed by others, would be sullen, dull, and irresponsible. A master of slaves was even more morally reprehensible—he became overbearing, brutish, arrogant, and dependent on the work of others. A merchant operated under quite different, but morally almost as unpropitious circumstances. Since he made his living by buying cheaply and selling dearly, he was exposed to the temptation to secure by fraud and dispose by misrepresentation. To stay in business he often had to lie and cheat, and even under the best of circumstances he was in danger of being wiped out by whims of a market beyond his control. Overall, his attention focused entirely on money. A factory operative, deadened by long hours of labor in dark, filthy places and trained to be an "appendage of a machine," was also unlikely to be a self-reliant citizen. The mobs that roamed the streets of Rome or London or Paris were likewise moral barbarians, entirely unfitted by their habits of idleness, beggary, and theft for self-government. The life of the barracks, the march, and the battlefield was also bereft of ennobling influences for either officers or men in the ranks. Though Jefferson's disdain for these occupations had significant economic foundations, he took his stand against them primarily because they did not sustain the personal qualities of the hypothetical "Cato" (in fact, they stifled them at every turn), and therefore did not yield the habits of the good life and of republican citizenship that were Jefferson's *summum bonum*.

Left, of course, was the life of the yeoman farmer, rhapsodized by Jefferson in his famous tribute to husbandmen, "the chosen people of God." They were, he declared, the "peculiar deposit for substantial and genuine virtue, . . . looking to their own soil and industry" for their livelihood. They possessed the admired qualities of "Cato" because implicit in the daily round of their lives was a reliance on their own fruitful labor in a healthy environment. On the other hand, Jefferson observed:

Dependence begets subservience and venality, suffocates the germ of virtue, and prepares fit tools for the designs of ambition. . . . Generally speaking, the proportion which the aggregate of the other classes of citizens bears in any State to that of its husbandmen, is the proportion of its unsound to its healthy parts. . . . While we have land to labor then, let us never wish to see our citizens occupied at a workbench, or twirling a distaff. . . . The mobs of great cities add just so much to the support of pure government as sores to the strength of the human body. It is the manners and spirit of a people which preserves a republic in vigor. A degeneracy in these is a canker which soon eats to the heart of its laws and constitution.[6]

Jefferson accepted the physiocratic doctrine that only those who labored to produce truly increased the wealth of a nation; his praise of farmers he therefore regarded as economically defensible, and it was politically astute as well in a nation 90 percent composed of farmers and possessed of vast unsettled lands. But it is also evident that he had a primary concern for cultivating the virtues of the good person and the good citizen. Thus, had he somehow been able to envision the hopeless, stupefying, degrading life of the countryside described by Hamlin Garland and Sherwood Anderson, he would have quickly set aside his agrarian predilections: if farmers weren't virtuous there was, in his thought, little reason to idolize them. Furthermore, if he had become persuaded in the manner of Sidney and Beatrice Webb or Frances Perkins that industrial workers—with proper job conditions, unions, and educational programs—could achieve daily lives of virtue and self-respect, Jefferson would surely have embraced the workshop. The crux for him, as he said over and over again, was "the manners and spirit of the people." The coming of the Industrial Revolution to America, so unwelcome to Jefferson, in a way made his vision irrelevant, but at a more fundamental level his central thesis retains its full force: for the United States (or any nation) to develop a virtuous citizenry and practice successfully the difficult art of self-government requires that its people have occupations and living conditions that enhance rather than destroy their humanity. Any observer of a modern city slum or assembly-line factory or *petit bourgeois* taxpayer's association can understand that proposition—and thus share Jefferson's concern that the circumstances of the common people be rendered benign rather than malignant.

Altogether, then, Jefferson bespoke a vivid, compelling, comprehensive, profoundly revolutionary vision of the nation's character and its future development. He explained what worthy character was, what the distinctive American qualities should be, how these were suited to republican government, the institutions required and the occupations appropriate to the society thus brought into being. Jefferson formed his opinion on constitutional interpretation, foreign policy, civil liberties, political parties, and a host of other questions in terms of the good or bad impact on his vision of the good society. Though many of his followers doubtless grasped but fragments of his social philosophy, though his political movement depended on powerful self-interests as well as on theoretical visions, and though he himself indulged a variety of compromises and even contradictions in forty years of public life, the overview, scarcely ever entirely absent from his thousands of letters and political acts, is the source of his towering position among his contemporaries and his standing as the preeminent philosopher of

American democracy ever since. He was, richly and fully, a nation-conceiver and a nation-builder.

II

The praise best bestowed on Jefferson's arch-foe, Alexander Hamilton, is that he was in every way a worthy opponent. Born in obscurity in the West Indies and uncommitted emotionally to any state or region, Hamilton related himself always to the national scene and to national purposes. He revealed most of the assumptions and goals of his public career in a letter of September 1780, when he was twenty-five and serving as aide to Washington during a dark moment of the Revolution. "The fundamental defect," he declared, "is a want of power in Congress." From this flowed the wretched condition of the army, the debilitating quarrels among the states, and the confused, demoralized spirit of the people. The remedy, in Hamilton's view, could only be applied from the top, by reforming the leadership and authority of the nation. Besides the lack of power in many particulars —to tax, to recruit the army, to regulate trade, and so on—Hamilton stressed the "want of method and energy in the administration" of the government under the Continental Congress. Phrases throughout his critique display his predilections about government. "Meddling too much with details of every sort," Hamilton noted, Congress bungled executive functions, "constantly fluctuating [and never] acting with sufficient decision or with system." With its rotating membership, there was little understanding of how present policy related "to what has been transacted on former occasions" or to what might be planned for the future. Furthermore, having boards instead of individuals head the departments of government resulted in too little "knowledge, . . . activity, . . . responsibility, . . . zeal, and attention. . . . Decisions are slower, energy less, [and] responsibility more diffused" than was consistent with effective administration. Finally, to persuade men of ability to enter government, Hamilton thought they should be offered a single appointment, not board membership, because only a "conspicuous, . . . important, . . . distinguished" post would "excite the ambition of candidates." Nor was Hamilton's view conservative. "There are epochs in human affairs," he concluded, "when *novelty* even is useful.

If a general opinion prevails that the old way is bad, . . . and this obstructs the operations of the public service, a change is necessary. . . . This is exactly the case now."[7]

The desire to plan and organize on a national scale with vigor and efficiency was ingrained in Hamilton. He believed that the matters which made a nation great and worthy—its prosperity, its dominion, its reputation in the world, its planned development, its cultural achievement, its splendor in the eyes of its citizens—could only be gained by skilled, systematic direction from a single authoritative source. The states he admired were the Athens of Pericles, the Rome of Augustus Caesar, and the France of Louis XIV, where the grandeur of the realm stood revealed for all the world to see. In a way Hamilton cared very little for the earnest arguments over the seat of sovereignty —as long as it was clearly *somewhere*, so *someone* would have both power and responsibility. He was indifferent whether the freemen of Athens, the conspirators of Rome, or the hereditary right of the Sun King placed the great leaders in authority—the point was that they possess authority and exercise it for the benefit of the nation.

Though this view of government is entirely tactical and seems not to have substance or moral commitment, there are implicit clear notions both of the admired personality and the kind of society Hamilton hoped to see come into being in the United States. He started oppositely from Jefferson, that is, with society at large, reasoning from there to the personal characteristics that would be appropriate to it. Hamilton's good society would be a bustling, dynamic place, full of the commerce and industry that would produce the means of power and prosperity. It would be orderly and purposeful as well, committed to integrated planning so that the nation might achieve national goals: an economy able to trade advantageously in the world, a credit and standing that would draw investment to it, an opportunity for profit that would encourage men to build and to invent, a government able unhesitatingly to maintain stability and to protect from without, a climate of steady long-range prospects so that men might plan effectively, and a civil service of capable, incorruptible, authoritative officials who would constitute a web of guidance and control throughout the nation. There would be riches and fame for men of towering talents, but there would also be opportunity for all men to advance and a general prosperity and orderliness that would be a blessing to all the people of the nation.

What kind of citizens would be most appropriate to such a nation? Jefferson's virtuous, self-reliant farmers would be acceptable as citizens, but they did not possess the greatness for leadership. To conceive the noble plans, to propel the innovations, and to do the work of Hamilton's good society would require ambitious entrepreneurs, disciplined administrators, creative engineers, and skilled workmen for the variety of enterprises that would sprout and grow as the nation achieved stage after stage of development. The center of attention for most men in such a society would be their own endeavors, whether they be those of the banker calculating loans on a national scale or of the shoemaker deciding which last would be most profitable. Thus occupied, a man's sense of his own self-interest would mobilize his energy and, to use a modern term Hamilton would have liked very much, increase the gross national product. As for the explicit duties of citizenship, Hamilton reserved only a modest function for the common man—not more than a periodic approval or disapproval of what the leaders were doing. Skilled administrators, of the sort Hamilton himself epitomized, would attend to the important activities of government and as much as possible be given a free hand to guide the national destinies. Hamilton's great reports, two on the public credit (1790 and 1795), on the national bank (1790), and on manufactures (1791), together with his opinion to President Washington on the constitutionality of the national bank (1791), embody the conceptions of national purpose and national character that he set so compellingly before his countrymen.[8]

Amid the now familiar arguments for national assumption and funding of war debts, for full establishment of the public credit, for a national bank to enlarge control over the economy, and for the support of manufacturing to accelerate and diversify national growth, Hamilton embedded guidelines for the national character. The creditors of the nation, Hamilton thought, "are, generally speaking, enlightened men." They had been "fair purchasers" of public securities when the risks were great, and had thus sustained what little remained of the public credit when the patriotic need to do so was desperate. Thus scorning the popular notion that creditors were devils, Hamilton sought further to "bind" them to the federal government by assuming debts owed the states. "If all the public creditors receive their dues from one source, distributed with an equal hand, their interest will be the same. And, having the same interests, they will unite in the support of the fiscal arrangements of the Government." Hamilton further revealed the critical relationship between men of wealth and the public welfare in explaining how the partly public but mostly private board of directors of the national bank would operate. "The keen, steady, and, as it were, magnetic sense of their own interest as proprietors, . . . pointing invariably to its true pole—the prosperity of the institution— is the only security that *can always be relied upon* for a careful and prudent administration." (Italics added.) That is, the self-interest of the directors in maintaining the strength of an institution in which they had a large stake would "invariably" dictate policies that would prevent default, wild speculation, inflation, and other threats to a stable economy. This reliance was preferable to public control, Hamilton asserted, because political pressures, under such a system, would often cause "calamitous abuse." This sophisticated blending of public and private interest gave wide scope to the fiscal dexterity Jeffersonians so much feared and abhorred—hence their incessant diatribes against "stock-jobbers."[9]

Hamilton denied categorically that this arrangement gave dominance to private interests: "Public utility is more truly the object of public banks than private profit." Therefore, it was "the business of government to constitute them" so that private interests were made subservient. This was assured in the national bank he had proposed because its charter depended occasionally on a need for public renewal, because the government through its fiscal policies "had it in its power to reciprocate benefits to the bank," and because the directors would usually be "discreet, respectable, and well-informed citizens" who would be attuned to public needs, and whose own interests rested upon the same steady policies vital to good government. Hamilton did favor giving businessmen tangible benefits in order to "cement" their support for a strong national government, but he always proposed as well tangible means to assure that, in the long run at least, the public interest would also be served. Since in his view the public interest consisted in large part of an expanding economy, it is not surprising that he saw businessmen as friends, not foes.[10]

Hamilton's readiness to use national policy for public, even moral, ends was evident in some of his proposals for tariffs and bounties. He urged duties "as high as will be consistent with . . . a safe collection on wines, spirits, . . . teas, and coffee" because they were "luxuries; the greater part of them foreign luxuries." Their "abundant" use was therefore "a source of national extravagance and impoverishment." "Ardent spirits" especially, if cheaply available, injured "the health and morals [as well as] the economy of the community," and also depressed the production and use of "cider and malt liquors" that ought instead to be encouraged to help American farmers. Hamilton also proposed a higher duty on imported books to protect American printers from the flood of books coming into the country from Great Britain. "The wealthier classes" and professional men who sought foreign books could afford to pay the higher price, while schools and public libraries should, Hamilton thought, be entirely exempted from paying any duty. Demand for books for "general family use" would be so large that domestic printers would fill it cheaply. Finally, "to encourage the printing of books is to encourage the manufacture of paper." Again, Hamilton supposed that wise governors could devise policies "good" for the public morality and also conducive to a rising prosperity. The opposite was, of course, equally true: without such leadership, a nation would drift aimlessly, prey to foreign aggression, plagued by factional strife at home, and derelict in its duty to promote the welfare of its citizens. Even more than Jefferson, Hamilton accepted the Aristotelean proposition that government itself was the prime moral agent, alone capable of providing the leadership that could result in a "good society."[11]

Hamilton's vision for the nation, then, was a grand design exhibiting a distinctive purpose and character that would give the nation a respectable place in the world. The people would be energetic and enterprising, intent on their own pursuits and content with them because each would have opportunity, be assured the fruits of his labor, and benefit from a rising prosperity in the nation at large. In such a society, of course, some would become very rich, largely because of superior capabilities. But since the vigorous, shrewd qualities that earned riches were on the whole admirable qualities, Hamilton saw little danger and much advantage in coupling rich men to the powers of government. That they would benefit from this he had no doubt (they would prosper with or without ties to the government, he was sure), but he thought that, properly controlled, their talents were uniquely valuable to government. If the government used the energies of ambitious men, and was attuned to the requirements of the general welfare, the whole dynamic society would run efficiently and fairly and great nationhood for the United States was possible. Though Hamilton thought varieties of proconsulship and monarchy proper forms of government, he also thought that republicanism in general and the federal Constitution in particular could be made to yield the firm leadership vital to a good society.

III

The many specific divergences between the Jeffersonian and Hamiltonian "visions" can properly be subsumed under these general differences. The economy favored by each, though important in their respective schemes, was not the *main* point. Jefferson extolled agriculture because it nourished vital personal qualities, while Hamilton encouraged commerce and industry because they furnished the means of growth and wealth and power. Jefferson was a "strict constructionist" because only under a restrained or "mild" government could "Cato's" brand of personal virtue and self-reliance flourish, while Hamilton urged broad construction because only such wide powers would permit firm, expansive leadership. Jefferson feared standing armies and shunned military adventurism because such tendencies encroached on provincial vitalities and corrupted personality, while Hamilton was perfectly willing to build armed strength and to encourage military virtues and ambitions because such power and energy fostered stability at home and expansion abroad. Skilled in the use of power, Hamilton had confidence that civilian leadership could control the usurping tendencies of military officers, while Jefferson, suspicious of power, doubted the capacities of civilian control and exaggerated the threat of "Cromwellism." In foreign relations, Jefferson responded sympathetically to republican France because she seemed likely to turn Europe from the corrupt, tyrannical ways that had for centuries suppressed humanity, while Hamilton favored England because her trade, sea power, and burgeoning factories could best underwrite the development he placed first among American needs. Neither man, of course, subordinated American national interest to a foreign power. Rather, they differed on what posture in the world would best suit the kind of nation they hoped the United States would become.

Their impressions of each other's world view further reveal the basic difference in values. To Jefferson, Hamilton seemed frankly to favor "the few," to offer the rich a program to become richer, while "the many" found themselves harnessed powerlessly to an economy perhaps materially useful, but morally debilitating. To Hamilton, Jefferson seemed hopelessly biased toward one segment of the population and entirely neglectful of the needs for growth and national leadership. Hamilton's admired entrepreneur seemed to Jefferson merely greedy, sharp-dealing, and dishonest, while Jefferson's valued yeoman seemed to Hamilton merely narrow-minded, provincial, and unimaginative. Jefferson's "trinity of immortals"—Bacon, Newton, and Locke —though in some ways admired by Hamilton, seemed to him only marginally relevant to the needs of statesmanship, while Hamilton's hero—Julius Caesar—was to Jefferson a dangerous tyrant and adventurer. So pervasive were their differences that the honest zeal of each to cooperate as cabinet colleagues under Washington turned first to perplexity and then to mutual abhorrence. Jefferson wrote late in life, for example, that Hamilton's financial system had two objects:

First, as a puzzle, to exclude popular understanding and inquiry; and second, as a machine for the corruption of the legislature, for he avowed the opinion that man could be governed by one of two motives only, force or interest; force, he observed, in this country was out of the question; and the interests, therefore, of the members must be laid hold of, to keep the legislature in unison with the executive. And with grief and shame it must be acknowledged that his machine was not without effect. . . . Some members were found sordid enough to bend their duty to their interests and to look after personal rather than public good. . . . Immense sums were thus filched from the poor and ignorant, and fortunes accumulated by those who had themselves been poor enough before. Men enriched by the dexterity of a leader, would follow, of course, the chief who was leading them to fortune, and become the zealous instruments of all his enterprises.

Hamilton, amid bitter cabinet quarrels, wrote that Jefferson, "whom I once *very much esteemed* but who does not permit me to retain that sentiment for him, is certainly a man of sublimated and paradoxical imagination, entertaining and propagating notions inconsistent with dignified and orderly Government." Jefferson could see in all of Hamilton's great plans only the design of a sinister engine that would go in the wrong direction and surely debauch the character of the people, while Jefferson was to Hamilton a whimsical nut who simply did not understand the needs of practical, systematic government.[12]

Repeatedly their careers exhibited their differing conceptions of nationhood. During the Revolutionary War *Mr.* Jefferson sought first to *legislate* reform of grass-roots institutions and then spent two years uneasily and ineffectively trying to govern a Virginia threatened and then mauled by British armies. *Colonel* Hamilton at once joined the army, served brilliantly as aide to Washington, and thirsted to *command* troops in battle. In "retirement," Jefferson went to his farm to write, think, and be with his grandchildren. His only "activity" was to found a university where young men might acquire the occupational, social, and moral skills vital to Jefferson's vision of the national future. Hamilton, on the other hand, returned to a thriving law practice, chartered banks, organized manufacturing societies, promoted foreign "filibusters," and managed political campaigns. In style of statesmanship Hamilton reminds us of leaders so dynamic and so sure of their own grasp of national needs that there is little for the people to do but follow and find fulfillment in the national grandeur—Bismarck, Churchill, and de Gaulle come to mind. Jefferson, on the other hand, reminds us of the occasional "moralists" who have achieved power and then seem somehow out of place amid geopolitical crosscurrents—Woodrow Wilson, Lester Pearson, and Jawaharlal Nehru, for examples.

In American history the Jeffersonian and Hamiltonian traditions are still invoked (often inappropriately) for political purposes. They have also persisted in more profound ways. In the 1830s and 1840s the Transcendentalists spoke in Jeffersonian tones, asking for moral revival and attention to personal virtue—paragraph after paragraph in *Walden* evokes Jeffersonian pieties. On the other hand Clay's American System, frontier "boosters," the Whig Magnates, and the Jacksonian entrepreneurs, condemned by Emerson but brilliantly high-

lighted in Daniel Boorstin's *The National Experience*, are energetically
Hamiltonian. Boorstin's admiring account of Frederic Tudor's genius
in shipping ice from Walden Pond all over the world, and Thoreau's
distaste for the bustling despoilers of the pond, capture the contrasting
values perfectly. Most clearly, though, the two main currents of Progressive reform, Theodore Roosevelt's New Nationalism and
Woodrow Wilson's New Freedom, restate the Hamiltonian and the
Jeffersonian visions. Wilson, consciously following Jefferson, insisted
repeatedly that society could be renewed only by a "constant rise of
the sap from the bottom, from the rank and file of the great body of
the people . . . not from above; not by the patronage of its aristocrats."
Roosevelt's "house intellectual," Herbert Croly, on the other hand, in
considering "the promise of American life," gave classic, if biased,
formulation to the two traditions:

Jefferson implied that society and individuals could be made better without
actually planning the improvement or building up the organization for that
purpose. . . . [His] policy was at bottom the old fatal policy of drift . . .
whose ugly face was covered by a mask of good intentions. Hamilton's
policy was one of energetic and intelligent assertion of the national good.
He knew that the only method whereby the good could prevail either in
individual or social life was by persistently willing that it should prevail
and by the adoption of intelligent means to that end.

Half a century later, in the 1960s, the polarity, though less clear politically, was nonetheless everywhere evident: "multiversities," Nelson
Rockefeller, the Export-Import Bank, and "urban redevelopment," for
example, are Hamiltonian, while liberal arts colleges, Eugene Mc-
Carthy, the Peace Corps, and community control are Jeffersonian.
Jefferson and Hamilton set forth the paradigms of American character
and national development that crystallized rival political parties in
their own day and have ever since infused reformulations of the national purpose.[13]

14. Albert Gallatin and John Marshall

I

IN THE EARLY NATIONAL PERIOD JEFFERSON AND HAMILTON EACH HAD THE GOOD FORTUNE TO HAVE A COLLEAGUE ABLE TO PROJECT HIS CONCEPTION OF NATIONAL NEED INTO PUBLIC POLICY. JEFFERSON'S SECRETARY OF THE TREASURY, ALBERT GALLATIN, SUCCEEDING TO THE OFFICE OF the despised Hamilton, worked out in detail what it meant to conduct government on the principles of his chief. Presiding over much the largest department of the federal government and responsible for the fiscal policy undergirding all its operations, Gallatin sought to "republicanize" the Hamiltonian machine—not by dismantling it but by giving it a new character. As keen as Hamilton on maintaining the public credit, solvency, and a stable currency, Gallatin also approved an efficient public service, a national bank, encouragement for investment, and promotion of economic growth by the government. His highly sophisticated "A Sketch of the Finances of the United States" (1796), though, challenged the Hamiltonian view that a public debt was a public blessing and that men of wealth should be "attached" to the Union by measures favorable to them. Such favoritism might "at times give useful support," Gallatin admitted, but he pointed out the danger that men of wealth might "at some future period lend [their] assistance to bad measures and to a bad administration." Since their interests were not identical with those of the public, their influence might "become as pernicious as it is supposed to have been useful." It was better, therefore, to restrain rather than to increase their power. Overall, Gallatin deflated Hamiltonian fiscal wizardry—there simply were no magic ways to wealth, to national growth, or to a stronger Union. Rather, prudence, debt reduction, and economy would lighten the burdens of the common man and thus enhance the prosperity of the nation—and at the same time infuse the federal government with a "mildness" in sharp contrast to the "high tone" favored by the Federalists.[1]

Gallatin devised the means for this redirection in fiscal plans submitted to the first Republican Congress in November 1801. He proposed that three-fourths or more of the $10,000,000 annual revenue be devoted to debt retirement under a plan that would entirely extinguish it in eighteen years. Since the debt had risen steadily under the Federalists, this was a major reversal. Furthermore, he proposed reduction of government employees by one-half (ministries in Berlin, Lisbon, and The Hague would be closed out, for example, leaving only London, Paris, and Madrid with full American diplomatic representation), and, striking at the major expenses, he slashed defense appropriations to about $1,500,000—half of what had been considered a peacetime minimum and but a quarter of the annual expenditures during the 1798–1800 war scare with France. Furthermore, by repealing internal taxes, Gallatin not only gained political popularity but was also able to discharge half of the federal tax gatherers, thus cutting costs and, more important, diminishing the "army of agents" potentially able to overawe the people. Without in the least undermining fiscal responsibility or indulging simplistic or agrarian nostrums, Gallatin applied a Jeffersonian regulator to the very engines of government Hamilton had created to pursue splendor and aggrandizement. There is a certain truth to charges that the Republicans were forced to adopt Federalist ways they had pledged themselves to overturn. Overall, though, they accomplished the substantial revolution in government "tone" they thought necessary to guide the national character toward the pastoral virtues, rather than letting it be trained in the hucksterism and vainglory they felt was implicit in the Hamiltonian design. That Gallatin, a sophisticated man who understood trade and finance and who, like Franklin, spent most of his life in the great cities of Europe and America, so effectively championed Jeffersonian agrarianism highlights its essentially moral character.[2]

Gallatin and Jefferson were willing to *use* government power for the general welfare when it was subordinated to clearly republican objectives. Gallatin regarded the Louisiana Purchase, for example, as constitutional because "the existence of the United States as a nation presupposes the power enjoyed by every nation of extending their territory by treaties," but, more important, he hoped "the Missouri Country" would be settled by the people of the United States. To have such an immense territory transformed into range on range of yeoman farms was a perfect Jeffersonian idyll, and therefore worthy of the sponsorship of the American government. The same assumption guided federal support for the Cumberland Road—"a national object . . . of primary importance" in Gallatin's opinion. In 1808 he even inspired the Senate to request from him, as Congress had done under impetus from Hamilton, a "Report on Roads and Canals." "Good roads and canals," Gallatin asserted, "will shorten distances, facilitate commercial and personal intercourse, and unite, by a still more intimate community of interests, the most remote quarters of the United States. No other single operation, within the power of Government, can more effectually tend to strengthen and perpetuate that Union which secures external independence, domestic peace, and internal liberty." But eighteen months later, when factions in Congress sought to use war scares to subvert the whole Republican program, Gallatin nearly resigned his office. "I cannot," he wrote Jefferson, "consent to act the part of a mere financier, to become a contriver of taxes, a dealer of loans, a seeker of resources for the purpose of supporting useless baubles, of increasing the number of idle and dissipated members of the community, of fattening contractors, pursers, and agents [of the army], and of introducing in all its ramifications that system of patronage, corruption, and rottenness which you so justly execrate." *Power in government* under republican guidance did not trouble Gallatin, but this power harnessed to grandiose ends and permeated with a spirit of speculation and fortune-making was profoundly disturbing. Power used to open thousands of square miles of the West to industrious farmers was benign, while power used to enrich dissipated financiers or would-be monopolists was quite a different thing. In devising fiscal policies and national plans to make these distinctions Gallatin was a model Jeffersonian public official.[3]

II

John Marshall was the consummate spokesman for the national dignity and authority deemed so essential by Hamilton. After sharing

Washington's tribulations during the Revolutionary War and defending the new Constitution in 1788, Marshall became in the 1790s the leading Virginia Federalist. Though he did not approve the Alien and Sedition Acts, he stoutly defended their constitutionality:

Government is instituted and preserved for the general happiness and safety; the people therefore are interested in its preservation, and have a right to adopt measures for its security, as well against secret plots as open hostility. But government cannot be thus secured, if, by falsehood and malicious slander, it is deprived of the confidence and affection of the people. . . . Therefore, in all the nations of the earth, where presses are known, some corrections of the licentiousness has been indispensable. . . . The will of the majority must prevail, or the republican principle is abandoned, and the nation is destroyed. If upon every constitutional question which presents itself, or on every question we choose to term constitutional, the constructions of the majority shall be forcibly opposed, and hostility to the government excited throughout the nation, there is an end of our domestic peace, and we may forever bid adieu to our representative government.

Marshall's assumption that "government" was a valued entity in its own right, a superintending body worthy of protection since it performed the indispensable offices of security and guidance for the people, was staunchly Hamiltonian—and precisely the presumption from which Jefferson sought to unburden the people.[4]

In decision after decision as Chief Justice (1801–1835) Marshall enunciated a conception of nationality suited to the Hamiltonian vision. In *Fletcher v. Peck* (1810) he declared a state law contrary to a clause of the federal Constitution null and void. In *Cohen v. Virginia* (1821) he affirmed the power of the Supreme Court to review and if necessary set aside decisions of state courts that challenged federal authority. In the *Dartmouth College Case* (1819) he denied the power of state legislatures to infringe the sanctity of contracts—a doctrine subsequently useful to large *national* corporations in resisting control by *local* jurisdictions and doubtless one Hamilton would have approved both in theory and in its projection. In *Worcester v. Georgia* (1832) Marshall pronounced a Georgia law contravening a federal treaty with the Cherokee Nation null and void. In *Gibbons v. Ogden* (1824) he both voided a state law granting a restrictive commercial monopoly and pointed toward a broad construction of the Interstate Commerce Clause, a power clearly necessary if the United States was to avoid a petty warfare of jurisdictions harmful to trade and growth.

In *McCulloch v. Maryland* (1819), however, Marshall best expressed the broad conception of national power vital to Hamiltonian dynamism. Drawing heavily on Hamilton's defense of the national bank (1791), which he had found among Washington's papers while writing his laudatory biography of the first President, Marshall noted it was "a *constitution* we are expounding," and that therefore the opinion would "essentially influence the great operations of the government." After insisting, as he had heard Madison do thirty years earlier at the Virginia ratifying convention, that the people and not the states had formed the Constitution, Marshall offered a proposition he hoped would "command the universal assent of mankind:

The government of the Union, though limited in its powers, is supreme within its sphere of action. This would seem to result, necessarily, from its nature. It is the government of all; its powers are delegated by all; it represents all; and acts for all. Though any one state may be willing to control its operations, no state is willing to allow others to control them. The nation, on these subjects on which it can act, must necessarily bind its component parts.

With supremacy within its sphere thus established, Marshall noted that though there was no enumerated power in the Constitution to charter banks, such power was implicit in "a fair construction of the whole instrument." To have enumerated specifically "all the subdivisions of which its great powers will admit, and all the means by which they may be carried into execution, would partake of the prolixity of a legal code, and could scarcely be embraced by the human mind. It would, probably, never be understood by the public." This argument, of course, reveals precisely how the Hamilton-Marshall idea of nationality differed from that of the Jeffersonians. Not having high-toned, elaborate notions of what the *government* would do for the people, Jefferson insisted that almost any "human mind" could "embrace" its functions. Indeed, to so construct and so conduct government was an essential element of republicanism. It was dangerous, therefore, to propound a broad construction that would extend to the unimaginable limits a vigorous government would always find it "necessary" to reach. Such reaches were exactly what Jefferson thought inadmissible. To Hamilton and Marshall, though, guided by expansive assumptions about the range of a government capable of leading a nation to greatness, it was humanly (or at least *commonly*) impossible to spell out the powers and functions it might have to grasp and use.

What was the only "sound construction of the Constitution," then? In *McCulloch v. Maryland* Marshall announced it:

To allow to the national legislature that discretion, with respect to the means by which the powers it confers are to be carried into execution, which will enable that body to perform the high duties assigned to it, in the manner most beneficial to the people. Let the end be legitimate, let it be within the scope of the constitution, and all the means which are appropriate, which are plainly adapted to that end, which are not prohibited, but consist with the letter and spirit of the constitution, are constitutional.

Once admitting the need for national power *to do* so many unforeseeable things, the argument for broad construction becomes inevitable and is sure to recur whenever new "needs" arise amid new circumstances. Hamilton's propositions of 1791, established in constitutional law by Marshall, are repeated without essential change by Webster and Lincoln in the nineteenth century and by the two Roosevelts and Lyndon Johnson in the twentieth. Marshall's great manifestoes, culminating in *McCulloch v. Maryland*, built firm legal foundations for the assumptions of national leadership and glory vital to the Hamiltonian conception of what might be the future of the new United States.[5]

In agreeing with Marshall's decision giving the Supreme Court the power to review state court actions, Madison revealed a critical, Jeffersonian distinction. If the state courts had final jurisdiction, he pointed out, "The Constitution of the U.S. might become different in every State, and would be pretty sure to do so in some; the State Governments would not stand all in the same relation to the General Government, some retaining more, others less of sovereignty, and the vital principle of equality, which cements their Union thus gradually deprived of its virtue." For Marshall and the Hamiltonians the "vital principle" was the *power* to act from above for national purposes, while for Madison and the Jeffersonians the "vital principle" was an equality of treatment at once assuring a key moral precept and generating affection for the Union. The Jeffersonians valued the Union for its capacity to promote *virtue* (a sentiment in the hearts of the people), while the Hamiltonians emphasized *authority*, legitimate, under law, and on behalf of the people, but less attentive to their personal qualities than to what Herbert Croly would call "the energetic and intelligent assertion of the national good."[6]

15. Religion and Science

WHILE THE ATTENTION OF THE COUNTRY CENTERED ON THESE LARGE ISSUES OF NEW NATIONHOOD, AND ITS INTELLECTUAL ENERGIES CONCENTRATED, IN THE MANNER OF JEFFERSON AND GALLATIN, HAMILTON AND MARSHALL, ON QUESTIONS OF PUBLIC POLICY, thoughtful men projected the implications of new nationhood everywhere—onto religion, science, race, literature, language, and the arts. Though there was no agreement on *what* the implications were for these various areas, there was a remarkable assent to the proposition that all would respond to the new status and that redefinitions were in order. As the political debate continued, and as American self-conceptions achieved greater sophistication, only myriad projections in arts, letters, and institutions, it seemed, could fully define the character of the new nation and its place in the world.

I

American religion during the Revolutionary and early national periods in many respects fulfilled the impetus provided both by the Great Awakening and by the growth of rational religion that accompanied the quest for political liberty (described in Part II, Chapter 2). The rationalist impulse found expression in the deism of Paine, Priestley, Franklin, Jefferson, Ethan Allen, Elihu Palmer, and many others. Unitarianism was the chief institutional result, though varieties of rationalism found their way into almost all the Protestant sects. The evangelicalism of the Great Awakening, on the other hand, kept alive in the theology of Edwards' disciples Joseph Bellamy and Samuel Hopkins and among the New Light graduates of the College of New Jersey, flourished fitfully in the last third of the eighteenth century—for example, in the Baptist-Presbyterian-Methodist revivals in Virginia between 1765 and 1790, and in the "visits of the Holy Spirit" to colleges such as Princeton in the early 1770s and Yale in the 1790s. These trends sustained the doctrinal and epistemological arguments that had raged between Edwards and Chauncy at mid-century, but added to them were efforts to find in religion manifestations of the new nationality—and to find in the new nationality embodiments of religious values.

American religion in the early national period received its most characteristic impulses from the series of "awakenings" that flourished on the frontier beginning in 1800–1801, broke out irregularly in the East during the first decades of the nineteenth century, and reached another peak in the preaching missions of Charles G. Finney in the "Burned-over district" of New York State during the 1820s. Like the Great Awakening of the 1740s, these revivals attended mainly to religious concerns transcending time and place—repentance of sins, spiritual renewal, establishing a communion of believers and so on—but preachers and laymen frequently projected their enthusiasms to national life itself. Frightened by the atheism, materialism, and amorality emanating from the French Revolution and concerned that American preoccupation with the physical exploitation of the West might secularize and corrupt the new nation, New England evangelists exhorted their audiences to save the country from these devilish dangers. Just as Nathaniel Niles and other followers of Edwards had linked independence with the coming of the Kingdom of God on earth, so leaders of the Second Awakening insisted that the political opportunities of new nationhood could be fulfilled only if its citizens, powerfully affected by spiritual renewal, purged it of decadence and barbarism and imbued it with the teachings of Christianity. Lyman Beecher's magazine would warn by 1831:

The government of God is the only government which will hold society, against depravity within and temptation without; and this it must do by the force of its own law written upon the heart. This is that unity of the Spirit and that bond of peace which alone can perpetuate national purity and tranquility—that law of universal and impartial love by which alone nations can be kept back from ruin. There is no safety for republics but in self-government, under the influence of a holy heart, swayed by the government of God.[1]

Though the evangelical fervor of American Protestantism spawned great denominational diversity in the first quarter of the nineteenth century, there was substantial agreement with the outlook expressed by Beecher in 1831. The revivalist methods, the zeal to Christianize the West, and the sense of a Christian duty to influence the conduct of government at all levels permeated dynamic elements within virtually all the churches. The evangelicals also joined in a series of associations designed to foster the right sort of Christian character in the nation. The American Education Society (1815), The American Bible Society (1816), The American Sunday School Union (1824), The American Tract Society (1825), and The American Home Missionary Society (1826) all sought to instill in Americans attitudes and beliefs vital to the nation as well as to the spread of Christianity. This double, inseparable conviction was for many Americans the way they hoped to give everyday, substantial meaning to the national character.[2]

The most dramatic and enduring part of the Second Awakening took place in the South, where following the great revivals of the Cumberland Valley and Cane Ridge, Kentucky, in 1800–1801, religious enthusiasm washed back over the Appalachians to affect the Piedmont regions between Richmond, Virginia, and Macon, Georgia. Catching fire from the huge camp meetings where five or ten thousand people were preached to by interdenominational teams of ministers, the revivals resulted in the evangelical churches—Methodist, Baptist, Presbyterian, and Disciples of Christ—doubling and tripling their memberships in a few years. The denominations had formal differences in doctrine and organization among themselves, and the stress and excitement of revival produced new schisms in the churches, but overwhelmingly the participants, clergy and laymen alike, felt themselves to be in Christian communion, united in the goal of salvation. Rice Haggard, for example, a Virginia Methodist in the 1790s and a deviant Presbyterian who helped found the Disciples of Christ in Kentucky in 1804, insisted that "the Church of Christ is *one body*, and one name is enough for the same body." Christians, he asserted, should accept the Bible as their one Confession of Faith and "consider themselves members one of another . . . [in the] religion of Jesus Christ." Anything else was superfluous and divisive, Haggard argued. Even so ardent a denomination-builder as Methodist Bishop Francis Asbury rejoiced in 1802 that the great camp meetings must "supply an addition of hundreds and thousands to the Methodists, Presbyterians, and Baptist Societies, . . . and oh that they may all be Christians." Thus, though the institutional aspect of the Second Awakening was a rapid growth of separately organized Protestant denominations, dynamically, as each group sought the conversion of individuals, there was an overwhelming sense of enlarging a single Christian communion.[3]

A Kentucky Presbyterian, David Rice, identified the theological agreement when he noted in revival appeals "a strange heterogeneous mixture of antinomianism, arminianism, and I may add, calvinism; calvinism, perhaps in the beginning, antinomianism in the middle, and arminianism at the end of a sermon." That is, the preachers often began with severe strictures on the damned state of the unregenerate in the congregation (Calvinism), then expiated on the wonderous workings of the Holy Spirit among those who repented (Antinomianism), and concluded urging everyone to accept salvation through Jesus Christ (Arminianism). Whatever chaos this made of centuries of theological polemics, the mixture was preached to hundreds of thousands of Americans in the first decades of the nineteenth century, giving them a remarkably unified sense of human nature and theory of providential deliverance in the New World. Though the revival preachers seldom mentioned public life and in fact often exhorted their audiences to shun politics and business lest they lose their souls, by creating vivid conceptions of the sanctified life they helped define fundamental aspects of the American character.[4]

The revivalists, then, like their counterparts during the Great Awakening, sought to affect society through the qualities of the individuals they led to salvation. Made sober, devout, honest, and charitable by his new faith, the argument went, the regenerate Christian as citizen (and as office-holder) would make the United States a Christian nation in the only acceptable post-Establishment meaning of that idea: that is, a nation whose people, in their hearts and in their daily lives, would make Biblical Christianity the touchstone of the public as well as the private life of the nation. A Georgia minister, preoccupied with the Second Awakening, observed conventionally in 1802 "that without religion there can be no virtue; and . . . without virtue, there can be no liberty," nor, of course, republican government. The revivalists redefined this ancient equation, accepted as readily by Jefferson and John Adams as by Bishop Asbury, only they insisted upon the conversion experience as the genuine way to bring virtue into human life. This reinforced the individualistic emphasis of American Protestantism, but it was neither new nor unrelated to the public life of the new nation.[5]

With a different ideological emphasis, the Unitarians saw the same linkage. In 1831, for example, William Ellery Channing, student of Samuel Hopkins but also heir to Charles Chauncy, leading American Unitarian but also an inspiration for Emerson, looked beyond doctrinal incongruities to consider how "the Essence of the Christian Religion" might relate to the "New World" he saw not only around him in the United States but also coming into being in Europe. The "great principle" of Christianity, Channing asserted, was "the perfection of human nature, the elevation of men into nobler beings." In the "torrent of revolution," in which by 1831 the United States was a leading, powerful current, Channing saw likewise "the promise of a freer and higher action of the human mind, the pledge of a state of society more fit to perfect human beings." The essence of Christianity, then, was akin to the character of the new nation already in being in America and, Channing hoped and expected, would be more and more evident in nations around the world. The revolutionary spirit would banish the despotism that had "enslaved men's faculties . . . [and] bowed and weighed down the soul." "The unintelligible and irrational doctrines, . . . uncouth and idolatrous forms and ceremonies, . . . [and the] terror, superstition, vanity, priestcraft and ambition" associated with traditional Christianity would also be swept away. If the betrayal and tragedy that so often followed revolution were to be avoided, however, the zeal to perfect human nature and a "conception of a BETTER STATE OF SOCIETY, under which the rights of human nature will be recognized, and greater justice be done to the mind in all classes of the community" would have to become a positive guide for the disenthralled society. Sounding the same theme that the followers of Jonathan Edwards had struck during the Revolution, Channing had a poignant sense of how new nationhood furnished an opportunity for Christianity to transform society—by giving the people new habits and new interests it might mold the *character* of a whole society. In the first decades of the nineteenth century American Christians sought ways to make their values become the flesh and blood of the skeleton of national existence, just as the Puritan Ethic or the pastoralism of Crèvecoeur and Jefferson offered substance to the framework.[6]

Also omnipresent was the sense that churches, like nations and social institutions, could ossify and thus betray themselves and become a curse to mankind. The corruption and stagnation imposed on colonial society by British rule, and the subsequent virtue and dynamism released by independence, had its religious counterpart in the contrast between the decadent church establishments of Europe (and America) and the vigorous faith of the independent sects of the United States.

David Ramsay, historian of the Revolution in South Carolina and no friend of revivalism, observed that to anyone acquainted with "the state of the country before and since [the Methodists] commenced their evangelisms, . . . great good has resulted. Drunkards have become sober and orderly—bruisers, bullies, and blackguards, meek, inoffensive and peaceable—profane swearers, decent in their conversation." The way of the evangelical churches was especially useful on the rural frontier, Ramsay thought, where the people could not support "learned stationary clergymen." "Multitudes" received religious instruction that "produced a great diminution of gross immoralities," and altogether the Methodists and Baptists had astonishing success "in civilizing and evangelizing remote and destitute settlements." James Madison, writing in 1819, saw a similar improvement and related it directly to the public philosophy of religious freedom:

That there has been an increase of religious instruction since the Revolution can admit of no question. . . . The old churches built under the establishment at public expense have in many instances gone to ruin, or are in a very dilapidated state, owing chiefly to the desertion of the flocks to other worships. . . . Among the other sects, meeting houses have multiplied and continue to multiply. . . . On a general comparison, of the present and former times, the balance is certainly and vastly on the side of the present as to the number of religious teachers, the zeal which activates them, the purity of their lives, and the attendance of the people on their instructions. It was the universal opinion of the century preceding the last, that Civil Government could not stand without the prop of a Religious establishment and that the Christian religion itself, would perish if not supported by a legal provision for its clergy. The experience of Virginia conspicuously corroborates the disproof of both opinions. The Civil Government, tho bereft of anything like an associated hierarchy, possesses the requisite stability . . . whilst the number, the industry, and the morality of the Priesthood, and the devotion of the people have been manifestly increased by the total separation of church and state.[7]

Writing from the perspective of the Old World, Tocqueville noted that he "had almost always seen the spirit of religion and the spirit of freedom pursuing courses diametrically opposed to each other, but in America I found that they were intimately united, and that they reigned in common over the same country." Thus, though religion in the United States had no formal connection with the state, "it directs the manners of the community, and by regulating domestic life it regulates the State." Tocqueville doubtless spoke more categorically than the facts warranted, but there were substantial foundations for his statement. American churches were far less bound to the established order than those of Europe; religion in America did exhibit a remarkable vitality many ascribed to its separation from the state; and indirectly, through the faith of its citizens and officials, religion was a powerful force in the life of the new nation. Though revivalism and denominationalism often created schisms, pandered to irrationalism, lurched about on emotional binges, and turned motivations away from public life, more importantly the religious awakenings spurred a buoyant individualism and a sense of mission that became a critical part of the emerging national character.[8]

II

The Revolution excited as much hope among American scientists as it did among those zealous for religion. Samuel Cooper, a Boston clergyman and leader in the resistance to British measures, wrote that only in America, where liberty "unfetters and expands the human mind, can science flourish." Francis Hopkinson, a signer of the Declaration of Independence and an important promoter of scientific societies, declared in 1792 that "the world looks toward us as a country that may become a great nursery of arts and science." Freed of many of the immemorial stultifications that smothered open inquiry in many parts of the world, the new nation did indeed seem well placed to advance science. The work of American scientists during the colonial period, aiding Linnaeus, Buffon, and others to classify the newly discovered plants and animals of the New World, was viewed as a propitious beginning. In fact, it seemed to many "natural philosophers" on both sides of the Atlantic that the new nation was somehow founded on precisely the same world view that since the time of Galileo, Bacon, and Harvey had stimulated the growth of scientific knowledge: a preoccupation with the physical environment, a sense of the irrelevance of many traditional ways, a willingness (indeed a need) to experiment, and the daily encountering of so many "new facts" that only an open-ended, inductive attitude seemed to make sense. In the 1780s Franklin, John Winthrop, Jr., Benjamin Rush, William Bartram, and David Rittenhouse, celebrating the Enlightenment ideals of free inquiry, reason, and progress, heralded a golden age of science as well as of society. A free country, abounding in nature's riches and peopled by energetic men seeking to improve their condition, should be the scene of amazing new discoveries and their ready application to the betterment of human life. Philip Freneau expressed the vision in poetry:

> . . . even now we boast
> a Franklin, prince of all philosophy,
> A genius piercing as the electric fire,
> Bright as the lightning's flash, explained so well,
> By him, the rival of Britannia's sage. [Newton]
> This is the land of every joyous sound,
> Of liberty and life, sweet liberty!
> Without whose aid the noblest genius fails,
> And science irretrievable must die.[9]

Aware of the patronage long given to science by some European countries and convinced that their new, free government had even more reason to promote the growth of useful knowledge, early American officials enthusiastically promoted science. State after state sponsored natural history surveys, both to participate in the excitement over the expansion of knowledge and to be sure they would be able to exploit their resources fully. The data thus collected, added to that obtained on private expeditions, provided a remarkable picture of the physical assets of the new nation and even led to such important discoveries as Thomas Say's use of fossils for stratigraphic correlation. Thomas Nuttall studied and collected rare plants from Florida to the far reaches of the Missouri and Columbia rivers, and compared fossil remains in Iowa with those of his native English Midlands. Benjamin Silliman's *American Journal of Science and Arts*, first published in 1818, epitomized its editor's view that the expansion of scientific knowledge and an increasing interest by the American people in science should be vital aspects of the new nation's public life. Silliman also believed, and persuaded a large public audience to believe, that the new scientific discoveries confirmed and enlarged religious faith by revealing to man the marvels of God's world. Thus, to Silliman, for fifty years professor of chemistry at Yale College, science, religion, education, and patriotism fitted neatly into an expansive, harmonious *Weltanschauung*.

In a discarded portion of his first inaugural address Washington urged Congress to "use your best endeavors to promote the education and manners of a people; to accelerate the progress of arts and sciences; to patronize the works of genius; to confer rewards for inventions of utility; and to cherish institutions favourable to humanity." Responding in 1790 to a request from Congress that he draw up a comprehensive plan of weights, measures, and currency, Jefferson plunged energetically into Enlightenment literature on uniform, rational schemes for such matters. He sought the help of Madison, Rittenhouse, and a Philadelphia watchmaker, Robert Leslie, in devising a decimal system that would, if adopted not only in the United States but all over the world, simplify every kind of exchange and vastly facilitate scientific research. A European scientist, on reading Jefferson's report (not acted upon by Congress), wrote him that "I believe you are the first nation that ever produced statesmen who were natural philosophers." A zeal for scientific information was also a prime reason for Jefferson's support of the Lewis and Clark expedition.[10]

When in 1820 Congress again asked a Secretary of State to prepare a report on weights and measures, John Quincy Adams responded in the Jeffersonian spirit, and in the nationalist mood of the time sought to repudiate the patchwork British system for the more rational metric or French system. Adams concluded with what can only be described as a peroration to the linkages between science and human improvement:

If man upon earth be an improveable being; if that universal peace, which was the object of a Savior's mission, which is the desire of the philosopher, the longing of the philanthropist, the trembling hope of the Christian, is a blessing of which the futurity of mortal man has a claim of more than mortal promise; if the Spirit of Evil is, before the final consummation of things, to be cast down from his dominion over men, and bound in the chains of a thousand years, the foretaste here of Man's eternal felicity; then this system of common instruments, to accomplish all the changes of social and friendly commerce, will furnish the links of sympathy between the inhabitants of the most distant regions; the metre will surround the globe in use as well as in multiplied extension; and one language of weights and measures will be spoken from the equator to the poles.

In his first annual message to Congress Adams translated this Whitmanesque vision into practical proposals. Since "the very first instrument for the improvement of the condition of men is knowledge," Adams recommended that Congress act upon Washington's proposal to found a "national seminary of learning." Furthermore, "in assuming her station among the civilized nations of the earth it would seem that our country has contracted the engagement to contribute her share of mind, of labor, and of expense to the improvement of those parts of knowledge which lie beyond the reach of individual acquisition, and particularly to geographical and astronomical science." The United States, Adams thought, should sponsor voyages of discovery such as those undertaken by Cook and La Pérouse. The President chided his countrymen that "on the comparatively small territorial surface of Europe there are existing upward of 130 light-houses of the skies [astronomical observatories], while in the whole American hemisphere there is not one." He urged the federal government therefore to build and maintain a national observatory, and to subsidize improvements in transportation and to aid inventors by stronger patent laws. It "would be treachery to the most sacred of trusts," Adams concluded, if the federal government failed to act to promote "the cultivation and encouragement of the mechanic and of the elegant arts, the advancement of literature, and the progress of the sciences, ornamental and profound."[11]

Neither Adams' *Report Upon Weights and Measures* nor his proposals to Congress resulted in positive action. In fact, nearly all the elaborate, officially sponsored plans for the advancement of science proved abortive. The nation's energies were absorbed by more immediate, more evidently practical promotions than an astronomical observatory or a rational system of weights and measures. Jefferson's moldboard plow, Eli Whitney's cotton gin and factory for inter-changeable parts, Robert Fulton's steamboat, and De Witt Clinton's Erie Canal, all quickly and obviously useful to growth and develop-ment, were the characteristic results of American technical ingenuity in an age when Lavoisier, Dalton, Humboldt, and Cuvier were the giants of science in Europe. Not only did the United States lack the laboratories, the sophistication, the channels of communication, and the support that sustained these great scientists, but it also had little use for what many of its people regarded as distractions or luxuries. Indeed, as men like Jefferson and John Quincy Adams, who thought of themselves as part of the European world of science, faded from the scene and were replaced by men more provincially American and more consumed by the practical tasks of continental development, the pursuit of pure science tended to retrogress in the United States. Far from being an aid to science, the demands of new nationhood seemed to turn talented men away from the inquiries so dear to the age of Enlightenment.

Furthermore, the beginning of American national life, and the attendant dream that it might be a unique boon to science, coincided with a sharp change in scientific style—the generalist was giving way to laboratory specialist. In the United States the way of the "natural philosopher," contemplating and understanding the whole physical world from astronomy, physics, and chemistry to geology, biology, and medicine as Franklin had done, remained an ideal well into the nineteenth century. Jefferson, Benjamin Silliman, John Winthrop, Jr., Benjamin Rush, David Rittenhouse, and Samuel Latham Mitchell, the luminaries of American science in the early national period, were "generalists" and, as such, increasingly obsolete. The great scientific discoveries in their day came more and more from highly skilled spe-cialists trained in the laboratories of Cavendish, Volta, and Davy rather than from men who, like Newton, considered the universe at large their field.[12]

In any event, by 1820 it was all too apparent that the advancement of science and its application to the improvement of human life re-quired much more than a free society and reiterated enthusiasm. There were dozens, perhaps even hundreds, of European scientists vastly superior to any the United States could claim. One great scien-tist, Benjamin Thompson (Count Rumford), was born in America, and another, Joseph Priestley, went there to live, but their shining contributions arose from stimulation and support in the Old World, not the New. Though the American Philosophical Society, the Philadelphia Academy of Natural Sciences, and other such organizations helped significantly to spread scientific knowledge, though American medical schools and societies slowly raised standards for physicians, and though rapidly multiplying agricultural societies encouraged scientific husbandry, taken together these hardly amounted to the dramatic breakthrough hoped for by John Quincy Adams. Louis Agassiz, Joseph Henry, and Asa Gray would in years to come demonstrate greatness among American scientists, but their achievements would result from an approach and a maturity but little evident in the first decades of the nineteenth century. Indeed, the modest accomplishments of American science in this period indicated again that the national genius was of a social-moral sort. Technical improvement, social growth, enhancement of daily life, and a new place for religion and morality in society were areas in which foreign and domestic observers saw something remarkable—there one found the distinctive marks of American national character. The ideals and achievements in these areas, of course, rested on concepts of natural law in turn heavily dependent on the study of nature undertaken so energetically by American scientists, but in the first decades of the nineteenth century the results were more notable in society at large and in a descriptive, practical, popularized enthusiasm for "natural philosophy" than in the sophisticated realms of scientific research.

16. Indians, Blacks, Race, and Slavery

IN AN AREA WHERE SCIENCE MIGHT HAVE OPENED HUMANE VISTAS, THAT
OF UNDERSTANDING RACE, CULTURAL DIFFERENCES, AND THE WHOLE
RANGE OF INSIGHTS NOW EXPLORED BY ANTHROPOLOGISTS, THE LEARN-
ING OF THE AGE OF REASON NOT ONLY FAILED TO AID LIBERALIZING TENDEN-
cies but it often supported enthnocentric attitudes of superiority and ex-
ploitation.

I

The paradox and ultimate tragedy of these attitudes is evident in
Jefferson's view of the native Indians. He insisted on their manly
virtues, intelligence, and essential nobility as human beings (especially
in defending the North American environment against Buffon's deficiency theories), but he also assumed that their "savagery" and their
"backwardness" could and must yield to the influence of "civilization."
That is, the Indian language, way of life, agriculture, morality, and
technology had to yield to that grandest creation of the human race,
civilization as it was understood and practiced by the Enlightened
eighteenth-century European. Progress required not an appreciation
of cultural pluralism, but a simple movement by all mankind toward
the values and way of life of learned men in Western Europe. The
same sense of superiority that led the *philosophes* to view the Turks
as bigoted tyrants, the Chinese as effeminate exotics, the blacks of
Africa as half-animals, and the Hindus of India as superstitious fanatics
led Jefferson to see the natives of America, however inherently noble,

as victims of severe cultural deprivation. He assumed, therefore, as did almost all his Enlightened colleagues, that philanthropy required Europeans to spread across the North American continent not only to expand the portion of the New World cultivated by yeoman farmers, but also to bring the yeoman's way of life to such natives as might already inhabit the wilderness.[1]

The pattern of European thought about the Indians illustrates classically the tragic fruits of mixing good intentions with misconceptions and overwhelming power. Under the influence of Lockean ideas on the state of nature and the efficacy of sense impressions, men of Jefferson's frame of mind supposed that only the degradation and impoverishment of the Indians' environment made them savages. Happily, the arrival of the Europeans gave them a chance to leap rapidly into civilization—they had only to adopt European technology, science, values, and living habits to become ornaments to the human race. Europeans had the philanthropic burden to aid the Indians in every way they could along this path. This attitude, widely held by thoughtful men during the Revolutionary and nation-building era, caused Europeans-in-America to believe that the barbarism of the Indians' way of life could be overcome by changes offered (or imposed) by white settlers. The inherently noble savage then might become a self-reliant, Christian yeoman farmer differing from the colonist only in the redness of his skin. Political leaders as diverse as Timothy Pickering and James Madison, missionary-educators as different as Jedidiah Morse and Samuel Stanhope Smith, and Indian agents from Benjamin Hawkins to Thomas L. McKenney worked earnestly for such "progress."

Malignant aspects appeared at once, aided, of course—indeed, made inevitable—by the chasm between these sentiments and the actual conditions and attitudes on the frontier. Hatred, violence, and suppression there more than cancelled out what little progress the well-intended made in incorporating the Indians into white society. Puzzled and appalled at the "failure" of the Indians to accept the proffered way of life, the philanthropists intensified their efforts, more and more using manipulation and coercion to rescue the Indians from savagery. Overwhelmed by the rush of the frontier and perhaps not allowed enough time to become assimilated, the surviving Indians were first encouraged and then forced to go westward. Out there in Oklahoma, the philanthropists supposed, the Indians might "settle down" and give up barbarous tribal customs. The tendency of the Indians to learn the white man's vices faster than his virtues, and the resulting rapid disintegration of Indian culture, persuaded sympathetic whites that incorporation had failed and that forced removal was justified to prevent the horrors of savages living amid civilized men. In this policy, of course, greedy, murderous, Indian-hating frontiersmen heartily concurred.

The flaws in the Jeffersonian attitude, in retrospect, are all too apparent: it lacked any sense that a different culture might be in itself valid and admirable, it miscalculated the complexity and persistence of cultural traits in the face of any attempted transformation, and it was blind to its complicity in the most nefarious intentions of grasping and violent men. Despite its striving for universality, the Enlightenment world view, even when embraced by such a thoughtful man as Jefferson, was pathetically narrow and ethnocentric. The effect, however liberating and expansive for "civilized" men, was exploitive and tragic for those who did not possess the sanctified culture. Though the philanthropist might sincerely admire the savage as a person, his savagery had to fall before the advance of civilization. If it did not, and instead threatened that advance, then coercion, removal, and even extinction seemed in order.

II

Different, though no less tragic, ironies surrounded Revolutionary attitudes toward black men and their enslaved status in America. Halting efforts were made to apply the ideals of freedom and equality to *all* men, but by the time of Jefferson's death regressive views were dominant. As the Revolution began, a first draft of the Declaration of Independence condemned the slave trade, Quakers stressed the moral wrong of black servitude, and New Light preachers proclaimed egalitarian principles inclusive of all men (see Part II, Chapter 3). Many white Americans were thus well aware that their struggle for liberty (and, as they asserted endlessly, against "slavery") and their projection of republican principles to all areas of life were inconsistent with black slavery.

In an abolitionist tract following the natural rights precept of John Wise that it is "a Command of the Law of Nature, that every Man Esteem and treat another as one who is naturally his Equal, [and] . . . that we all Derive our Being from one stock, the same Common

Father of [the] human Race," Benjamin Rush declared that "Human Nature is the same in all Ages and Countries, and all the difference we perceive in its Characters in respect to Virtue and Vice, Knowledge and Ignorance, may be accounted for from Climate, Country, Degrees of Civilization, form of Government, or other accidental causes." Thus, he asserted unequivocably, black slavery, based on ideas of innate inferiority or of social necessity, was inadmissible in general and blatantly inconsistent in a nation proclaiming itself governed by the laws of "nature and nature's god." Those opposing the Revolution saw the same incongruity: Americans treated Negroes, wrote Admiral Lord Howe's secretary, "as a better kind of cattle . . . while they are bawling about the Rights of *human nature*."[2]

Petitions, resolutions of churches, and even state action bespoke the plain logic, as James Madison put it in opposing a 1780 plan to offer black slaves as a bounty to recruit white soldiers, of adhering to "the principles of liberty . . . in a contest for liberty." In 1777 "A Great Number of Blacks" in Massachusetts, petitioning for the abolition of slavery, noted that "every principle from which America has acted in the course of her unhappy difficulties with Great Britain, pleads stronger than a thousand arguments in favor of your Petitioners." In 1784 Methodists in Virginia, adopting resolves already accepted by Quakers there, declared "the Practice of holding our Fellow-Creatures in Slavery . . . [is] contrary to the Golden Law of God on which hang all the Law and the Prophets, and the unalienable Rights of Mankind, as well as every principle of the Revolution." A Rhode Island law prohibiting the importation of slaves (1774) had as a preamble: "Whereas, the inhabitants of America are generally engaged in the preservation of their own rights and liberties, among which, that of personal freedom must be considered the greatest; as those who are desirous of enjoying all the advantages of liberty themselves, should be willing to extend personal liberty to others." Thomas Paine's preamble to a Pennsylvania abolition law of 1780 declared simply that "all are the works of the Almighty hand." A Massachusetts judge, noting that the state's 1780 constitution declaring "all men are born free and equal [was] . . . totally repugnant to the idea of [persons] being born slaves," ruled that "slavery is inconsistent with our own conduct and constitution." Such sentiments, together with the relatively informal status of servitude and the small number of blacks in the North, led there to laws first against the importation of slaves and then for general abolition. Between 1771, when Connecticut forbade the slave trade, and 1804, when New Jersey passed a gradual emancipation law, slavery as an institution disappeared north of the Mason-Dixon line.[3]

When the injustice of slavery was projected into the enlarging debate over national identity and character, the chasm between republican principles and black bondage seemed even more baneful. Franklin had pointed out in 1751 that the institution of slavery, by robbing slaves of the fruits of their labor, made them lazy, neglectful, and untrustworthy, and at the same time made those who held slaves arrogant and proud of their idleness (see Part II, Chapter 1). To Poor Richard, encouraging a life-style in America founded on self-reliance, personal virtues, hard work, and opportunity, slavery was entirely out of place. This sense grew rapidly during the 1770s and 1780s among Americans who saw the goals of the Revolution in broad terms requiring a transformation of ancient practices of hierarchy and degradation into new values leading eventually to a new society. An anonymous writer made the vital connections in 1789, declaring:

Persons of opulence in Virginia and the Carolinas treat their unhappy slaves with . . . the most deliberate indifference. Surrounded with a numerous train of servants, to contribute to their personal ease, and wallowing in all the luxurious plenitude of riches, they neglect the wretched source whence they draw this profusion. . . . While those miserable degraded persons thus scantily subsist, all the produce of their unwearied toil, is taken away to satiate their rapacious Master. . . . Thus, he sets up two carriages instead of one; maintains twenty servants, when a fourth part of that number are more than sufficient to discharge the business of personal attendance.[4]

How could the good, Jeffersonian society of self-reliant yeomen able to govern themselves virtuously come into being in the presence of an institution that took from some men what they had labored to produce in order to sustain an opulent class in dissipated luxury? How could men be raised to an ethic of diligence and equal opportunity when slavery denied opportunity to some men and trained others in habits of indolence, overbearance, and rapacity? In the first halfcentury of national existence every earnest effort to articulate and bring into being a nationhood embodying the trumpeted republican virtues was mocked by the curse of slavery.

In Jefferson's own thought and writings the obstacles in the way of any effective action for the ending of slavery, to say nothing of the even more complex task of eliminating the pervasive race prejudice of white Americans, were all too apparent. In the same *Notes on Virginia* (1782) that contained fervent denunciations of the moral evil of slavery and a plan for its gradual abolition in the state, Jefferson revealed his own deep feelings about race. The most apparent of the physical and moral differences between the races, he noted, was that of color, "and is this difference of no importance?" he asked. "Is it not the foundation of a greater or lesser share of beauty in the two races? Are not the fine mixtures of red and white, the expressions of every passion by greater or less suffusions of color in the one, preferable to that eternal monotony, which reigns in the countenances, that immovable veil of black which covers the emotions of the other race?" Jefferson also thought whites had a "superior beauty" in their "flowing hair, [and] a more elegant symmetry of form," while blacks had "a very strong and disagreeable odor." Intellectually, though blacks seemed "equal to whites" in memory, in reason they were so inferior that "I think one could scarcely be found capable of tracing and comprehending the investigations of Euclid; and in imagination they are dull, tasteless, and anomalous." Furthermore, Jefferson noted, he had heard Indians speak "the most sublime oratory, but never yet could I find a black that had uttered a thought above the level of plain narration; never saw even an elementary trait of painting or sculpture." To prove that these deficiencies were inherent in blacks rather than entirely the result of their bondage, Jefferson declared that the white slaves of antiquity, though treated more harshly than "blacks on the continent of America," nonetheless often excelled in science and were the "rarest artists." Jefferson concluded that perhaps nature had formed the blacks as a distinct race, "inferior to the whites in the endowments both of mind and body," and therefore destined to be forever separate and lesser in accomplishment. It is perfectly evident from these remarks that while Jefferson regarded the Indians as savages in dire need of "civilization," he saved his indelible *racial* prejudices for blacks. Jeffersonian anthropology made room for civilized Indians fully incorporated into white society, but his deep conviction of inherent black inferiority, combined with his sense of the demands of republican citizenship, made black incorporation impossible.[5]

Though Jefferson used this discussion of race as an argument for *release* of blacks from bondage and for *removal* of them to an asylum in the West or in Africa where they could develop their own strong moral qualities and distinctive folkways free from domination and invidious comparison with whites, he nonetheless had given powerful support to those who used "evidence" of black inferiority as grounds for retaining slavery. He was, in fact, caught in the web that had entangled and perverted European thought on race for three centuries: "The ideas of laziness, vice, blackness, and slavery, are so blended, so twisted together," wrote a West Indian foe of slavery in 1770, that slaveowners "may be supposed as utterly incapable of separating them." Though Jefferson admitted, after acquaintance with the black mathematician Benjamin Banneker and after seeing examples of black literature, that his earlier doubts of black capacities "were the result of personal observation on the limited sphere of my own State, where the opportunities for the development of their genius were not favorable, and those of exercising it less so," he nonetheless retained biases that made it impossible for him to conceive of a color-blind republic devoted to the rights of *all* men.[6]

During the Revolution many men, lacking Jefferson's sense of justice, used views like his to challenge the antislavery movement. They argued that the "lack of capacity" of blacks and their "uncivilized" African heritage rendered them not really human, and therefore they were "by nature" destined to be slaves. For example, a West Indian "history" of 1774, reprinted in a Philadelphia magazine in 1788, elaborating on the physical differences between "Europeans and Negroes," concluded that the races were "different species of the same GENUS." The "history" then repeated the ancient mythology that classified the African as a species intermediate between the "oran-outang" (chimpanzee) and the European, a link in the divinely ordained structure of nature. Thus "the Negro race will rise progressively in the scale of intellect, the further they mount above the oran-outang," and the system of slavery "will seem more consistent . . . and analogous to the harmony and order that are visible in every other line of the world's stupendous fabric." The British anatomist, Dr. John Hunter, dramatized the chain-of-being argument when he arranged a variety of skulls to show that white skulls were most upright, oriental skulls slightly less so, Africans more slanted, and orangutans and then monkeys even more so. Another English physician widely read in

America, Dr. Charles White, after further detailed study of physical differences, found the Negro skull not only flatter but of smaller capacity than the European. He rhapsodized at "the beautiful gradation that subsists among created beings. . . . Nature exhibits to our view an immense chain of beings, endowed with various degrees of intelligence and active powers, suited to their stations in the general system." At the top, of course, was "the white European; who being most removed from brute creation, may, on that account, be considered as the most beautiful of the human race. No one will doubt his superiority in intellectual powers. . . . Where shall we find, unless in the European, that nobly arched head, containing such a quantity of brain?"[7]

Following these precedents, in 1808 a young American physician, Dr. John A. Smith, declaring it a duty to lay before medical students "all the facts which are relevant," demonstrated, to his satisfaction at least, that the European was "farther removed from the brute creation" than the other races. Taking high facial angle as the crux, Smith remarked on the very high facial angles of the noble Greeks and Romans preserved in their statuary, and even speculated that the owl was the symbol of wisdom because of its exceedingly upright face. The meaning of such treatises for the American debate over race and slavery was all too obvious—and ominous. Black men were different, inferior, and therefore legitimately held in slavery, or, at best, destined to be otherwise subordinated or separated from white society. The still unsophisticated, imprecise state of eighteenth-century science, combined tragically with its high prestige and the inability of even honest, able investigators to transcend their preconceptions, strengthened the argument for black inferiority.[8]

The voices raised against the "evidence" of the doctors were increasingly lonely and futile. A New York Federalist, aiming especially at President Jefferson in 1804, wondered that "modern philosophy herself could . . . have the face to declare the wretch who is driven out to labour at the dawn of day, and who toils until evening with the whip flourishing over his head, ought to be a poet." Does impartiality, he asked, "command us to criticise the talents and literary productions of a few negroes who have escaped the unhappy lot of their brethren; and because they fall far short of European excellence, to degrade their whole race below the standard of mankind?" A young Marylander put down the arguments for degradation concisely when he declared "the ignorance and the vices of [blacks] are solely the result of situation, and therefore no evidence of their inferiority." A learned Princetonian, however, Samuel Stanhope Smith, most eloquently held up "the doctrine of one race" as an indispensable part of both Enlightenment philosophy and the founding beliefs of the new United States. Writers who "attempt to deny the unity of the human species," he declared, didn't realize the confusion and absurdity their ideas entailed. Under them, "the law of nature and nations would be annihilated; no general principles of human conduct, of religion, or of policy could be framed; for, human nature, originally infinitely various, and, by the changes of the world, infinitely mixed, could not be comprehended in any system. . . . Such principles tend to confuse all science, as well as piety; and leave us in a world uncertain whom to trust, or what opinion to frame of others." To men who took seriously the words of freedom and equality in the Declaration of Independence and, especially, who understood the universalizing implications of *Common Sense* and other Revolutionary manifestoes, the doctrines of racial gradation and of fixed inequalities among men contradicted every hope for human dignity and social progress. Instead, however, of being able to sustain "the principles in favor of human nature," as they put it, they were overwhelmed by prejudices such as Jefferson's, the wrenching social demands of considering *all* men equal, and the revived economic advantages of slavery resulting from the exploitation of new lands in the old Southwest and the invention of the cotton gin (1793). Enlightenment-spawned condemnation of black slavery increasingly gave way to rationalizations for it.[9]

III

Some consequences of otherwise progressive and humane aspects of the Revolution, ironically, helped assure the continuation of slavery, or, at least, of black degradation. The emphasis on personal property rights, for example, which in a Lockean context of resistance to arbitrary seizures by tyrannical governments was useful to a free society, when applied to slaveholders, had the effect of supporting their *right* to *own* men. Even antislavery advocates recognized the "rights" of slaveowners by calling for some kind of compensation to them should abolition commandeer their "property." Moreover, the legalistic quality of much Revolutionary rhetoric did not carry beyond the *formal* end of bondage under law. In the North, once slavery was abolished, no attention was paid to the condition of the freed blacks. The combination of white prejudices and the continuing effects of former servitude on freedmen made it seem that blacks were "not ready" for integration into society. The result was second-class citizenship for free blacks and reinforcement for the arguments against emancipation. If blacks were so difficult to "fit into free society" and seemed so ill suited to full political rights, the line went, was it really wise to end slavery? A related rationalization followed the general relaxation of slave codes during the Revolutionary era. If slavery was made "more humane," it was argued, was it not true that a well-treated slave was at least as well off as a despised, neglected free Negro, or even an ill-treated white factory operative? And therefore was not the plantation system "better" than the insensitive, irresponsible "free society" of England or of the North? What actually happened was that as Revolutionary ideals raised the possibility that black men might not only be emancipated but also live among whites in a more or less equal state, it seemed urgent that their nature and potentialities be fully understood. Faced with this prospect, categorical statements about freedom gave way to "practical" commentaries on sociology, human capacities, "reality," and the like.[10]

The ironies and incongruities were further heightened as the end of the foreign slave trade and the specter of slave rebellion impinged together on the American consciousness between 1787 and 1812. In the first place, the prohibition of the international slave trade, initially by the states and then by the national government in 1808, satisfied many people that black slavery, cut off from its African sources, would slowly die out. Feeling they had "succeeded," many abolitionist societies lost their zeal and faded away in the early years of the nineteenth century. At the same time, the fear of slave rebellions, made real by events in the West Indies from 1792 on and brought home especially by Gabriel's plot in Virginia in 1800, introduced a fateful compromise into the antislave-trade movement. Those anxious to *preserve* the slave system as it already existed in the United States opposed the slave trade in order to stop an influx of blacks that might make rebellion on the continent as calamitous as it had been in Haiti. So, humanitarians and slave-owners found themselves in a strange alliance—one group seeking to help the slaves and the other desperate to reduce the prospect of bloody insurrection. The same alliance then turned to emigration as the only solution to the race and slavery problem. Abolitionists saw removal of blacks, first to an asylum in the American West and then to the west coast of Africa, as the only real means of freedom for them, given the prejudices against them among whites. Southern liberals such as Jefferson and Madison saw removal as the only way to prevent endless racial strife in their society. Some friends of slavery supported it as a means for getting rid of free blacks (who were a "bad example") and troublemaking slaves. The net effects of this strange alliance were to blunt any sustained movement for total abolition of slavery and to afford rationalizations for various degrees of black subordination inside and outside of chattel slavery.

Finally, the frankly conservative ideology spawned by a horrified reaction to the excesses of the French Revolution and nostalgia for an ordered, hierarchical society offered further ways to justify slavery and racial subordination. Those disillusioned or frightened by the course of revolutionary events in France found reason to draw back from doctrines of liberty, fraternity, and equality. Perhaps as Burke, John Adams, Fisher Ames, John Randolph of Roanoke, and others argued, order, stability, and tradition were vital elements of social peace—perhaps even more vital than a hasty extension of freedom to black men. Before 1830 the conservative writers seldom defended slavery outright, but clearly their arguments dampened the reforming ardor of the antislavery movement of the 1770s and 1780s and nourished a social philosophy unlikely to resist either the apologies for slavery or the imposition of an inferior status on free blacks.

By 1820, then, as the controversy over the Missouri Compromise revealed so ominously, American thought on questions of race and slavery was both confused and polarized. The Revolution's ideals called unequivocally for the end of slavery and the equality of *all* men, and in New England and in much of the rapidly filling areas of New York, Pennsylvania, and the old Northwest, an egalitarian yeoman society with no place for slavery was fast becoming dominant in numbers, in economic power, and in "opinion"—the Jacksonian America described by Tocqueville. At the same time, a pervasive ethnocentrism, even among the new breed of Americans typified by Lincoln, acquiesced in second-class citizenship for blacks in their midst and in the existence of slavery in a large portion of their own nation. In the South itself the revived utility of slavery in a cotton economy and a growing conviction that white and black men could not live together after abolition foreshadowed the positive defense of a slave society undertaken by Calhoun and his followers in the thirty-five years before the Civil War. As many Americans realized, these incongruities and polarities dangerously, perhaps fatally, flawed the quest for a worthy national character. How could a nation stand for freedom when two million blacks were slaves in its midst? How could its society rest on the virtues of an independent yeomanry when legalized servitude degraded the slave and debauched the master? How could genuinely humane attitudes of equality undergird a new nation such as that envisioned by Crèvecoeur when crude notions of racial gradation infected virtually the entire population? The inconsistency implicit in these questions dramatized the failure of Americans in one vital way to fulfill the promise of their new nation.

17. The Search for
an American Literature

A DIFFERENT SET OF DIFFICULTIES ATTENDED THE EAGERLY SOUGHT-FOR FLOWERING OF AN AMERICAN LITERATURE. AMERICAN WRITERS SEEMED FRANTIC TO TELESCOPE JOHN ADAMS' THREE GENERATIONS OF CULTURAL GROWTH INTO A FEW YEARS WITH ODES AND essays expressing the spirit of the new nation even while its best energies were focused upon founding a government. However hard they tried, though, they could not match the achievements of Wordsworth and Goethe—or even dozens of lesser authors who graced the European literary scene as the Romantic Age began. Only partially successful in his own efforts as an author, Philip Freneau explained the difficulty in 1788:

In a country which two hundred years ago was peopled only by savages and whose government has ever . . . been no other than republican, it is really wonderful there should be any polite authors at all in any line, especially when it is considered, that according to the common course of things, any particular nation or people must have arrived to, or rather passed, their meridian of opulence and refinement before they consider the professors of the fine arts in any other light than a nuisance to the community. This is evidently the case at present in our age and country.

Another struggling author, Charles Brockden Brown, expressed much the same view fourteen years later. The practical habits of Americans, he wrote, grew

out of the necessities of their situation, while engaged in the settlement of a new country, in the means of self-preservation, in defending their possessions, in removing the obstacles and embarrassments arising from their colonial condition, and in forming and establishing independent systems of government. . . . A people much engaged in the labors of agriculture, in a country rude and untouched by the hand of refinement, cannot with any tolerable facility of success, carry on, at the same time, the operations of imagination and indulge in the speculations of Raphael, Newton, or Pope.

The two aspiring authors hoped to overcome these unpropitious circumstances by nourishing a unique American literature and by finding a suitable patronage for it. But competing with the sophisticated, well-supported literary circles in London proved to be a major problem. Brown lamented that the United States was "united by language, manners, and taste, by the bonds of peace and commercial intercourse, with an enlightened nation, the centre of whose arts and population may be considered as much *our* centre, as much the fountain whence *we* draw light and knowledge through books, as that of the inhabitants of Wales and Cumberland. In relation to the British capital as the centre of English literature, arts and science, the situation of *New* and *Old-York* may be regarded as the same." He hoped that his new magazine, *The American Review and Literary Journal*, would free the United States from this thralldom and set up instead American literary canons. Freneau proposed a duty on the flood of imported books, to give American authors a chance to earn a living. "Imported authors," he declared, "do twice as much mischief with their rumbling pindaric odes and gorgeous apparatus of strophes, antistrophes and recitatives" as did the importing of elegant British carriages, heavily taxed at the custom houses. Freneau also proposed to eliminate such servile devices as the dedicatory epistle that had for so long degraded European literature. "I would not give a farthing more for a book on account of its being patronized by all the noblemen or crowned heads in christendom," he declared. Brown and Freneau had identified the traditions and liabilities from which generations of American authors would suffer in attempting to create a respectable national literature.[1]

I

Freneau's own writings reveal almost pathetically the immense difficulties. For the Princeton graduation exercises in 1771 he collaborated with his classmate, Hugh Henry Brackenridge, in writing a long poem, "The Rising Glory of America." The form and meter came entirely from Pope and other masters of England's neoclassical age— an imitativeness not surprising in a twenty-year-old poet but indicative of Freneau's lifelong dependence on a British style of poetry. The theme—the expansion of English glory and freedom across the continent—was by 1771 commonplace on both sides of the Atlantic. Franklin had expressed it in his 1751 *Observations concerning the Increase of Mankind* and William Pitt had announced it repeatedly in great orations in Parliament. The young poets celebrated "Britannia's warlike troops, choice spirits of her isle," and made British soldiers— General Braddock, Sir William Johnson, and General Wolfe—the principal heroes. Again, in 1771 this was conventional, evidence only of the still-intense loyalty to England. But when Freneau republished the poem after the Revolution he only substituted a few references to American glory for those praising English glory, added some charges against "cruel . . . unrelenting Britain," and substituted the name and deeds of Washington for those of the British warriors. The idea of the national ode (so admired in the Augustan age), the heroic couplets of Pope, and the "chaste" style approved in *The Spectator* were still with him. The ease with which Freneau could make his substitutions betrays that both the "before" and "after" versions are imitative verse, not genuine poetry, for one could hardly render the national experience or vision by merely patching over the fabric of an earlier, derivative form. Freneau's prophecy that

> A second Pope, like that Arabian bird
> of which no age can boast but one, may yet
> Awake the muse by Schuylkill's silent stream,

revealed a hope that *English* poetry would flourish in America, not that an indigenous literary tradition would come into being. American poetry would happen only when the American character was distinctive enough to require its own new forms, and American speech its own cadences.[2]

During half a century Freneau wrote dozens of poems commemorating events in the new nation's history: "General Gage's Confession" (1775), "A Poem on the memorable victory obtained by the gallant

Capt. Paul Jones of the Good Man Richard" (1781), "On the fall of General Earl Cornwallis" (1781), "Verses on General Washington's Retirement" (1783), "Stanzas on the Emigration to America, and peopling the Western Country" (1785), "On the American and French Revolution" (1790), "Stanzas occasioned by the Death of Dr. Franklin" (1790), "Ode to Liberty" (1793), "Parody on the attempt to enforce the British Treaty on the People of the United States" (1796), "Lines on the Federal City" (1800), "Lines Addressed to Mr. Jefferson, on his approaching Retirement (1809), "To the Squadrons on the Lakes" (1814), "Stanzas written on the Grand Western Canal of the State of New York" (1821), "General Lafayette: on his expected visit to America" (1824), and many more. The subjects were patriotically American or partisanly Republican, but the style and mood were conventionally English. In his best poems—"The Wild Honey Suckle," "The Indian Burying Ground," and "The House of Night," for example —Freneau attained lyrical excellence, but it was never sustained. More characteristic was a critical debate in essay and verse between Freneau and proponents of the Connecticut Wits that occupied the pages of the New York *Daily Advertiser* in 1791. Though far inferior in quality to the countless such "literary wars" that filled the English reviews in the eighteenth century, the genre was entirely familiar. Freneau the poet was enthralled by London coffeehouses long after Freneau the republican had freed himself from London ministries.

Like Paine's, Franklin's, and many others', Freneau's American patriotism was international: the ideals he admired were the universal ones of the Enlightenment, applicable, he thought, to all men everywhere. He would have understood the underlying agreement between Franklin and Paine when, to the older man's remark that any nation where liberty dwelt was his country, Paine responded that any nation where liberty *was not* was his country—the linking of Enlightenment idealism to nationality implied both a sense of paradise and a strenuous mission. Though in a way such a posture exalted Freneau's standing as an *American* poet, it also continued his dependence on English neoclassicism. He often made the usual connections between the spread of science and reason and the new society coming into being in America, but his couplets blossomed with classical allusions, slavishly followed neoclassical conventions, and scarcely ever touched an original theme. Only in celebrating the unique opportunities in America for Enlight-

enment rationalism did he go beyond his British roots. He matched the
enthusiasm of Tom Paine for the orderliness of nature, the age of
reason, and the rights of man, and then made more explicit his sense of
a special American contribution:

> On one fix'd point all nature moves,
> Nor deviates from the track she loves;
> Her system drawn from reason's source,
> She scorns to change her wonted course.
>
> .   .   .
>
> No imperfection can be found
> In all this, above, around,—
> All, nature made, in reason's sight
> Is order all and all is right.
>
> *   *   *
>
> So shall our nation, form'd on Virtue's plan,
> Remain the guardian of the Rights of Man,
> A vast Republic, famed through every clime,
> Without a king, to see the end of time.
>
> *   *   *
>
> Joy to the day, when all agree
> On such grand systems to proceed,
> From fraud, design, and error free,
> And which to truth and goodness lead:
> Then persecution will retreat
> And man's religion be complete.[3]

Even in writing deistic poems Freneau remained something less than
the bard of the American spirit he so fervently wanted to be. His
"religious" poetry is indistinguishable from, often inferior to, and
clearly derivative of the works of dozens of English poets in the
tradition of Alexander Pope. The neoclassical vogue indeed remained
so vigorous through the first third of the nineteenth century that
Pope's *Essay on Man* went through 105 editions in the United States

between 1790 and 1830, and American poets unable to rise above imitating him had difficulty gaining either critical or popular acclaim.[4]

Freneau's life (1752–1832) illustrates the perilous currents that swirled about a man of letters during the Revolutionary era. He began, unsuccessfully, to publish poems the year he graduated from college. At the same time he considered a career as a schoolteacher, clergyman, or lawyer—all considered, one suspects, as ways of making a living that would allow him to be a writer and poet. During the Revolution he sought poetic refuge in the West Indies, fought as a militiaman in New Jersey, went to sea as third mate on a privateer, languished on a British prison ship, and edited a fervently anti-British newspaper. He turned from the lyrical nature verses written in the West Indies to the patriotic odes of the 1780s, for which he gained some fame and the title "Poet of the American Revolution." The infusion of politics into his verse, however, made his writing more didactic and less poetic. After some years as a sea captain Freneau returned to political journalism, first in New York and then in Philadelphia where, with the encouragement of Jefferson and Madison, he edited the zealously Republican *National Gazette* (1791–1793) For this vigorous partisanship Washington dubbed the editor "that rascal Freneau," while Jefferson declared that "his paper has saved our constitution which was galloping fast into monarchy." In any case Freneau became more a propagandist than a poet and discovered again, when the newspaper went bankrupt during the terrible yellow fever epidemic of 1793, how hard it was to earn a living with his pen. Thereafter he lived most of the time on his New Jersey farm, editing country newspapers and writing widely published poems and essays, but nonetheless generally poor and neglected.

Freneau was frustrated as a poet because he could not free himself from the influence of a British literary tradition that by 1776 had lost its creativity and was ill-suited to the new, *American* themes he so much wanted to express; because the lure to lend his pen to political purposes, laudable and doubtless useful in a public sense (as Jefferson testified), was harmful to the quality of his poetry; and because the American public, preoccupied with politics and intent on fulfilling a vast continent, simply did not feel a need to patronize or even respect its native men of letters. The limitations so evident in Freneau's career were the general causes of the low state of American literature during his lifetime.[5]

II

Other American writers struggled with the same difficulties, many surmounting some of them to some degree, but, before the time of Cooper, Melville, Hawthorne, Poe, and the Transcendentalists, no talent of the first rank appeared. Royall Tyler's play *The Contrast* (1787), was based on an upper-class hero-defends-heroine situation in post-Revolutionary New York and showed the superiority of the honest, democratic American over the artful European aristocrat. It developed as well the character of a practical, homespun Yankee, Jonathan, who was in many ways the real hero of the play. But Tyler followed slavishly the spirit and style of popular stage comedies by Sheridan and Goldsmith, and except for the American setting and the character of Jonathan, *The Contrast* was entirely English. Tyler advertised that his play was "the first essay of American genius in a difficult species of composition," and had a prologue speaker proclaim that

> Our Author pictures not from foreign climes
> The fashions, or the follies of the times;
> But has confin'd the subject of his work
> To the gay scenes—the circles of New York.

Yet the very form of the proclamation (heroic couplets) and every other device and convention of the play were derivative. Even the noble American hero, Colonel Manly, seems to hope only that the United States will come to exemplify all the conventional refinements and courtesies of the Old World. Though Tyler produced a play *set* in America, he did not give Americans a drama that would illuminate their national character.[6]

Hugh Henry Brackenridge (1748–1816) and Charles Brockden Brown (1771–1810), rightly regarded as the first American novelists, displayed much the same shortcomings. Brackenridge proclaimed in his *United States Magazine* (1779) an intention to show that Americans were not "so many Ouran-Outans of the wood [but were] . . . able to cultivate the belles lettres, even disconnected with Great Britain." As with his Princeton classmate, Freneau, however, public life repeatedly distracted Brackenridge from his literary efforts: much of his energy went into being a propagandist, a politician, and a judge. In his best work, *Modern Chivalry*, a long satirical novel in the mode of Cervantes published serially over a period of twenty-three years, Brackenridge commented scathingly on the deficiencies and vulgarities of republican America. He wrote solely of the scene in the United States, and he meant both to reveal realities of American society and to urge a more refined way of life on his compatriots, but his polemical intent overshadowed his literary achievement. His leading character, Captain Farrago, and his servant, Teague, resembled Don Quixote and Sancho Panza in prototype if not in biography, and Brackenridge's conventions, such as the stupid Irishman and the man of culture disdaining boorish peasants, had long been staples of English literature. Brackenridge revealed nothing profound or scarcely even indigenous about American character.[7]

Brown published a half-dozen notable novels between 1798 and 1800. He wrote skillfully in the English Gothic tradition exemplified by Walpole and William Godwin, but managed to bring American themes and contexts into his novels. In the preface to one of his best, *Edgar Huntly, or, Memoirs of a Sleep-walker* (1799), Brown declared his desire "to exhibit a series of adventures growing out of the condition of our country," to set aside the "puerile superstition and exploded manners, Gothic castles and chimeras" of European novels, and to use instead "the incidents of Indian hostility, and the perils of the western wilderness" as more suitable themes for an American literature. In *Alcuin, a Dialogue* (1798), following Mary Wollstonecraft, he defended the rights of women by asking that Enlightenment ideals of social justice be applied to their degraded condition, thus implying that in republican America immemorial inequities and stultifications could at last be overcome. Ironically, the simple, undramatic quality of American life seemed often to be an obstacle to the novelist. As Brown explained through a character in *Ormond* (1799) who had lived on both sides of the Atlantic:

I found that the difference between Europe and America lay chiefly in this: that in the former, all things tended to extremes, whereas in the latter, all things tended toward the same level. Genius, and virtue, and happiness, on these shores, were distinguished by a sort of mediocrity. Conditions were less unequal, and men were strangers to the heights of enjoyment and the depths of misery to which the inhabitants of Europe are accustomed.

Such plainness hardly spawned poems and novels likely to suit tastes used to the pathos and chivalry of European romance.[8]

Brown nonetheless wrote on, avoiding the explicit, didactic compulsion to be American, and helped develop a literature that would be intrinsically worthy as well as indigenous. Before realizing the considerable promise of his brief career as a novelist, however, he fell victim to the same forces that thwarted Freneau. He failed to gain the critical acclaim or popularity from his countrymen that could earn him a living as a man of letters, he felt compelled to edit (and write) an American literary journal, and he found his energy drained by political pamphleteering.

Another problem was that Brown's writings, and nearly all other American efforts in *belles-lettres* in the first decades of the nineteenth century, were overwhelmed by the vogue of Sir Walter Scott—a half-million volumes of his works were sold in the United States before 1823, far exceeding the total sale of all American fiction writers. Scott's stories of romance, history, legend, adventure, patriotism, and feudalism captivated the American imagination. Only a few cross-grained reviewers complained that Scott had "a diseased and perverted taste for the luxurious and aristocratic" that ill-suited the readers of a republic. Though they could scarcely deny Scott's genius, they could and did condemn the "habit of servile imitation" that caused thirty-five Southern towns to be named "Waverley." In 1842 Charles Dickens even found a Choctaw Indian who could recite whole sections of *The Lady of the Lake*. Why, James Kirke Paulding asked, should Americans abide such a ludicrous sight as that of their own noble aborigines mouthing feudal sentimentalities? Rather, "the peculiarities of [American] character, the motives which produced the resolution to emigrate to the wilderness, the courage with which they consumated this gallant enterprise, and the wild and terrible peculiarities of their intercourse, their adventures, and their contests with the savages," Paulding declared, were "amply sufficient for all those higher works of imagination" he so earnestly wanted Americans to write.[9]

Yet, for all his self-conscious nationalism, Paulding was more a victim of the vogue of Scott than a victor over it. Twenty years of polemics with scornful British critics so occupied him that his own talent failed to mature into a work of literature capable of confounding the English reviewers. He so much admired the nationalism and use of historical materials that characterized Scott's work that he wanted Americans to do likewise in an American context. But the spell of the master was too strong. Americans attempting to write in this vein— William Wirt and John Pendleton Kennedy, for example—could write of American circuit riders or Patrick Henry or Southern plantations, but their style was still so derivative that they often seemed to be merely substituting American names and places for British. The values, the attitudes toward life, and the social conventions remained somehow foreign and incongruous. Paulding's own writing, in such works as *Letters from the South* and *Westward Ho!*, was so infused with a sentimentalized Southern ethic actually borrowed from Scott's celebrations of chivalry that Paulding deserved to be called "A Northern Man of Southern Principles." Though he hated Northern materialism and was a Jacksonian democrat in politics, Paulding did not even begin to be the genuinely American, profoundly indigenous writer he and his fellow literary nationalists wanted so much to call forth and acclaim.[10]

"Surely the descendants of Englishmen in America are not absolutely degenerate," a discouraged Boston critic wrote in 1806. Why, then, did American authors do so little "to spread the glory of the English language?" "We may say that we have spice ships at the Philippines, and that our cannon has echoed among ice islands at either pole," he noted, but "we boast of no epic, tragedy, comedy, elegies, poems, pastoral or amatory, but this field is all desert, a wide African sand garden, showing brambles, and rushes, and reeds." Cultivated men of letters felt the anguish of not being able to fulfill the Revolution with works of art as well as with material accomplishments.[11]

III

The best American writer of this period, Washington Irving, accomplished what in retrospect seems about all that was possible in the insecure, too-self-conscious literary climate of the early nineteenth century. Using the Addisonian style with skill and charm, Irving wrote easily and even brilliantly on American themes in his *Knicker-bocker's History of New York* and *The Sketchbook*. His handling of this witty, urbane mood gained him recognition in England, and by writing of the Hudson Valley he familiarized thousands of readers with an American landscape and folklore. He declared that "never need an American look beyond his own country for the sublime and beautiful of natural scenery" and he poked fun at "the comparative importance and swelling magnitude of many English travellers" who looked condescendingly at Americans. At the same time, he admired a "Europe . . . rich in the accumulated treasures of age." Irving's ambivalence, comfortable as he himself was with it, often compromised his art. *The Alhambra*, for example, a romance set in Spain, was contrived and ill executed, and his biography of George Washington was stilted and lifeless, hardly an epic worthy of the hero or a fitting display to the world of the character of the nation he had founded. Irving was a mature author, capable of describing scenes and personalities with a wit and deftness admirable in any age, and fully deserving his fame on both sides of the Atlantic, but he remained always a skilled craftsman of the English language rather than a master artist of the American spirit.[12]

Writing the year before Emerson's 1837 "American Scholar" address, Edgar Allan Poe noted the two unhappy stages through which American literature had suffered and indicated the path toward maturity it was so soon to achieve. "There was a time," Poe wrote, thinking of the first generation after independence, "when we cringed to foreign opinion—let us even say when we paid a most servile deference to British critical dicta." A work by an American was approved "only after repeated assurances from England that such productions were not altogether contemptible." There was, Poe thought, "a slight basis of reason for a subservience so grotesque." During that period American writing was indeed poor compared to that of a great age of English literature. Given the comparative political and cultural circumstances, the dependent state of American writing seemed inevitable and perhaps even useful, since literary productions were measured against "a supremacy rarely questioned but by prejudice or ignorance." But even more dreary was the next stage, heralded by Paulding's *The Diverting History of John Bull and Brother Jonathan* (1812), a slashing reply to British criticism. Americans, Poe wrote, became "boisterous and arrogant in the pride of a too speedily assumed literary freedom. We throw off, with the most presumptuous and unmeaning hauteur, *all* deference whatever to foreign opinion. . . . We thus often find ourselves involved in the gross paradox of liking a stupid book the better, because, sure enough, its stupidity is American." In focusing too overtly and too narrowly on the *Americanness* of a poem or a novel, Poe insisted, native critics destroyed both their canons of judgment and the possibility of American writers' achieving really valued works of art. "We forget, in the puerile inflation of vanity, that *the world* is the true theatre of the *biblical histrio*—we get up a hue and cry about the necessity of encouraging native writers of merit—we blindly fancy that we can accomplish this by indiscriminate puffing of good, bad, and indifferent, without taking the trouble to consider that what we choose to denominate encouragement is thus, by its general application, rendered precisely the reverse."[13]

A great American literature could not be cajoled, proclaimed, or defined into existence—it had to *arise*, at once worthy in its own right and measuring up to standards recognized the world around. It would then be esteemed as profoundly *national* as the writings of Shakespeare, Cervantes, Pushkin, Goethe, Tagore, or Kawabata—but it would at the same time have universality. The delineations of American character that would come with Cooper's evocation of the pioneer in the wilderness, Hawthorne's revelation of Puritanism, Melville's insight into ambition and egotism, Thoreau's portrayal of nature and individuality, and Whitman's celebration of American vigor and diversity succeeded in revealing to mankind what the human species in the United States was like and what its contributions might be. In the period before 1820, though, American literature simply failed, as Poe explained so painfully, to offer such depth of insight.

18. American Art

I

EVEN MORE THAN THE WRITERS, AMERICAN ARTISTS FOUND IT DIF-
FICULT TO ACHIEVE AN INDEPENDENCE FROM GREAT BRITAIN THAT
WOULD ENCOURAGE A PECULIARLY AMERICAN STYLE AND AT THE
SAME TIME MEASURE UP TO HIGH AESTHETIC STANDARDS. BENJAMIN WEST
(1738–1820), though American-born, received much of his training in
Europe and took up residence in England to find stimulation and
patronage. He was, therefore, an American artist only in the technical-
ity of his birth, and his work contributed virtually nothing to the
expression of American character and nationality in the visual arts.
Even West's role as a teacher of American painters, important as it
was for their artistic growth, had the effect, since he was largely
European in his own themes and techniques, of training them in conventions in many ways alien to the New World.

The same pattern generally holds for Gilbert Stuart (1755–1828),
though he did work most of the time in the United States and did find
an ample patronage there for the hundreds of portraits he painted in
the last thirty years of his life. Trained in Britain before the Revolution and a "neutralist" who fled to England during the war in order to
pursue his craft (which he did successfully), Stuart returned to the
United States about 1792 for exactly the same reason: to earn a living
painting. His art, therefore, though attaining excellence in fresh, lively
portraiture, reveals very little about a fledgling American culture and

made no significant contribution toward defining its peculiar thrusts or meaning.

John Singleton Copley (1738–1815) achieved notable success as a portrait painter in Boston before the Revolution, and his paintings have a realistic, perhaps even indigenously American, quality, but caught between Whig and Tory animosities in 1775, he moved permanently to England where, consciously rejecting his distinctive traits, he mastered the techniques of West, Gainsborough, and other English painters.

Two other artists, John Trumbull (1756–1843) and Charles Willson Peale (1741–1827), contended much more directly with their new nationality. Though strongly tied to colonial painting traditions and trained in London under West, each returned to America eager to portray the events and personalities of the Revolution on canvas. Trumbull sought, he said, to be the "graphic historiographer" of the new nation. Influenced by West, he painted large, stirring scenes such as "The Death of General Montgomery," "Bunker's Hill," "The Surrender of Cornwallis," and "The Declaration of Independence." These works showed considerable talent and received wide acclaim in the United States, but a warning by Trumbull's patriotic father, Governor Jonathan Trumbull of Connecticut, advising his son to become a lawyer rather than an artist, bespoke the central problem: "You appear to forget, sir, that Connecticut is not Athens." Trumbull failed to receive the patronage he felt was his due, and as his capacities declined in old age, his energies were more and more dissipated in efforts to found and dominate an American academy of the arts. He thought, perhaps not without reason, that his work and that of other American artists ought to receive support like that enjoyed by Reynolds, West, and others in London. When this was not forthcoming, he became embittered and discouraged about the future of the visual arts in the nation to which he had returned with such enthusiasm in the 1780s. Like Samuel F. B. Morse, he had believed that American art would share in the millennial hopes of the Revolution. Morse supposed "a golden age is in prospect, and art is probably destined to again revive as in the fifteenth century," and that he himself might be "among those who shall . . . rival the genius of a Raphael, a Michel Angelo, or a Titian." The failure of such dreams to materialize revealed both the foolishness of exhorting art into existence and the enormous obstacles confronting the establishment of even a modestly respectable artistic tradition in America.[1]

II

Charles Willson Peale nonetheless undertook vigorously to exalt art in America and to exalt America through the arts. As a child of the Enlightenment, he saw art, science, society, nationality, religion, and philosophy as parts of a rational world view, harmonious, reflecting the order of nature, and altogether pointing toward a life of freedom, dignity, and progress for mankind. Peale was the artist of this outlook, just as Franklin was its sage, Jefferson its statesman, Rush its physician, Paine its pamphleteer, and Freneau its poet. Alike they considered that the United States had a supreme opportunity to rest society on rational precepts and expected its people to show in their character the traits admired by the Age of Reason. Insofar as art could promote the ideals of the Enlightenment, and these ideals become guideposts for the new nation, Peale was *the* American artist.

After studying in London, Peale returned to enlist in the Revolution. He fought at White Plains and Trenton, and he found time to paint at least forty portraits at Valley Forge. Later in the war he painted portraits of most of the leading generals and politicians and also participated in Philadelphia's radical politics. Thus committed publicly, he developed an eclectic, republicanized aesthetic. Though he sought patronage and fees in the conventional way from wealthy people, he sought as well to *popularize* art—both to bring art to the people and to derive from them a support that would release artists from their traditional dependence on an aristocracy. His chief means for accomplishing this, the famous museum of art and natural history housed in Independence Hall itself, revealed Peale's view of how art, science, and nationality intertwined. He collected and preserved specimens of hundreds of flowers, birds, animals, and reptiles from all over the world (but especially from the United States), and placed them according to the orderly systems of Linnaeus and Buffon in front of numerous natural landscapes he himself painted. Mineral specimens, utensils of civilized and savage peoples, wax figures, and "arms and clothing of various nations" filled other rooms. Peale had no objection to his thousands of visitors (admission was twenty-five cents, or one dollar for a yearly pass) being merely curious about the bizarre or terrifying, but he did seek also to instruct them by the rational arrangement of his exhibits and by lectures either in an assembly room or as groups walked around the museum. He himself often greeted visitors, explained the exhibits enthusiastically, and occasionally spotting an especially curious youth, would talk to him at length about the joys of art and science. A gallery of one hundred or more portraits of distinguished Americans by Peale and his sons added an element of deliberate patriotism. Peale's excavation, assembly, and exhibition in 1801 of the bones of a mammoth, or mastodon, ten feet high and fifteen feet long, excited the nation and the world, especially because it convincingly refuted Buffon's theory of animal degeneracy in the New World. This discovery, coming as it did just as a distinguished bone collector and paleontologist had been elected President of the United States, seemed to vindicate the combining of science, reason, and republicanism as the foundation of American nationality. "A knowledge of the wonderful and various beauties of Nature," Peale wrote Jefferson, was "more powerful to humanize the mind, promote harmony, and aid virtue, than any other school yet imagined."[2]

Better than any other American artist, Peale understood both the opportunities and the limitations imposed by trying deliberately to adjust art, traditionally associated only with privileged leisure classes, to the circumstances of a republic. He lacked the talent, the training, and the nourishment of an aesthetic tradition that made West, Copley, and Stuart his technical superiors as artists, and he understood less well than Trumbull the value of a sophisticated patronage, but he did perceive his novel situation in a new world among a new people. He wanted *the people* to appreciate and learn from art, science, and nature—in Peale's aesthetics, parts of a harmonious whole, not concepts in tension. He regretted that this goal sometimes resulted in pandering to popular tastes or even vulgarity, but he endured such things serenely, trusting that the tastes of the people, as they gained in wisdom, would rise and thus encourage ever higher standards for artists. Peale's persistent gadgeteering (he invented a stove and a polygraph, and designed a bridge and General Washington's dentures), like Franklin's and Jefferson's, was characteristically American, showing the tendency to merge "art" and technology in the interests of utility. Altogether Peale's career and aesthetic theory had little to do with, in fact perhaps even discouraged, the creation of great works of art, but his varied efforts display the pervasive impact of a new nationality on every aspect of its life. Art, like religion, science, and literature, was to enhance the growth of an American culture and character and to receive its distinctive mark from the new nationality.

III

By 1820, then, the attempt to realize a new American character appropriate for the new nation had yielded uncertain and uneven results. The strongest theme was overt and political: a new nation founded on republican principles never before fully tested, would, it seemed clear, have to possess unique characteristics to begin with and would surely exhibit more remarkable qualities as it worked out its special genius and destiny. This sense dominated all aspects of American thought for generations after the Declaration of Independence. Since the crucial fact was the political entity created between 1774 and 1789, speculation about the character and future of the American people had a public orientation. Individual growth and social maturation were thought to result from benign laws and institutions. The dreams and hopes of Benjamin Rush, Noah Webster, the Adamses, and others were tied to *political* programs—national academies, copyright laws, and diplomatic moves, for example. Barlow and Stiles likewise supposed that liberated public opinion would be mobilized by government to introduce the millennium. Unlettered William Manning proposed a *political* society for informing and organizing the common people that would fulfill the republican experiment. Crèvecoeur's celebration of the opportunities for immigrants in America and Jefferson's emphasis on "mild" government, though not positive programs, emphasized the *kind* of government exercising authority. Andrew the Hebridean and Jefferson's yeoman farmer fulfilled human potentials because *their* political society made that possible in a way most others did not. Even those who abhorred the course of events in the United States, such as Fisher Ames and John Taylor of Carolina, blamed the government and offered contrary political philosophies as the way out.

Thus it was that the most creative, influential considerations of the nation's character were one way or another proposals for law and public policy. The Jeffersonian and Hamiltonian visions for the nation's future, freighted as they were with conceptions of worthy personal qualities, were nonetheless political programs. Each saw the spirit and character of the new nation depending upon encouragement by law of this or that institution or occupation or foreign connection. The genius of Gallatin and Marshall was their ability to sustain postures of government that would bring into being a society of a particular quality. Overwhelmingly, it seemed that the meaning of the American experiment was tied closely to the impact of its republicanism. Foreign travelers again and again remarked on the relationship between the lives of the people and the nature of their government—a connection so critical that Tocqueville was transfixed by it when he wrote his classic interpretation of American society. Even the most egregious incongruities of American republicanism—the continued existence of black slavery and the iniquitous racial attitudes that sustained it—were founded on *political* compromise and clearly in part required political action for their elimination.

From these basically political speculations there emerged, often indirectly, some fort of consensus on what the essential features, the character, of the new nation and its citizens were. Following the observations of Crèvecoeur, Franklin, and others in the 1780s, it became increasingly clear that the essence was embodied in traits encouraged in the lives of the ordinary citizen. For the first time a nation was to receive its identity not from the splendor of a court, the courage of an army, the beauty of a capital, the devotion of saints, or the life-style of an aristocracy, but from a way of life shared by most of the people. America meant farmers able to enjoy the fruits of their own labor, merchants able to gain (or lose) a fortune in developing a continent, citizens exercising sway over the direction of government (as occurred in Jefferson's election in 1801), religion spreading across the land on its own merit and vitality rather than under government auspices, and the simple, priceless probability that a man by his own effort and ingenuity would be able to live a life of dignity and self-respect. Thus equality, self-reliance, practical skills, productivity, social cooperation, and other qualities associated with the ordinary citizen, rather than traits reserved for a few spectacular personages, became the hallmarks of American character.

Propitious as this was for the farmer or artisan, it seemed a mixed blessing at best for sophisticated Americans accustomed to European standards of "high culture." What of art, literature, "society," beauty, and science in the United States? To those with this anxiety, Sidney

Smith's taunt of 1820 was humiliating: "In the four quarters of the globe, who reads an American book? or goes to an American play? or looks at an American picture or statue? What does the world yet owe to American physicians or surgeons? What new substances have their chemists discovered? or old ones have they analyzed? What new constellations have been discovered by the telescopes of Americans?— what have they done in mathematics?" Though American achievements in the century to come would be substantial in these fields, in 1820 the new nation had not yielded much of value according to traditional standards of cultural greatness. To take a respectable place in the world as it was two generations after independence, the United States had to persuade mankind not so much that the old standards of national greatness were wrong, or that the United States fully measured up to them, but that new standards, more relevant to the everyday life of the people, should be added. It was in realizing these new dimensions that America found its meaning and that its people received their character in the "opinion of mankind" to which Jefferson had appealed in 1776.[3]

V

The American Mind

I

I

N RENEWING CORRESPONDENCE with John Adams in 1812, Jefferson's mind was carried "back to the times when, beset with difficulties and dangers, we were fellow laborers in the same cause, struggling for what is most valuable to man, his right of self-government." The retired President at Monticello noted that he and the retired President at Quincy had "labored always at the same oar, with some wave ever ahead threatening to overwhelm us and yet passing harmless under our bark, we knew not how, [and] we rode out the storm with heart and hand, and made a happy port." After detailing the hazards and crises of each of their Presidencies, Jefferson predicted, "And so we have gone on, and so we shall go on. . . . I do believe we shall continue to grow, to multiply and prosper until we exhibit an association, powerful, wise and happy, beyond what has yet been seen by man." Looking sadly at the failure of "pre-eminence in science" to banish "tyranny, murder, rapine and destitution of national morality" in Europe, Jefferson concluded, "I would rather wish our country to be ignorant, honest and estimable as our neighboring savages are" than in a state of sophisticated decadence or tyranny. John Adams replied, agreeing that "your life and mine for almost half a century have been nearly all of a Piece," and adding, as he winced at threats of disunity in New England at the approach of the War of 1812, that "the Union is to me an object of as much anxiety as ever Independence was."[1]

Almost four years later, as Adams observed the reactionary decisions of the Congress of Vienna, he asked, "When will the Rights of mankind and the Liberties and Independence of Nations be respected?" Reflecting more generally on the cycles of history, Adams declared that "the Eighteenth Century, notwithstanding all its Errors and Vices has been, of all that are past, the most honourable to human Nature. Knowledge and Virtues were increased and diffused, Arts, Sciences useful to Men, ameliorating their condition, were improved, more than in any former equal period." Now, it seemed, "the Nineteenth Century [sought] to extinguish all the lights of its Predecessor." Jefferson agreed with all Adams' "eulogies on the 18th century." "The sciences and arts, manners and morals, [had] advanced to a higher degree than the world had ever before seen. . . . To the great honour of science and the arts," Jefferson added, was their "natural effect" of, "by illuminating public opinion, to erect it into a Censor, before which the most exalted tremble for their future, as well as present fame." Though Jefferson accepted all of Adams' strictures on the regressions and tumult of the Napoleonic era, he nonetheless had faith that the "glimmering of their rights and their power" experienced by the people could not be erased and that "the idea of representative government had taken root and growth among them."[2]

Speculation on the prospects of freedom and republican government in the world led Adams and Jefferson to their most congenial subject, reflection on the nature and meaning of the American Revolution. Adams reiterated his idea that the real revolution was that effected "in the Minds of the People . . . from 1760 to 1775." Jefferson thought that it was as difficult to fix the moment when the Revolution began "as to fix the moment that the embryo becomes an animal." Adams replied that "in my opinion it began as early as the first plantation of the Country." They agreed, though, that the "external facts," however faithfully recorded, could never reveal "the life and soul of history" that had happened in the United States during their lifetimes. Jefferson accused an Italian historian of the Revolution of putting "his own speculations and reasonings into the mouths" of the American leaders, and he labeled John Marshall's huge biography of Washington a mere "party diatribe." The two philosopher-statesmen were sure that the purpose and character of the new society they had helped to bring into being in America were complex in their origins, unprecedented in human history, and full of meaning for the future. The

contours of "the idea of representative government," the arguments
that surrounded it, and its impact in all areas of thought and culture,
they thought, delineated the history of the American mind during the
years 1750–1820.[3]

. Long life, a position at the center of events, and a philosophizing
tendency placed Adams and Jefferson in a unique position for experi-
encing and understanding what had happened during those years. Jefferson agreed with a young Southern abolitionist in 1814, for example,
that it was "a moral reproach" that there had been neither a significant
effort nor even a "serious willingness" to end black slavery in the
nation. His generation, accustomed to "the quiet and monotonous
course of colonial life, . . . and nursed and educated in the daily habit
of seeing the degraded condition" of slaves, assumed unquestioningly
"that they were as legitimate subjects of property as . . . horses or
cattle." Thus Jefferson felt little could be expected from old men, but
he hoped "the younger generation, receiving their early impressions
after the flame of liberty had been kindled in every breast, and had
become as it were the vital spirit of every American; . . . would have
sympathized with oppression wherever found, and proved their love
of liberty beyond their own share of it." Though the failure of Jefferson's hope and the consequent survival of black slavery demonstrated
that revolutionary rhetoric is not always effective in changing powerfully entrenched institutions, he was certain that the ideals of the new
nation were inconsistent with slavery. He felt further that there had
been a substantial shift of thought and sentiment in the country since
the "quiet and monotony" had been shattered by the Revolution. In
this sense the intellectual history of the Revolutionary era has a peculiar importance. Though compromise often characterized the course
of events, though social and economic change were often slow and
trifling, and though counterrevolutionary ideas were often expressed
and widely held, concepts of "the Rights of Mankind and the Liberties
and Independence of Nations" took shape at that time that have ever
since prodded or reproved the United States and the rest of the world.
The fact that those unjustly treated have generally in American history pleaded simply that the nation live up to the ideals of 1776 is
perhaps the surest testimony to the intellectual vitality of the Revolutionary and nation-building generations.[4]

II

To grasp the remarkable changes in American thought during the years 1750–1820 one need only notice the *range* of transformations that took place. The revolution in loyalty, for example, required a substantial discarding of immemorial, deeply held, profoundly important attitudes, attachments, and values that taken together added up to English nationality. Whether one looked to religious rituals, to literary conventions, to geopolitical axioms, to means of government, or to aesthetic tastes, the pattern in 1750 was the same: the English colonies were both *English* and *colonies*. Britons in North America could scarcely perceive themselves except as compatriots of Addison, Pitt, and Whitefield. The British flag, the seal of the Crown, and the power of the Royal Navy were at once the symbols and the reality of the English nationality of the colonials. The process described in Part II, wherein John Adams and Benjamin Franklin threw off their English loyalty, the followers of Jonathan Edwards awakened their listeners to the blessings of a transcending union, and the controversy over British authority in the colonies generated new conceptions (or at least clearer perceptions) of the meaning of self-government, began the decolonizing of the American psyche and the American mind. By 1776 the colonies had divested enough of their British loyalty to be ready for, indeed, in need of, new accoutrements. To have come to such a state had required traumatic change.

Then, the no-longer-Britons had to formulate their own national purposes. The proclamations of *Common Sense* and the phrases of the Declaration of Independence about "unalienable rights," the just powers of government, the need for "consent," and the right to resist tyranny set forth the basic purposes, but they were the beginning, not the end, of a process of self-conscious "goal formation." Though Paine, Jefferson, Adams, and others derived their ideas from a rich heritage of classical, English Whig, and libertarian thought, they had the further challenge of implanting them in frames of government. Stimulated by this unprecedented opportunity of deciding whether government could derive, in Hamilton's words, from "reflection and choice" rather than from "accident and force," first the several states and then the federal union adopted constitutions. In state after state publicists filled the newspapers with speculations about and projections of the basic propositions of government: Could the republican form instill virtue? How could the government be made truly responsible to the people? Were representatives to act for special interests or for the public good? How could executive power be exercised in a republic? Could enlarged powers be safely entrusted to a national government resting on the people? And so on. In debating these questions, and in devising constitutions embodying answers to them, Americans not only greatly enhanced their understanding of their purposes in throwing off British rule, but they also exposed practically every future prospect and difficulty of republican government. In the discussions at the Constitutional Convention of 1787, and in the ratification controversy that followed, a sustained concern for the direction the new nation would take vied with the compromises compelled by competing interests in molding the government. After approval of the Bill of Rights by the first Congress under the Constitution in September 1789, in a formal sense at least the new nation had set forth its national purposes.

But this was by no means enough. Somehow the nation still had to *become* something. It had to have a character, a way of life, an approach to civilization that would both distinguish it among the peoples of the world and fulfill in rich color the design of the Declaration and the Constitution. It was necessary to conceive and then work toward a political economy, a moral philosophy, and a social system that would give substance to the new structures. Jefferson proposed a yeoman society depending on grass-roots impulses to guide a "mild" government manned by an "aristocracy of talent and virtue," while Hamilton advocated a dynamic, commercial nation led by vigorous men whose entrepreneurial genius and sense of the public good would result in a prosperous society useful to all its members and able to play an active role on the international stage. Within each conception were postulates about personal virtue, the good society, and the distinctive dynamic of the new nation. Jefferson and Hamilton bespoke visions of the national future that in profound but opposed ways could give the United States the meaning and character as a nation it so earnestly, sometimes pathetically, sought. It seemed as well that the Union might transcend the differences and somehow derive both virtue and vitality from the coexistence within it of the two conceptions.

The varieties of cultural experience within the new nation further underscored how complex, difficult, and mysterious it was to achieve a national character. In religious life, where changes in organization and in the experience of spiritual insight could have a profound effect, the emergence of new national patterns was relatively swift and meaningful. The evangelical churches preached that a moral and spiritual transformation had to be at the center of the new national character, not through the authority of an established and hierarchical church but through the personal rebirth of all the people. In science, on the other hand, which required a sophistication and a specialization difficult to sustain in a still rough society, the results were disappointing. Social science failed, too, in a way, when Enlightenment confidence that the Indians could be made over ("civilized") into yeoman farmers instead merely added to the frontier pressures steadily extinguishing Indian culture. In a further irony the wave of Revolutionary idealism favorable to the rights of black men receded in the first decades of the nineteenth century under pressure from economic imperatives and a depth of white prejudice unrecognized before the institution of slavery itself was seriously challenged. In this area, at least, the intellectual impact of the Revolution was at best a legacy of unfinished business, and at worst a replacement of unquestioned acceptance of an institution with a more explicit theory of racial superiority as blacks demanded recognition as men, not property.

At the same time, the painful, self-conscious effort to bring into being a national art and a national literature floundered in the face of a debilitating inferiority complex, a national preoccupation with "more practical tasks," and an utterly inadequate understanding of the patronage, the institutional encouragement, and the reciprocal stimulation required in those areas. American writers and artists knew that they had to gain cultural independence from Europe and to express the genius of their own land rather than, for example, slavishly follow the romantic conventions of Sir Walter Scott, but the images and metaphors from the New World experience that would inform the creative impulse simply had not worked deeply and distinctively enough on America's artists as yet. Characteristically, perhaps, the most significant publication by an American writer during the years 1789–1820 was Franklin's *Autobiography*, the record not of a grand hero on the scale of Frederick the Great or Napoleon, or of an elegant writer like Milton or Pope, but of a man whose achievement was to offer a life-style at once humble and of great integrity. The acclaim accorded this autobiography seemed to say that America was to *be-*

come a land whose meaning was at that level, whose character was to be found in the habits of Poor Richard and other ordinary citizens, rather than in the adventures of the mighty. Furthermore, given the preoccupation of talents on the order of those of Franklin, Jefferson, and Adams, it is not surprising that the notable achievements are in moral and public philosophy rather than in artistic or literary creativity. The great works of the American imagination would not come until the generation of Hawthorne and Melville and Poe, of Thoreau and Whitman, but the foundation they needed had been built: an ingenious polity that would release new human energies and insure freedom for growth.

III

A comparison of Franklin's *Observations concerning the Increase of Mankind* written in 1751 (see Chap. 1), and President James Madison's last Annual Messages to Congress delivered in December of 1815 and 1816 reveals that during those sixty-five years what had changed was not the general sense of a unique potential for the people of North America but the perception of what laws, institutions, and habits would help realize that potential. Franklin and Madison both believed, for example, that America's basic strength was a free, rapidly increasing, vigorous population spreading across a rich land. In Franklin's vision this prospect meant a vast "Accession of Power to the British Empire." English expansion in North America (sure to overwhelm tiny, stagnant French colonies and spread across the Mississippi Valley) would soon result in countless settlements of self-reliant people closely tied to the mother country by bonds of affection, trade, and self-interest. The real power, Franklin understood, inhered in the people—if they were numerous, prospering, and energetic, they would over the long run be irrepressible.[5]

Three generations later Madison not only substituted American for British sovereignty, but he grasped as well the details of how the growth had been achieved and how it could be extended in the future. To Franklin's urging, for example, that commerce and industry, as well as agriculture, be encouraged in North America, Madison added specific proposals: temporary tariffs that would give American industries started during the Napoleonic Wars a chance to gain a surer hold, a national system of finance to stimulate orderly investment, and a network of internal improvements "executed under the national authority" to supplement private and state-sponsored enterprises. In Franklinesque phrases, Madison noted that no other country in the world "presents a field where nature invites more the art of man to complete her own work for his accommodation and benefit," and that a stronger transportation system would "facilitate intercommunication" and thus "bring and bind more closely together the various parts of our extended confederacy." By 1816 the United States had expanded to the Pacific, Jackson's victory at New Orleans had defeated the last serious threat to American independence, the admission of new, equal states to the Union had applied the principle of government by consent to the new territories, and the national economy had achieved a remarkable size and diversity. Madison was even able to report, fulfilling Franklin's insight that rapid growth would overwhelm many nagging problems of the Old World, that there was "a surplus in the treasury" that would generate "an ample fund for the effectual and early extinguishment of the public debt." By the end of Madison's Presidency a nation existed that embodied in itself, that gave a dramatic sense of presentness to, Franklin's observations of 1751. Madison stated what Franklin's general anticipations meant in terms of peoples, resources, and institutions. This awareness of bursting reality and the consequent self-confidence, of course, were vital elements in American thought throughout the Revolutionary era.

Speculating on the new character and the new society coming into being in North America, Franklin argued that the availability of land and the absence of Old World restraints had not only transformed demography (the peoples of the colonies multiplied at least twice as fast as was common in Europe, he calculated), but had also transformed habits, attitudes, and self-conception. Self-reliant, hardworking families became the rule—the indolent, underemployed, dissipated, shiftless, drifting people of all classes, apparently without function in the rigid societies of Europe, were largely nonexistent in the colonies. This fecundity, impelled by a purposeful, creative way of life, in Franklin's opinion made many traditional national enterprises unwise: conquest became incongruous because it required useful workers to become destructive soldiers, made necessary a host of overseeing officials, and created in the subjugated population all the wrong qualities—subservience, irresponsibility, and sloth. Restraints on trade became unwise because they hindered the free exchange on which the new families depended for opportunity. Heavy taxes and arbitrary seizure of property, by discouraging enterprise and effort to improve one's circumstances, were similarly unwise. Finally, since slavery deprived free laborers of jobs, made wasteful thieves of those held in bondage and arrogant, lazy, incompetent tyrants of those who were masters, it was in every way hostile to the values and needs of a dynamic, open society.

Madison offered ways the new national government might encourage the qualities Franklin saw emerging in the society of the New World. He recommended vigorous American support of international action to suppress the slave trade from Africa. He labeled "unworthy" those Americans who colluded in any way to sustain the "great evil" of this now forbidden traffic. Furthermore, he spoke favorably of "the encouraging progress" among many Indian tribes in "the culture and improvement of the soil," a sign they were making "a transit from the habits of the savage to the arts and comforts of social life." Though Madison was painfully aware that in 1816 blacks and Indians were the ill-treated outcasts of American society, he was aware as well that a government resting on the Declaration of Independence had no choice but to seek the end of slavery and a fair participation of all peoples in what he unhesitatingly regarded as the supreme virtues of a yeoman republic. He sought additionally to sustain republican virtue by establishing a "national seminary of learning [dedicated to] . . . the advancement of knowledge, without which the blessings of liberty cannot be fully enjoyed or long preserved." Such a seminary would nourish and spread "those national feelings, those liberal sentiments, and those congenial manners, which contribute cement to our Union and strength to the great political fabric of which that is the foundation." The willy-nilly, half-formed contours of New World society Franklin had noted became for Madison circumstances to be sustained by the powers of a national government that had no other reason for existence. The creation of a political instrument able to serve that purpose had in fact been the major preoccupation of the American mind during the Revolutionary era.

Nothing, in fact, better illustrated the maturing of national self-confidence than the transformed conception of political parties. The suspicions of the very idea of party and the near universal conviction of the baneful effects of factious politics current in the 1780s (see Part

III, Chap. 6, sec. iv) had by 1820 given way to radically revised views
of the uses of public opinion, of appeal to it by political parties, and of
the prospect for the survival of republican government itself. The
Federalists under Hamilton's direction in the 1790s, deeply skeptical of
republicanism, sought to strengthen *government* through fiscal policies tying key groups to it, by acceptance of the British commercial
system, and by adroit political manipulations to maximize support for
Washington's administration. They hoped thus to enact programs the
public would approve, but they saw only danger in appealing to public
opinion to gain support for their policies. The Republicans, on the
other hand, believed in appeals to the public and saw in them the
best, the most inherently appropriate, way to resist the Federalists,
though they did not think of this as partisan activity. In seeing the
Republicans nearly succeed in blocking Jay's Treaty by arousing
public opposition to it, the Federalists learned an unwelcome lesson.
They themselves made such an appeal in 1798 when they mobilized
public indignation over the XYZ affair to push through their war
preparation measures. Subsequently the Federalists grudgingly accepted the seemingly inexorable tendency for appeals to the public,
and they indulged when necessary, but they never reconciled this with
their elitist view of who should govern, their preference for behind-
the-scenes politics, and their deep fear that such appeals led to degeneracy and mob rule. The Republicans, on the other hand, more and
more worked out the logic of aroused public opinion, welcomed, in
theory at least, its impact on policy (through elected representatives),
and generally accepted, even in office, the irritation of having their
policies criticized and even calumniated by their opponents. Thus,
during the War of 1812 Madison fumed privately about disloyal Federalist obstruction, but he never sought repressive measures similar to
the Alien and Sedition Acts. By the end of the war, regarded as a
vindication of republican government and thus a momentous victory
despite the status-quo character of the Treaty of Ghent, Jefferson
assured Lafayette that "our government is now so firmly on its republican tack, that it will not be easily monarchised by forms," a statement no one would have thought of making in 1790. Political parties,
henceforth, could be safely condoned, the press could be allowed to
criticize as it pleased, and the people could be encouraged to take
every active role in formulating and influencing public policy. In

short, the republic was secure enough to welcome the reality as well as the form of self-government.[6]

Madison was sure, then, that the vast changes he had observed in the half-century between his college days and his impending retirement from the Presidency in December 1816 in some profound way had *political* causes: the essence was "a Government pursuing the public good as its sole object, . . . a Government which watches over the purity of elections, the freedom of speech and of the press, the trial by jury, . . . a Government which avoids intrusions on the internal repose of other nations, and repels them from its own, . . . a Government, in a word, whose conduct within and without may bespeak the most noble of all ambitions—that of promoting peace on earth and good will to man." Such a government, Madison believed, had led to the "tranquillity and prosperity at home and the peace and respect abroad" the nation enjoyed in 1816, and only it could fulfill "the character of the American people." He was especially pleased that the Constitution, "the offspring of the undisturbed deliberations and the free choice" of the people, had reconciled the principles "of public strength with individual liberty, of national power for the defense of national rights with a security against wars of injustice, of ambition, and of vainglory in the fundamental provision which subjects all questions of war to the will of the nation itself, which is to pay its costs and feel its calamities." If republican government could abolish unjust, vainglorious war itself, for centuries the scourge of mankind, then, Madison argued, many lesser virtues might come easily and usher the world into an unprecedented era of human fulfillment. He saw in 1816, in short, national institutions embodying and sustaining the social qualities and individual virtues Franklin had seen arising in the New World. Madison knew as well, of course, that a multitude of unfulfillments, misconceptions, and inconsistencies clouded the landscape. An atomistic, merely material individualism pressed hard against the constructive polity intended by Jefferson as well as by Hamilton. A greedy, self-righteous expansionism paid little heed to the rights of the Indians on the Western frontier. A cultural vulgarity threatened to stifle the civilizing arts. Worst of all, slavery and race prejudice remained. The widespread recognition of these cancers, though, revealed both the transition American thought had achieved since 1750 and the unfinished agenda of the future.

IV

A sense of great change and a pregnant future was also evident during visits to Quincy by two of Jefferson's grandchildren during the last year of John Adams' life. Ellen Randolph Jefferson, newly married to Bostonian Joseph Coolidge, found the ninety-year-old man "afflicted with bodily infirmities, lame, and almost blind, but . . . as full of life as he could have been fifty years ago." Jefferson's last letter to Adams in March 1826 was delivered by Thomas Jefferson Randolph who, his grandfather wrote, "wishes to be able, in the winter nights of old age, to recount to those around him what he has heard and learnt of the Heroic age preceding his birth, and which of the argonauts particularly he was in time to have seen. It was the lot of our early years," the sage of Monticello observed, "to witness nothing but the dull monotony of colonial subservience, and of our riper ones to breast the labors and perils of working out of it. Theirs [Jefferson's grandchildren] are the Halcyon calms succeeding the storm which our Argosy had so stoutly weathered." Though the grandchildren of the old patriots lived through the scarcely "Halcyon" days of Civil War and Reconstruction, the mood of vast transitions accomplished and great fulfillments in prospect captured the central features of American thought during the Revolutionary era.[7]

More specifically to the point were Ellen Coolidge's report to her grandfather of her wedding journey north and the old man's cogent reply. Ellen was especially delighted with the trip through "the fairest and most flourishing portion of New England," the Connecticut River valley. The healthy, busy, self-reliant people, the neat farms and villages, the well-supported schools and churches, and the plain, generous manners she found everywhere seemed to her the perfect embodiment of the yeoman society she had so often heard her grandfather extoll. This seemed especially remarkable, she observed, when one remembered that the New Englander had "wrung" this virtue and prosperity "from the hard bosom of a stubborn and ungrateful land" bereft of "the immense advantages of soil and climate" possessed by her native Virginia. Only the presence of "the canker slavery" in Virginia, which "eats into the hearts and diseases the whole body by this ulcer at the core," Ellen thought, could explain the vastly greater blessings of New England society. Jefferson, of course, was delighted with his granddaughter's perceptions, despite his regret of her all-too-true comparison. He had taken the same trip through New England in 1791 with Madison, he noted, when much of the countryside was unsettled. "Now it is what 34 years of free and good government have made it. It shews how soon the labor of man would make a paradise of the whole earth, were it not for misgovernment, and a diversion of all his energies from their proper object, the happiness of man, to the selfish interests of kings, nobles, and priests." Whatever the unfinished business or the perils and disappointments the future might hold, Adams and Jefferson bespoke the dominant theme of American consciousness in the 1820s when they emphasized the redirection of human thought and energy they had witnessed in their lifetimes and the prospects this achievement held out for any people who would undertake, persistently and in good faith, to improve themselves and their society. This conviction defined the transition in loyalty, purpose, and character undergone in America from the time of Franklin's thorough Britishness of 1750 to Madison's self-confident American outlook of 1816.[8]

Notes and Bibliography

Source Notes

PART I

1. Franklin to W. Strahan, February 12, 1745 (*The Papers of Benjamin Franklin*, L. W. Labaree and others, eds., III, 13).
2. "Observations concerning the Increase of Mankind" (*Papers of Franklin*, IV, 227–230).
3. "Address of the House of Burgesses," May 8, 1769 (*The Writings of Thomas Jefferson*, Paul L. Ford, ed., I, 369); Franklin to Samuel Mather, July 7, 1773 (*The Writings of Benjamin Franklin*, A. H. Smyth, ed., 10 vols. [New York, 1905–1907], VI, 86).
4. *The American Magazine*, printed by W. Bradford, Philadelphia, March, 1758, 293–294.
5. To Lord Kames, January 3, 1760 (*Papers of Franklin*, IX, 7).
6. Felix Gilbert, *The Beginnings of American Foreign Policy* (New York, 1965), 19–32.
7. Daniel J. Boorstin, *The Americans: The Colonial Experience, passim.*
8. Brooke Hindle, *The Pursuit of Science in Revolutionary America, 1735–1789*, 11–36.
9. Carl Bridenbaugh, *Mitre and Sceptre* (New York, 1962), *passim*; Boorstin, *Colonial Experience*, 123–139.

PART II

1. Adams to Hezekiah Niles, February 13, 1818; first printed in *Nile's Weekly Register*, March 7, 1818; "Diary," July 22, 1756 (*Diary and Autobiography of John Adams*, L. H. Butterfield and others, eds., I, 36); Adams to Shelton Jones, March 11, 1809 (*The Works of John Adams*, C. F. Adams, ed., IX, 611).
2. C. P. Smith, *John Adams*, I, 32–35.
3. Adams to Thomas Jefferson, July 18, 1818 (*The Adams-Jefferson Letters*, L. J. Cappon, ed., II, 527).

4. *Diary and Autobiography of John Adams*, III, 262–275; Smith, *John Adams*, I, 52–56.
5. "Dissertation" (*The Political Writings of John Adams*, G. A. Peek, ed., 18–21); *Diary and Autobiography of John Adams*, I, 281.
6. Abigail Adams to Mercy Otis Warren, December 5, 1773, John to Abigail Adams, September 20, 1774, and July 3, 1776 (*Adams Family Correspondence*, L. H. Butterfield and others, eds., I, 88, 161; II, 28–31.

Chapter 1

1. *The Papers of Benjamin Franklin*, L. W. Labaree and others, eds., IV, 227–234.
2. Franklin to Whitefield, July 2, 1756 (*ibid.*, VI, 468–469).
3. Franklin to William Shirley, December 3, 4, and 22, 1754 (*ibid.*, V, 443–451).
4. Article signed "Pensylvanus," *Pennsylvania Journal*, supplement, March 25, 1756 (reprinted in R. L. Ketcham, ed., *The Political Thought of Benjamin Franklin* [Indianapolis, 1965], 134–138).
5. To William Franklin, February 19, 1772, and to Mary Stevenson, March 25, 1763 (*The Writings of Benjamin Franklin*, A. H. Smyth, ed., 10 vols. [New York, 1905–1907], V, 414; IV, 194).
6. To Joseph Galloway, February 17, 1758, and April 12, 1766 (*Political Thought of Franklin*, 144–145); to Isaac Norris, March 10, 1757, and Thomas Penn to Richard Peters, May 14, 1757 (*Papers of Franklin*, VIII, 291–297; VII, 110–111*n*).
7. To Joshua Babcock, January 13, 1772 (*Political Thought of Franklin*, 244–245).
8. To Joseph Priestley, July 7, 1775 (*Writings of Franklin*, VI, 408–409).
9. Winston S. Churchill, *A History of the English-Speaking Peoples: The Age of Revolution* (New York, 1957), 182.
10. Michael Kammen, *People of Paradox*, see especially 102–113, 117–148.

Chapter 2

1. Alan Heimert, *Religion and the American Mind*.
2. Heimert, *ibid.*, 33–34, cites sources for the works of Edwards quoted here.
3. *Ibid.*, 140–142.
4. Tennent, "The Danger of an Unconverted Ministry" (reprinted in Perry Miller and Alan Heimert, eds., *The Great Awakening* [Indianapolis, 1967], 72–99); Edwards, sermon on "The Church's Marriage," and *Freedom of the Will* (quoted in Heimert, *Religion and the American Mind*, 163–165).
5. Edwards, "An Humble Attempt to Promote . . . Visible Union" (1747) (reprinted in Miller and Heimert, eds., *The Great Awakening*, 566);

Noah Welles, "The Divine Right of Presbyterian Ordination Asserted" (1763) (quoted in Heimert, *Religion and the American Mind*, 119).

6. Joseph Montgomery, "Sermon Preached at Christiana Bridge . . . the 20th of July, 1775," Samuel Sherwood, "Churches Flight into the Wilderness" (1776), and David Avery, "Lord to Be Praised" (1778) (quoted in Heimert, *Religion and the American Mind*, 396, 404, 410).

7. Whitaker, "An Antidote Against Toryism" (quoted in Heimert, *Religion and the American Mind*, 504).

8. Robert B. Semple, *A History of the Rise and Progress of the Baptists in Virginia* (John Lynch: Richmond, 1810), 21–27 (Early American Imprints No. 21322).

9. Rhys Isaac, "Evangelical Social Revolt: The Challenge of the Baptists to the Traditional Order in Virginia, *c.* 1765–1775" (typescript of a paper presented at Twenty-ninth Conference on Early American History, Williamsburg, Va., March 31, 1973). This and the following two paragraphs depend heavily on Professor Isaac's paper, which he kindly loaned to the author.

10. John Leland, *The Virginia Chronicle* (1790), 26–27, and *Journal and Letters of Philip Vickers Fithian 1773–1774: A Plantation Tutor of the Old Dominion* (Charlottesville, Va.: 1968), 72 (quoted in Isaac, "Evangelical Social Revolt," 12, 18).

11. Niles, "Two Discourses on Liberty" (1774); quoted in Heimert, *Religion and the American Mind*, 514–517.

12. This and the next two paragraphs depend on Robert D. Meade, *Patrick Henry*, I, 65–74, 130–134; II, 48–50.

13. *Sibley's Harvard Graduates* (Boston, 1942), VI, 74–77; *The Life and Public Service of Samuel Adams*, W. V. Wells, ed., I, 24–25.

14. *Independent Advertiser*, March, 1749 (quoted in Wells, *Samuel Adams*, I, 17, 22); J. C. Miller, *Sam Adams, Pioneer in Propaganda*, 85, 18–19.

15. *Massachusetts Gazette*, October 29, 1767 (quoted in Miller, *Sam Adams*, 195); Heimert, *Religion and the American Mind*, 359; Adams to John Scollay, April 30, 1776, and to Samuel Savage, October 6, 1778 (*The Writings of Samuel Adams*, H. A. Cushing, ed., 4 vols. [New York, 1904–1908], III, 286; IV, 67–68); E. S. Morgan, "The Puritan Ethic and the American Revolution," *William and Mary Quarterly*, XXIV, 27–28, 1967.

16. *Peter Oliver's Origin and Progress of the American Rebellion*, Douglass Adair and J. A. Schutz, eds., 41; *Diary of William Bentley*, 4 vols. (Salem, Massachusetts, 1905–1914), III, 49.

17. Chauncy, "Ministers Exhorted . . . to Take Heed to Themselves" (1744), and Mayhew, "Seven Sermons" (1749) (quoted in Heimert, *Religion and the American Mind*, 175, 177).

18. Rush letter of 1800 (*The Letters of Benjamin Rush*, L. H. Butterfield, ed., II, 799, 820–821); quoted in Heimert, *Religion and the American Mind*, 529.

19. This and the two following paragraphs from Mayhew, "Discourse . . ." (1750) in Bernard Bailyn, ed., *The Pamphlets of the American Revolution, 1750–1765,* 215–247.

Chapter 3

1. Bernard Bailyn, "Introduction," *The Pamphlets of the American Revolution,* 29–31.
2. Loudoun to Lord Halifax, December 26, 1756, and to William Hardy, September 16, 1756 (quoted in Stanley Pargellis, *Lord Loudoun in North America* [New Haven, 1933], 183–185); Lord Dunmore, "Proclamation," May 13, 1775 (quoted in R. D. Meade, *Patrick Henry,* I, 338–339).
3. "Silence Dogood," No. 9 (*The Papers of Benjamin Franklin,* L. W. Labaree and others, eds., I, 30–32); Leonard Levy, *Legacy of Suppression: Freedom of Speech and Press in Early American History,* 118–119, 130–131; Milton Klein, ed., *The Independent Reflector* (Cambridge, 1963), 21–28, 365, 450–454.
4. Bailyn, "Introduction," *Pamphlets,* 81; G. Steiner, ed., *Korrespondenz des Peter Ochs* (Basil, 1927), I, 102, 104 (quoted in R. R. Palmer, *The Age of Democratic Revolution,* I, 242).
5. Bailyn, "Introduction," *Pamphlets,* 91–99.
6. *Ibid.,* 99–115.
7. Hicks, "The Nature and Extent of Parlimentary Power Considered . . ." (Philadelphia, 1768); (Merrill Jensen, ed., *Tracts of the American Revolution, 1763–1776* [Indianapolis, 1967], 170–173).
8. Bailyn, "Introduction," *Pamphlets,* 131–138.
9. Sidney's *Discourses,* Locke's *Second Treatise,* and Gordon's *Works of Tacitus,* all quoted in Pauline Maier, *From Resistance to Revolution: Colonial Radicals and the Development of American Opposition to Britain, 1765–1776,* 41–42.
10. *Ibid.,* 51–112, quoting, on 96 and 112, Silas Downer to New York Sons of Liberty, July 21, 1766, and *New York Gazette,* November 14, 1765.
11. Bailyn, "Introduction," *Pamphlets,* 172, 175–190; Paine, *Common Sense* (1776) (Jensen, *Tracts,* 402–418); *Diary and Autobiography of John Adams,* L. H. Butterfield and others, eds., III, 330.
12. Bailyn, "Introduction," *Pamphlets,* 190–191; Jefferson, "Autobiography" (1821) (*The Life and Selected Writings of Thomas Jefferson,* Adrienne Koch and William Peden, eds., 51–52).
13. T. B. Chandler, "A Friendly Address to All Reasonable Americans" (New York, 1774), and "Four Letters on Interesting Subjects" (Philadelphia, 1776) (quoted in Bailyn, "Introduction," *Pamphlets,* 194–198).
14. "Toleration . . . ," first printed in the *London Packet,* June 3, 1772 (A. H. Smyth, ed., *Writings of Franklin,* V, 399–405).

15. Eugene Rich, "John Witherspoon in Scotland, 1723–1768" (Ph.D. dissertation, Syracuse University, 1964), and R. Ketcham, "James Madison at Princeton," *The Princeton University Library Chronicle*, 38–41, Autumn 1966.

16. Mayhew, "Observation on the Charter and Conduct of the Society for the Propagation of the Gospel in Foreign Parts . . ." (Boston, 1763) (quoted in Bailyn, "Introduction," *Pamphlets*, 157–159); Madison to W. Bradford, April 1, 1774, and Prince Edward County petition, October 1776 (*The Papers of James Madison*, W. T. Hutchinson and others, eds., I, 112–113); Madison to Jefferson, January 22, 1786 (*The Papers of Thomas Jefferson*, J. P. Boyd and others, eds., IX, 194).

17. Parsons, "Freedom from Civil and Ecclesiastical Slavery . . ." (1774), and Hart, "Liberty Described and Recommended" (1774) (quoted in Alan Heimert, *Religion and the American Mind*, 121, 390, 395).

18. Moses Mather, "America's Appeal to the Impartial World . . ." (1775), Dickinson, *Letters* (1768), and Hopkins, "The Rights of Colonies Examined" (1765) (quoted in Bailyn, "Introduction," *Pamphlets*, 140–142, 516–517).

19. John Camm, "Critical Remarks on a Letter Ascribed to Common Sense" (1765) (quoted in Bailyn, "Introduction," *Pamphlets*, 143); Jefferson, *A Summary View of the Rights of British North America* (1774); *Notes on Virginia* (*Selected Writings*, 261).

20. Otis, "Considerations Upon the Act of Parliament" (1764), Samuel Cooke, "A Sermon Preached at Cambridge . . . 1770," Allen, "The Watchman's Alarm" (1764), and Hart, "Liberty Described and Recommended" (1775) (quoted in Bailyn, "Introduction," *Pamphlets*, 144–148).

21. Quoted in Bailyn, "Introduction," *Pamphlets*, 148–149.

Chapter 4

1. This and the following two paragraphs from David Ramsay, *The History of the American Revolution*, 2 vols. (Philadelphia, 1789), II, 310–325; extract in E. S. Morgan, ed., *The American Revolution: Two Centuries of Interpretation* (Englewood Cliffs, N.J., 1965), 6–15.

2. To Lord Kames, April 11, 1767 (*Writings of Franklin*, V, 21–22).

3. *Writings of Franklin*, IX, 261.

PART III

1. Jefferson to Henry Lee, May 8, 1825 (*The Life and Selected Writings of Thomas Jefferson*, A. Koch and W. Peden, eds., 719).

2. Martin Diamond, "Democracy and *The Federalist*: A Reconsideration of the Framers' Intent," *American Political Science Review*, LIII, 52–68, 1959.

Chapter 5

1. *Common Sense,* (Philadelphia, January 1776) (*Tracts of the American Revolution,* Merrill Jensen, ed., 400–446).
2. Trenton *New Jersey Gazette,* May 20, 1778, and T. B. Chandler, "A Friendly Address to All Reasonable Americans . . ." (New York, 1774) (quoted in Gordon S. Wood, *The Creation of the American Republic, 1776–1787,* 55, 66).
3. John to Abigail Adams, July 10, 1776 (*Adams Family Correspondence,* L. H. Butterfield and others, eds., II, 42); "Loose Thoughts on Government" (1776) and Thomas Dawes, *Oration Delivered March 5th 1781,* (quoted in Wood, *American Republic,* 73).
4. Charles Thomson to John Dickinson, August 18, 1776 (*Pennsylvania Magazine of History and Biography,* XXXV, 499, 1911); Samuel Adams ("Valerius Poplicola"), Boston *Gazette,* July 28, 1771; John to Abigail Adams, July 3, 1776, and Abigail to John Adams, July 14, 1776 (*Adams Family Correspondence,* II, 28, 46).
5. West, *Sermon Preached May 29th 1776,* (quoted in Wood, *American Republic,* 120).
6. John Adams, *Thoughts on Government* (Philadelphia, April 1776) (reprinted in *The Political Writings of John Adams,* G. A. Peek, Jr., ed., 84–92).
7. Letter of December 6, 1773 (quoted in Pauline Maier, *From Resistance to Revolution,* 289–290).
8. George Washington to J. A. Washington, May 31, 1776 (*The Writings of George Washington,* J. C. Fitzpatrick, ed., 39 vols. [Washington, D.C., 1931–1940], V, 20); Pendleton to Jefferson, August 26, and August 10, 1776 (*The Letters and Papers of Edmund Pendleton,* D. J. Mays, ed., 2 vols. [Charlottesville, Va., 1967], I, 200, 198); Jefferson "Autobiography" (1821) (*Selected Writings of Jefferson,* 39, 42).

Chapter 6

1. *Journal of the Continental Congress,* 34 vols. (Washington, D.C., 1904–1937), IV, 342.
2. John to Abigail Adams, May 17, 1776 (*Adams Family Correspondence,* L. H. Butterfield and others, eds., I, 410–411).
3. G. S. Wood, *The Creation of the American Republic,* 227–229; broadside dated Philadelphia, July 26, 1776 (Evans No. 15115) (quoted in Merrill Jensen, "The American People and the American Revolution," *Journal of American History,* LVII, 29, June 1970).
4. F. N. Thorpe, ed., *The Federal and State Constitutions . . .* V, 3081–3084; Wood, *American Republic,* 226–227; Philadelphia broadside (1776, Evans No. 14984) (quoted in Jensen, "The American People and

the American Revolution," *Journal of American History*, LVII, 29–30, June 1970).

5. Thorpe, *State Constitutions*, V, 3084–3092.

6. "Autobiography of John Adams," February–April 1776 (written in 1805) (*The Diary and Autobiography of John Adams*, L. H. Butterfield and others, eds., III, 333); Francis Allison to "Cozen Robert," August 20, 1776, Sarah to Jasper Yeates, September 14, 1776, and St. Clair to James Wilson, October 21, 1776 (all quoted in C. Page Smith, *James Wilson, Founding Father, 1742–1798*, 108–109); Rush to Anthony Wayne, September 24, 1776 (quoted in Wood, *American Republic*, 233).

7. "Thirty one Resolves," October 17, 1776 (quoted in Smith, *Wilson*, 110–111).

8. Madison to W. Bradford, May 9, 1775 (*The Papers of James Madison*, W. T. Hutchinson and others, eds., I, 144–145); T. L. Lee to R. H. Lee, June 1, 1776 (quoted in D. J. Mays, *Edmund Pendleton, 1721–1803*, II, 120–122); Charles S. Syndor, *American Revolutionaries in the Making* (New York, 1952, 1962).

9. Thorpe, *State Constitutions*, VII, 3812–3014.

10. Mays, *Pendleton*, II, 120–122.

11. "Article on Religious Freedom" (*Papers of Madison*, I, 160–161, 170–179).

12. Jefferson, "Autobiography" (1821) (*The Life and Selected Writings of Thomas Jefferson*, A. Koch and W. Peden, eds., 55–56, 50 51).

13. "Act for Establishing Religious Freedom" (1779; passed in 1786) (*Selected Writings of Jefferson*, 311–313); Madison to Jefferson, January 22, 1786 (*The Papers of Thomas Jefferson*, J. P. Boyd and others, eds., IX, 194).

14. "Notes on Virginia" (1782) (*Selected Writings of Jefferson*, 265–266).

15. "Autobiography" (1821) (*Selected Writings of Jefferson*, 51).

16. Documents of the town of Pittsfield, Massachusetts (quoted in Wood, *American Republic*, 285–286).

17. Wood, *American Republic*, 339–341.

18. This and the following four paragraphs based on "Massachusetts Constitution of 1780" (Thorpe, *State Constitutions*, VIII, 1888–1911); and "Address of the Convention . . ." signed by James Bowdoin but drafted by Samuel Adams (W. V. Wells, *The Life and Public Services of Samuel Adams*, III, 90–96).

19. Jefferson to W. S. Smith, November 13, 1787 (*Selected Writings of Jefferson*, 436).

20. Richard Hofstadter, *The Idea of a Party System*, 53.

21. Madison to Caleb Wallace, August 23, 1785 (*The Writings of James Madison*, G. Hunt, ed., II, 166–167).

22. Madison to Monroe, October 5, 1786 (*ibid.*, II, 272–273); Jefferson, "Notes on Virginia" (*Selected Writings of Jefferson*, 237).

Chapter 7

1. "Of Ancient and Modern Confederacies" (1786) (*The Writings of James Madison*, G. Hunt, ed., II, 306–390).
2. "Vices of Political System of the United States" (1787) (*ibid.*, II, 361–369).
3. To Randolph, April 8, 1787, and to Washington, April 16, 1787 (*ibid.*, II, 336–349).
4. Wilson, "Lectures on Law," delivered in 1790, but not published until 1804 (quoted in G. S. Wood, *The Creation of the American Republic*, 598).
5. Wood, *American Republic*, describes in detail the evolving political concepts, 1776–1787, especially the shift to the sovereignty of the people (pp. 519–615); *The Federalist*, Jacob E. Cooke, ed., No. 51, 349.
6. Debates, May 31, 1787 (Max Farrand, ed., *The Records of the Federal Convention of 1787*, I, 48–55).
7. *The Federalist*, No. 62, 418–419.
8. Debates, June 1, 2, 1787, resolves of June 13, 1787 (Farrand, *Records*, I, 64–69, 81–82, 232–237).
9. Debates, July 25, 1787, committee report, September 14, 1787 (*ibid.*, II, 106–108, 496).
10. Debates, July 23, 1787 and June 5, 1787 (*ibid.*, II, 93, and I, 123).
11. Debates, June 6, 1787 (*ibid.*, I, 134–136).
12. *Ibid.*, II, 666–667.

Chapter 8

1. Hamilton to George Clinton, February 13, 1787 (*The Papers of Alexander Hamilton*, H. C. Syrett and others, eds., I, 425–428).
2. *The Federalist* No. 1.
3. *The Federalist* Nos. 4, 9, 18–20.
4. *The Federalist* Nos. 11, 12, 25, 23.
5. *The Federalist* Nos. 68, 70.
6. *The Federalist* No. 78.
7. *The Federalist* No. 45.
8. *The Federalist* No. 57.
9. "The Objections of the Honorable George Mason to the Proposed Federal Constitution" (October 1787); Anonymous, *Letters from the Federal Farmer*, No. II (October 9, 1787); and Samuel Bryan, "Centinel" No. I (October 5, 1787) (all reprinted in Cecelia Kenyon, ed., *The Antifederalists*, 192, 209–214, 7).
10. "John DeWitt," Letter No. III (November 5, 1787) (reprinted in *ibid.*, 105, 108).
11. Henry, speech of June 5, 1788 (reprinted in *ibid.*, 250–256).
12. "Cato," November 22, 1787 (reprinted in *ibid.*, 309).

13. "Brutus" letters, December 27, 1787, and March 20, 1788 (reprinted in *ibid.*, 326–329, 352, 357).
14. Melancton Smith, speech in July 1788 (reprinted in *ibid.*, 382–385).
15. Thomas Tredwell, speech in July 1788 (reprinted in *ibid.*, 404).
16. This and the following two paragraphs from John to Samuel Adams, September 12 and October 18, 1790, and Samuel to John Adams, October 4 and November 20, 1790 (reprinted in *The Life and Public Service of Samuel Adams*, W. V. Wells, ed., III, 297–314).

Chapter 9

1. Adapted from R. Ketcham, *James Madison: A Biography*, 288–303, which summarizes Madison's political thought in 1789.
2. Adams to Timothy Pickering, August 6, 1822 (*The Works of John Adams*, C. F. Adams, ed., II, 514); Jefferson to Henry Lee, May 18, 1825 (*The Writings of Thomas Jefferson*, P. L. Ford, ed., X, 343).
3. Preface to notes on "Debates in the Convention of 1787" (Max Farrand, ed., *The Records of the Federal Convention of 1787*, III, 551); speech in the Virginia Constitutional Convention of 1829 (*The Writings of James Madison*, G. Hunt, ed., IX, 361).
4. Madison, speech on June 20, 1788 (*Writings of Madison*, V, 223); Aristotle, *Politics*, Book IV, Chapter 9 (Barker translation, cited in Paul Eidelberg, *Philosophy of the American Constitution* [New York, 1968], 130).
5. Madison to Jefferson, October 24, 1787 (*The Papers of Thomas Jefferson*, J. P. Boyd and others, eds., XII, 276–277).
6. Essay on "Majority Government" (1833) (*Writings of Madison*, IX, 523).
7. Niebuhr, *The Children of Light and the Children of Darkness* (New York, 1944), viii.
8. Aristotle, *Politics*, Book III, Chapter 9; Book VII, Chapters 1 and 2 (Jowett translation, Modern Library, 1943), 147–149, 278–281.
9. To Jefferson, October 24, 1787 (*Papers of Jefferson*, XII, 275).

PART IV

1. John to Abigail Adams, 1780 (C. F. Adams, ed., *Familiar Letters of John Adams and his Wife* . . . [New York, 1876], 206–207); Belknap to Ebenezer Hazard, February 4, 1780 (quoted in Linda Kerber, *Federalists in Dissent*, 3n.).
2. Price, *Observations on the Importance of the American Revolution* (Dublin, 1785), 85 (quoted in G. S. Wood, *The Creation of the American Republic*, 396); Rush to Price, May 25, 1786 (*The Letters of Benjamin Rush*, L. H. Butterfield, ed., I, 388–389).
3. Webster to Connecticut General Assembly, October 24, 1782, and to John Canfield, January 6, 1783 (*The Letters of Noah Webster*, Harry

Warfel, ed., 1–4); Webster to Joel Barlow, November 12, 1807 (Emily
E. F. Ford, *Notes on the Life of Noah Webster* [New York, 1912], II,
97).

Chapter 10

1. August 23, 1774 (*The Diary and Autobiography of John Adams*, L. H.
   Butterfield and others, eds., I, 109); John to Abigail Adams, October 9,
   1774 (*Adams Family Correspondence*, L. H. Butterfield and others, eds.,
   I, 166–167).
2. To Abigail Adams, March 7, 1777, and October 29, 1775 (*Adams Family
   Correspondence* II, 169–170; I, 318–319); July 16 and July 21, 1786
   (*Diary of John Adams*, III, 194–195).
3. April 2–6, 1778 (*Diary of John Adams*, IV, 35–40).
4. December 27, 1779 to February 5, 1780 (*Diary of John Adams*, II, 415–
   434).
5. Samuel Adams to Arthur Lee, October 31, 1771, Resolves of Bristol,
   Rhode Island, March 21, 1774, and Henry Marchant to Ezra Stiles,
   1772 (all quoted in E. S. Morgan, "The Puritan Ethic and the American
   Revolution," *William and Mary Quarterly*, XXIV, 16–17, January 1967.
6. Franklin, "Comparison of Great Britain and the United States" (1777)
   (*The Political Thought of Benjamin Franklin*, R. L. Ketcham, ed.,
   298).
7. Thomas to Martha Jefferson, March 28 and May 5, 1787 (*The Papers
   of Thomas Jefferson*, J. P. Boyd and others, eds., XI, 250–251, 349);
   Morgan, "The Puritan Ethic and the American Revolution," *William
   and Mary Quarterly*, XXIV, 29–30, January 1967, quoting Laurens to
   R. Lowndes, May 18, 1778, and David Ramsay, *The History of South
   Carolina* . . . (Charleston, 1809), II, 484–485.
8. November 1775 (*Autobiography of John Adams*, III, 340); William
   Stinchcombe, *The American Revolution and the French Alliance*, 77–90.
9. Franklin to Samuel Mather, May 12, 1784, to Charles Thomson, May
   13, 1784, and to R. R. Livingston, July 22, 1783 (*Writings of Franklin*,
   IX, 210, 213, 262); Deane to John Jay, November 1780 (quoted in
   Morgan, "The Puritan Ethic and the American Revolution," *William
   and Mary Quarterly*, XXIV, 27, January 1967); Ketcham, "France and
   American Politics, 1763–1793," *Politcal Science Quarterly*, LXXVIII,
   198–223, June 1963.
10. "Notes on Virginia" (*The Life and Selected Writings of Thomas Jeffer-
    son*, A. Koch and W. Peden, eds., 205–214).
11. To Sarah Bache, January 1, 1784 (*Writings of Franklin*, IX, 161–167).
12. *Information to Those Who Would Remove to America* (1782);
    Writings of Franklin, VIII, 603–614.
13. To Charles Bellini, September 30, 1785, and to Eliza Trist, August 18,
    1785 (*Selected Writings of Jefferson*, 383, 372).
14. To J. Bannister, October 15, 1785 (*ibid.*, 386–387).

15. Preface to *The Algerine Captive* (Walpole, New Hampshire, 1797) (reprinted in R. E. Spiller, ed., *The American Literary Revolution, 1783–1837* [Garden City, N.Y., 1967], 23).

Chapter 11

1. Crèvecoeur, *Letters from an American Farmer* (London, 1782) (Dolphin Books ed., n.d.), 49–50.
2. *Ibid.*, 12, 18, 24, 52, 58.
3. *Ibid.*, 73–91.
4. *Ibid.*, 208–209, 222.
5. May 8, 1789, E. S. Maclay, ed., *Journal of William Maclay* (New York, 1890), 23; C. P. Smith, *John Adams*, II, 753–755.
6. *Annals of Congress*, May 11, 1789.
7. Dumas Malone, *Jefferson the President, First Term, 1801–1805*, 376–392, 499–500.
8. Pendleton, *The Danger Not Over*, October 5, 1801 (David J. Mays, ed., *The Letters and Papers of Edmund Pendleton*, 2 vols. [Charlottesville, Va., 1967], II, 695–699); charge of Associate Justice John Dudley (quoted in Richard E. Ellis, *The Jeffersonian Crisis*, 115).
9. Ellis, *Jeffersonian Crisis*, especially 109–229.
10. "Introduction" reprinted in Spiller, ed., *American Literary Revolution*, p. 15.
11. Barlow, *Advice to the Privileged . . .* , *passim*, but especially 4–5, 25, 45–50; *Prospectus of a National Institution, to be Established in the United States* (Washington, D.C., 1806), 35, 5 (quoted in Linda Kerber, *Federalists in Dissent*, 107).
12. Stiles, *A History of the Three Judges of Charles I* (Hartford, Connecticut, 1794), 272–290 (reprinted in E. S. Morgan, ed., *Puritan Political Ideas* [Indianapolis, 1965], 373–392).
13. F. B. Dexter, ed., *Literary Diary of Ezra Stiles*, 3 vols. (New York, 1901), III, 124–126.
14. This and the following two paragraphs from S. E. Morison, ed., "William Manning's 'The Key of Libberty,'" *William and Mary Quarterly*, XIII, 210–254, 1956.

Chapter 12

1. John Adams, "Discourses on Davila" (1790) (*The Works of John Adams*, C. F. Adams, ed., VI, 274); Arthur M. Walter, in the *Monthly Anthology and Boston Review*, II, 199–200, April, 1805 (reprinted in L. P. Simpson, ed., *The Federalist Literary Mind* [Louisiana State University Press, 1962], 49).
2. Ames, in the *Monthly Anthology and Boston Review*, II, 563–566, November, 1805 (reprinted in *ibid.*, 52, 54); Ames, "The Dangers of

American Liberty" (reprinted in E. H. Cady, ed., *Literature of the Early Republic* [New York, 1961], 108–110).

3. Cady, *Literature of the Early Republic*, 111–115.

4. Ames, "American Literature" (1809) (reprinted in Spiller, ed., *American Literary Revolution*, 73–75); *New England Quarterly Magazine*, 125, September, 1802 (quoted in Linda Kerber, *Federalists in Dissent*, 118).

5. Kerber, *Federalists in Dissent*, *passim*, but especially 173–215, and quoting the *New England Palladium* (1802).

6. From Dennie's magazine, *The Port Folio*, III, Philadelphia, 1803 (reprinted in Cady, *Literature of the Early Republic*, 477–481).

7. Taylor, *An Inquiry into the Principles and Policy of the Government of the United States*, 1814 (reprinted, New Haven, Conn., 1950), 231.

8. Jefferson to John Adams, October 28, 1813 (*The Adams-Jefferson Letters*, L. J. Cappon, ed., II, 392).

9. *Annals of Congress*, December 10, 1811; Gallatin to Jefferson, September 6, 1815 (Henry Adams, ed., *The Writings of Albert Gallatin*, 3 vols. [Philadelphia, 1879], I, 651); Madison to Lafayette, November 25, 1820 (*The Writings of James Madison*, G. Hunt, ed., IX, 35–36).

10. Richard B. Davis, *Intellectual Life in Jefferson's Virginia, 1790–1830*, 378–382, 403–406, 415–420.

Chapter 13

1. Jefferson quoted in Merrill Peterson, *Thomas Jefferson and the New Nation*, 923.

2. Franklin, "Busy-Body No. 3," *American Weekly Mercury*, February 18, 1729 (reprinted in *The Papers of Benjamin Franklin*, L. W. Labaree and others, eds., I, 118–120).

3. Jefferson to Joseph Priestley, March 21, 1801 (quoted in Malone, *Jefferson the President*, 27).

4. Madison, "Annual Message," December 5, 1815 (J. D. Richardson, *Messages and Papers of the Presidents*, II, 551–554).

5. Jefferson to L. W. Tazewell, January 1805 (quoted in Peterson, *Thomas Jefferson*, 964); Jefferson, "Report of Commissioners for the University of Virginia," August 4, 1818 (*Early History of the University of Virginia As Contained in the Letters of Thomas Jefferson and Joseph C. Cabell* [Richmond, 1856], 445).

6. "Notes on Virginia" (1782) (*The Life and Selected Writings of Thomas Jefferson*, A. Koch and W. Peden, eds., 280–281).

7. Hamilton to James Duane, September 3, 1780 (*The Papers of Alexander Hamilton*, H. C. Syrett and others, eds., II, 400–418).

8. Hamilton's reports are reprinted in Samuel McKee, Jr., ed., *Alexander Hamilton's Papers on Public Credit, Commerce and Finance* (New York, 1957).

9. *Ibid.*, 83.

10. *Ibid.*, 76, 84–85.
11. *Ibid.*, 38, 270–271.
12. Jefferson, "Anas" (1818) (*Selected Writings of Jefferson*, 121); Hamilton to C. C. Pinckney, October 10, 1792 (Broadus Mitchell, *Heritage from Hamilton* [New York, 1957], 142–143.
13. Wilson, *The New Freedom*, 1913 (Englewood Cliffs, N.J., 1961), 6; Croly, *The Promise of American Life*, 1909 (Indianapolis, 1965), 45.

Chapter 14

1. "Sketch" (reprinted in part in *Selected Writings of Albert Gallatin*, E. James Ferguson, ed., 32–41).
2. Raymond Walters, Jr., *Albert Gallatin, Jeffersonian Financier and Diplomat* (New York, 1957), 142–152.
3. Gallatin to Jefferson, December 13, 1803, and November 8, 1809, and "Report," April 19, 1808 (*Selected Writings of Albert Gallatin*, E. James Ferguson, ed., 212–218, 240–263, 325–326).
4. "Address of the Minority of the Virginia Legislature" (1800) (*John Marshall: Major Opinions and Other Writings*, John P. Roche, ed., 43, 48).
5. *Ibid.*, 171–187.
6. Madison to Spencer Roane, June 29, 1821 (*The Writings of James Madison*, G. Hunt, ed., IX, 60–68).

Chapter 15

1. Richard Carwardine, "The Second Great Awakening in the Urban Centers: An Examination of Methodism and the New Measures," *Journal of American History*, LIX, 327–340, 1972; Lyman Beecher, *The Spirit of the Pilgrims*, 1831 (quoted in Perry Miller, *The Life of the Mind in America from the Revolution to the Civil War* [New York, 1965], 36).
2. Miller, *Life of the Mind in America*, 3–95; H. Richard Niebuhr, *The Kingdom of God in America* (New York, 1937), 99–119, 150–163.
3. Haggard, *An Address to the Different Religious Societies on the Sacred Import of the Christian Name* (Lexington, Ky., 1804) (quoted in John B. Boles, *The Great Revival, 1787–1805*, 155); *The Journals and Letters of Francis Asbury*, E. T. Clark and others, ed., III, 253, letter to Ezekiel Cooper, December 23, 1802; Donald G. Mathews, "The Second Great Awakening as an Organizing Process, 1780–1830," *American Quarterly*, XXI, 23–43, 1969.
4. Boles, *Great Revival*, 66, 25–35.
5. Henry Holcombe, "Address to the Friends of Religion in the State of Georgia, on their Duties, in Reference to Civil Government," *Georgia Analytical Respository*, 1802 (quoted in Boles, *Great Revival*, 176).
6. Channing, "The Perfect Life," (1831) (Sidney Ahlstrom, ed., *Theology in America* [Indianapolis, 1967], 206–210).

7. David Ramsay, *The History of South-Carolina from its First Settlement in 1670, To the Year 1808* (Charleston, 1809) (quoted in Boles, *Great Revival*, 188); Madison to Robert Walsh, March 2, 1819 (*The Writings of James Madison*, G. Hunt, ed., VIII, 430–432).

8. *Democracy in America*, H. S. Commager, ed. (New York, 1947), 195, 204.

9. Statements by Cooper and Hopkinson quoted in R. B. Nye, *The Cultural Life of the New Nation, 1776–1830*, 55; Freneau, "The Rising Glory of America" (1771) (H. H. Clark, ed., *Major American Poets* [New York, 1936], 6–7).

10. J. C. Fitzpatrick, ed., *Writings of Washington*, XXX, 307; M. D. Peterson, *Thomas Jefferson and the New Nation*, 402–405.

11. J. Q. Adams, *Report Upon Weights and Measures* (Philadelphia, 1821) (reprinted in Charles Sanford, ed., *Quest for America, 1810–1824* [Garden City, N.Y., 1964], 208–209); "Annual Message," December 6, 1825 (J. D. Richardson, *Messages of the Presidents*, II, 876–882).

12. Nye, *Cultural Life, 1776–1830*, 93–95.

Chapter 16

1. Bernard W. Sheehan, *Seeds of Extinction: Jeffersonian Philanthropy and the American Indian*, explains and carefully documents attitudes toward the Indians during the half-century following the Declaration of Independence.

2. Wise, "Vindication of the Government of New England Churches" (1717), Rush, "Address on the Slavery of the Negroes" (1773), and "Journal of Ambrose Serle" (1776) (all quoted in Winthrop Jordan, *White Over Black: American Attitudes Toward the Negro, 1550–1812*, 293–294, 287, 291).

3. Massachusetts petition, 1777; Minutes of Methodist Conference, 1784; *Records of Colonial Rhode Island*, VII, 251; Philip Foner, ed., *Writings of Paine*, II, 21 (all quoted in Jordan, *White Over Black*, 291–294); decision of Judge William Cushing, 1781 (Herbert Aptheker, *The American Revolution: 1763–1783* [New York, 1960], 210–213).

4. "Essay on Negro Slavery, By Another Hand," Philadelphia, 1789 (quoted in Jordan, *White Over Black*, 333).

5. Jefferson, "Notes on Virginia" (1782) (*The Life and Selected Writings of Thomas Jefferson*, A. Koch and W. Peden, eds., 256–262).

6. Anonymous antislavery address, *c.* 1770 (quoted in Jordan, *White Over Black*, 280); Jefferson to Banneker, August 30, 1791, and to H. Grègoire, February 28, 1809 (*Selected Writings of Jefferson*, 508–509, 594–595).

7. Edward Long, *The History of Jamaica* (3 vols., London, 1774); extract reprinted in *Columbian Magazine*, II (1788); Charles White, *An Account of the Regular Gradation in Man . . .* (London, 1799) (all quoted in Jordan, *White Over Black*, 491–501).

8. J. A. Smith, "A Lecture," *New York Medical and Philosophical Journal and Review*, I (1809) (quoted in *ibid.*, 505–506).
9. C. C. Moore, *Observations on Certain Passages in Mr. Jefferson's Notes on Virginia* (New York, 1804), 24–25, William Pinkney, speech in Maryland House of Delegates, November 1789, and S. S. Smith, *An Essay on the Causes of the Variety of Complexion and Figure in the Human Species* (Philadelphia, 1787), 109–110 (all quoted in *ibid*, 447–448, 487).
10. This and the following three paragraphs depend heavily on Jordan, *White Over Black*, chapters VIII–XI.

Chapter 17

1. Freneau, "Advice to Authors by the Late Mr. Robert Slender" (Philadelphia, 1788); C. B. Brown, "Preface," *The American Review and Literary Journal for the Year 1801* (New York, 1802) (reprinted in Spiller, ed., *American Literary Revolution*, 6–12, 32–37).
2. *The Poems of Philip Freneau*, Fred L. Pattee, ed., I, 49–84.
3. "On the Uniformity and Perfection of Nature" (1815), "On Mr. Paine's *Rights of Man*" (1792), and "On the Religion of Nature" (1815) (H. H. Clark, ed., *Major American Poets*, [New York, 1936], 54–57).
4. R. B. Nye, *The Cultural Life of the New Nation, 1776–1830*, 247–249.
5. Lewis Leary, *That Rascal Freneau, A Study in Literary Failure, passim.*
6. *The Contrast* (New York, 1787) (reprinted in Cady, ed., *Early Republic*, 392–451).
7. Benjamin T. Spencer, *The Quest for Nationality*, 12, quotes from Brackenridge's 1779 magazine.
8. Preface to Edgar Huntley (1799) (reprinted in Spiller, ed., *American Literary Revolution*, 24–25); *Ormond* (1963 reprint), 229.
9. Nye, *Cultural Life, 1776–1830*, 254–255; Paulding, "National Literature" (1819–1820) (reprinted in Spiller, *American Literary Revolution*, 381–385.
10. William R. Taylor, *Cavalier and Yankee* (New York, 1961), 225–259.
11. Arthur M. Walter in the *Monthly Anthology and Boston Review*, III (November 1806), 579 (reprinted in Simpson, ed., *Federalist Literary Mind*, 69).
12. Irving, "The Author's Account of Himself," in *The Sketchbook* (1819) (reprinted in Spiller, *American Literary Revolution*, 378–380).
13. E. A. Poe, "A Review of the Poems of Drake and Halleck," *Southern Literary Messenger* (April 1836) (reprinted in *ibid.*, 417–418).

Chapter 18

1. John Trumbull, *Autobiography, Reminiscences, and Letters, 1776–1841*, 89–90; E. L. Morse, ed., *The Letters and Journals of Samuel F. B. Morse*, 2 vols. (Boston, 1914), I, 23, 177.

2. Charles C. Sellers, *Charles Willson Peale, passim,* but especially II, 1–14, 84–93, 124–153; Peale to Jefferson, January 12, 1802 (quoted in Dumas Malone, *Jefferson the President,* 184).

3. Sidney Smith, *Edinburgh Review,* XXXIII (1820) (reprinted in Sanford, ed., *Quest for America, 1810–1824,* 308).

PART V

1. Jefferson to Adams, January 21, 1812, and Adams to Jefferson, February 3, 1812 (*The Adams-Jefferson Letters,* L. J. Cappon, ed., II, 291, 294–295).

2. Adams to Jefferson, August 24 and November 11, 1815, and Jefferson to Adams, January 11, 1816 (*ibid.,* II, 455–460).

3. Adams to Jefferson, August 24, 1815, and May 29, 1818, and Jefferson to Adams, August 10, 1815, and May 18, 1818 (*ibid.,* II, 452–455, 524–525).

4. Jefferson to Edward Coles, August 25, 1814 (*The Life and Selected Writings of Thomas Jefferson,* A. Koch and W. Peden, eds., 641–642).

5. This and the following three paragraphs from Franklin, "Observations Concerning the Increase of Mankind" (1751) (*The Papers of Benjamin Franklin,* L. W. Labaree, ed., IV, 227–234); and Madison, "Annual Message," December 5, 1815, and December 3, 1816 (J. D. Richardson, *Messages of the Presidents,* II, 547–554, 558–565).

6. Richard Buel, Jr., *Securing the Revolution: Ideology in American Politics, 1789–1815* (Ithaca, N.Y., 1972); see esp. pp. 17, 26–27, 85, 122–123, 131, 185–186, 203, and 285–286. Jefferson to Lafayette, November 23, 1818, is quoted on p. 292.

7. Adams to Jefferson, January 22, 1825, February 25, 1825, December 1, 1825, January 14, 1826, and April 17, 1826, and Jefferson to Adams, February 15, 1825, January 18, 1825, and March 25, 1826 (*Adams-Jefferson Letters,* II, 606–614).

8. Ellen Coolidge to Jefferson, August 1, 1825, and Jefferson to Ellen Coolidge, August 25, 1825 (E. M. Betts and J. A. Bear, eds., *The Family Letters of Thomas Jefferson* [Columbia, Mo., 1966], 454–458).

Selected Bibliography

Primary Sources

The Diary and Autobiography of John Adams. L. H. BUTTERFIELD and others, eds. 4 vols. Cambridge, Mass.: Harvard University Press, 1961.

Adams Family Correspondence. L. H. BUTTERFIELD and others, eds. 2 vols. Cambridge, Mass.: Harvard University Press, 1963.

The Political Writings of John Adams. G. A. PEEK, JR., ed. Indianapolis: Bobbs-Merrill Co., 1954.

The Works of John Adams. C. F. ADAMS, ed. 10 vols. Boston: Little, Brown and Co., 1856.

The Adams-Jefferson Letters. L. J. CAPPON, ed. Chapel Hill, N.C.: University of North Carolina Press, 1959.

The Life and Public Service of Samuel Adams. W. V. WELLS, ed. 3 vols. Boston: Little, Brown and Co., 1888.

The Journal and Letters of Francis Asbury. E. T. CLARK and others, eds. 3 vols. London: Epworth Press, 1958.

BAILYN, BERNARD, ed. *The Pamphlets of the American Revolution, 1750–1765.* Cambridge, Mass.: Harvard University Press, 1965.

BARLOW, JOEL. *Advice to the Privileged Orders in the Several States of Europe . . .* [1792]. Ithaca, N.Y.: Cornell University Press, 1956.

CADY, E. H., ed. *Literature of the Early Republic.* New York: Holt, Rinehart and Winston, 1961.

CRÈVECOEUR, J. HECTOR ST. JOHN. *Letters from an American Farmer* (1782). Garden City, N.Y.: Doubleday and Co., n.d.

FARRAND, MAX, ed. *The Records of the Federal Convention of 1787.* 4 vols. New Haven, Conn.: Yale University Press, 1937.

The Federalist [1788]. J. E. COOKE, ed. Cleveland: World Publishing Co., 1961.

The Autobiography of Benjamin Franklin. L. W. LABAREE and others, eds. New Haven, Conn.: Yale University Press, 1964.

The Papers of Benjamin Franklin. L. W. LABAREE and others, eds. 16 vols. New Haven, Conn.: Yale University Press, 1959–1972.

The Political Thought of Benjamin Franklin. R. L. KETCHAM, ed. Indianapolis: Bobbs-Merrill Co., 1965.

The Poems of Philip Freneau. F. L. PATTEE, ed. Princeton, N.J.: Princeton University Press, 1902.

Selected Writings of Albert Gallatin. E. J. FERGUSON, ed. Indianapolis: Bobbs-Merrill Co., 1967.

The Papers of Alexander Hamilton. H. C. SYRETT and others, eds. 17 vols. New York: Columbia University Press, 1961–1972.

The Papers of Thomas Jefferson. J. P. BOYD and others, eds. 18 vols. Princeton, N.J.: Princeton University Press, 1950–1971.

The Life and Selected Writings of Thomas Jefferson. ADRIENNE KOCH and WILLIAM PEDEN, eds. New York: Random House, 1944.

The Writings of Thomas Jefferson. P. L. FORD, ed. 10 vols. New York: G. P. Putnam's Sons, 1892–1899.

JENSEN, MERRILL, ed. *Tracts of the American Revolution, 1763–1776.* Indianapolis: Bobbs-Merrill Co., 1967.

KENYON, C. M., ed. *The Antifederalists.* Indianapolis: Bobbs-Merrill Co., 1966.

The Papers of James Madison. W. T. HUTCHINSON and others, eds. 8 vols. Chicago: University of Chicago Press, 1962–1973.

The Writings of James Madison. GAILLARD HUNT, ed. 9 vols. New York: G. P. Putnam's Sons, 1900–1910.

"William Manning's 'The Key of Libberty.' " S. E. MORISON, ed. *The William and Mary Quarterly*, XIII, 202–254, 1956.

John Marshall: Major Opinions and Other Writings. J. P. ROCHE, ed. Indianapolis: Bobbs-Merrill Co., 1967.

MILLER, PERRY, and ALAN HEIMERT, eds. *The Great Awakening.* Indianapolis: Bobbs-Merrill Co., 1966.

MORGAN, E. S., ed. *Puritan Political Ideas, 1558–1794.* Indianapolis: Bobbs-Merrill Co., 1965.

Peter Oliver's Origin and Progress of the American Rebellion: A Tory View. D. ADAIR and J. A. SCHUTZ, eds. San Marino, Calif.: Huntington Library, 1961.

RICHARDSON, J. D., comp. *Messages and Papers of the Presidents.* 20 vols. Washington, D.C.: Government Printing Office, 1897–1917.

The Letters of Benjamin Rush. L. H. BUTTERFIELD, ed. 2 vols. Princeton, N.J.: Princeton University Press, 1951.

SANFORD, C. L., ed. *Quest for America, 1810–1824.* Garden City, N.Y.: Doubleday and Co., 1964.

SIMPSON, L. P., ed. *The Federalist Literary Mind, Selections from the Monthly Anthology and Boston Review, 1803–1811* . . . Baton Rouge, La.: Louisiana State University Press, 1962.

SPILLER, R. E., ed. *The American Literary Revolution, 1783–1837.* Garden City, N.Y.: Doubleday and Co., 1967.

THORPE, F. N., ed. *The Federal and State Constitutions* . . . 7 vols. Washington, D.C.: Government Printing Office, 1909.

TRUMBULL, JOHN, *Autobiography, Reminiscences, and Letters, 1776–1841.* New York: Wiley and Putnam, 1841.

The Letters of Noah Webster. HARRY WARFEL, ed. New York: Library Associates, 1953.

Secondary Sources

BAILYN, BERNARD. *Ideological Origins of the American Revolution.* Cambridge, Mass.: Harvard University Press, 1967.

BECKER, CARL. *The Declaration of Independence.* New York: Alfred A. Knopf, Inc., 1922.

BOLES, JOHN B. *The Great Revival, 1787–1805: The Origins of the Southern Evangelical Mind.* Lexington, Ky.: The University Press of Kentucky, 1972.

BOORSTIN, D. J. *The Americans: The Colonial Experience,* and *The Americans: The National Experience.* New York: Random House, 1958, 1965.

BROWN, S. G. *Thomas Jefferson.* New York: Washington Square Press, 1963.

BUEL, RICHARD, *Securing the Revolution: Ideology in American Politics, 1789–1815.* Ithaca, N.Y.: Cornell University Press, 1972.

COLBOURN, H. T. *The Lamp of Experience: Whig History and the Intellectual Origins of the American Revolution.* Chapel Hill, N.C.: University of North Carolina Press, 1965.

DAVIS, R. B. *Intellectual Life in Jefferson's Virginia, 1790–1830.* Chapel Hill, N.C.: University of North Carolina Press, 1964.

DIAMOND, MARTIN. "Democracy and *The Federalist*: A Reconsideration of the Framers' Intent." *American Political Science Review,* LIII, 52–68, 1959.

ELLIS, RICHARD. *The Jeffersonian Crisis: Courts and Politics in the New Republic.* New York: Oxford University Press, 1971.

GILBERT, FELIX. *To the Farewell Address: Ideas of Early American Foreign Policy.* Princeton, N.J.: Princeton University Press, 1961.

J. E. GRAUSTEIN. *Thomas Nuttall, Nationalist: Explorations in America, 1808–1841.* New York: Cambridge University Press, 1967.

J. C. GREENE, "American Science Comes of Age, 1790–1820." *Journal of American History,* LV, 22–41, 1968.

NEIL HARRIS. *The Artist in American Society: The Formative Years, 1790–1860.* New York: George Braziller, 1966.

HEIMERT, ALAN. *Religion and the American Mind: From the Great Awakening to the Revolution.* Cambridge, Mass.: Harvard University Press, 1966.

HINDLE, BROOKE. *David Rittenhouse.* Princeton, N.J.: Princeton University Press, 1965.

HINDLE, BROOKE. *The Pursuit of Science in Revolutionary America, 1735–1789.* Chapel Hill, N.C.: University of North Carolina Press, 1956.

HOFSTADTER, RICHARD. *The Idea of a Party System: The Rise of Legitimate Opposition in the United States, 1780–1840.* Berkeley and Los Angeles: University of California Press, 1969.

JORDAN, W. D. *White Over Black: American Attitudes Toward the Negro, 1550–1812.* Chapel Hill, N.C.: University of North Carolina Press, 1968.

KAMMEN, MICHAEL. *People of Paradox: An Inquiry Concerning the Origins of American Civilization.* New York: Alfred A. Knopf, 1972.

KERBER, LINDA. *Federalists in Dissent: Image and Ideology in Jeffersonian America.* Ithaca, N.Y.: Cornell University Press, 1970.

KETCHAM, RALPH. *James Madison: A Biography.* New York: The Macmillan Co., 1971.

KOCH, ADRIENNE. *Jefferson and Madison: The Great Collaboration.* New York: Alfred A. Knopf, 1950.

LARKIN, OLIVER. *Art and Life in America.* New York: Holt, Rinehart and Winston, 1960.

LEARY, LEWIS. *That Rascal Freneau: A Study in Literary Failure.* Brunswick, N.J.: Rutgers University Press, 1941.

LEVY, L. W. *Legacy of Supression: Freedom of Speech and Press in Early American History.* Cambridge, Mass.: Harvard University Press, 1960.

MC KELVEY, S. D. *Botanical Exploration of the Trans-Mississippi West, 1790–1850.* Jamaica Plains, Mass.: Arnold Arboretum, 1955.

MAIER, PAULINE. *From Resistance to Revolution: Colonial Radicals and the Development of American Opposition to Britain, 1765–1776.* New York: Alfred A. Knopf, 1972.

MALONE, DUMAS. *Jefferson and His Time* (to 1805). 4 vols. Boston: Little, Brown and Co., 1948–1970.

MAYS, D. J. *Edmund Pendleton, 1721–1803.* 2 vols. Cambridge, Mass.: Harvard University Press, 1952.

MEADE, R. D. *Patrick Henry.* 2 vols. Philadelphia: J. B. Lippincott Co., 1957, 1969.

MILLER, J. C. *Sam Adams, Pioneer in Propaganda.* Boston: Little, Brown and Co., 1936.

MILLER, L. B. *Patrons and Patriotism: The Encouragement of the Fine Arts in the United States, 1790–1860.* Chicago: The University of Chicago Press, 1966.

MITCHELL, BROADUS. *Alexander Hamilton.* 2 vols. New York: The Macmillan Co., 1957, 1962.

MORGAN, E. S. "The Puritan Ethic and the American Revolution." *William and Mary Quarterly,* XXIV, 3–43, 1967.

NYE, R. B. *The Cultural Life of the New Nation 1776–1830.* New York: Harper and Bros., 1960.

PALMER, R. R. *The Age of Democratic Revolution.* 2 vols. Princeton, N.J.: Princeton University Press, 1959, 1964.

PETERSON, M. D.. *Thomas Jefferson and the New Nation.* New York: Oxford University Press, 1970.

REINGOLD, NATHAN. *Science in Nineteenth Century America: A Documentary History.* New York: Hill & Wang, 1964.

ROSSITER, CLINTON. *Seedtime of the Republic.* New York: Harcourt, Brace and Co., 1953.

SELLERS, C. C. *Charles Willson Peale.* 2 vols. Philadelphia: American Philosophical Society, 1939, 1947.

SHEEHAN, B. W. *Seeds of Extinction: Jeffersonian Philanthropy and the American Indian.* Chapel Hill, N.C.: University of North Carolina Press, 1973.

SMITH, C. P. *John Adams.* 2 vols. Garden City, N.Y.: Doubleday and Co., 1962.

SMITH, C. P. *James Wilson, Founding Father, 1742–1798.* Chapel Hill, N.C.: University of North Carolina Press, 1956.

SPENCER, B. T. *The Quest for Nationality.* Syracuse, N.Y.: Syracuse University Press, 1957.

STEARNS, R. P. *Science in the British Colonies of America.* Champaign-Urbana, Ill.: University of Illinois Press, 1970.

STINCHCOMBE, W. C. *The American Revolution and the French Alliance.* Syracuse, N.Y.: Syracuse University Press, 1969.

VAN DOREN, CARL. *Benjamin Franklin.* New York: The Viking Press, 1938.

WOOD, G. S. *The Creation of the American Republic, 1776–1787.* Chapel Hill, N.C.: University of North Carolina Press, 1969.

Index

Key

AH — Alexander Hamilton
TJ — Thomas Jefferson
JM — James Madison
JA — John Adams
BF — Benjamin Franklin

WITHDRAWN,
PUBLIC LIBRARY
BRC

Public Library of Brookline

COOLIDGE CORNER BRANCH
31 Pleasant Street
Brookline, Mass. 02146

I M P O R T A N T

Leave cards in pocket

DEMCO